The Art of C++

About the Author

Herbert Schildt is a leading authority on the C, C++, Java, and C# languages, and is a master Windows programmer. His programming books have sold more than 3 million copies worldwide and have been translated into all major foreign languages. He is the author of numerous C++ bestsellers, including *C++: The Complete Reference*, *C++ From the Ground Up*, *C++: A Beginner's Guide*, and *STL Programming From the Ground Up*. His other bestsellers include *C: The Complete Reference*, *Java 2: The Complete Reference,* and *C#: The Complete Reference*. Schildt holds a master's degree in computer science from the University of Illinois. He can be reached at his consulting office at (217) 586-4683.

The Art of C++

Herbert Schildt

McGraw-Hill/Osborne

New York   Chicago   San Francisco
Lisbon   London   Madrid   Mexico City   Milan
New Delhi   San Juan   Seoul   Singapore   Sydney   Toronto

The **McGraw·Hill** *Companies*

McGraw-Hill/Osborne
2100 Powell Street, 10th Floor
Emeryville, California 94608
U.S.A.

To arrange bulk purchase discounts for sales promotions, premiums, or fund-raisers, please contact **McGraw-Hill**/Osborne at the above address. For information on translations or book distributors outside the U.S.A., please see the International Contact Information page immediately following the index of this book.

The Art of C++

1234567890 CUS CUS 01987654

ISBN 0-07-225512-9

Publisher	Brandon A. Nordin
Vice President & Associate Publisher	Scott Rogers
Editorial Director	Wendy Rinaldi
Project Editor	Jenn Tust
Acquisitions Coordinator	Athena Honore
Technical Editor	Fahad Gilani
Copy Editor	Sally Engelfried
Proofreader	Marian Selig
Indexer	Sheryl Schildt
Composition	Carie Abrew, Lucie Ericksen
Illustrator	Melinda Lytle, Kathleen Edwards, Gregg Scott
Series Design	Roberta Steele
Cover Design	Jeff Weeks

This book was composed with Corel VENTURA™ Publisher.

Contents at a Glance

Contents

Preface

Since the early days of FORTRAN, the on-going development of computer languages has followed what can best be described as an evolutionary path, with the efforts of the past shaping developments in the future. In this process, weak features fell away and misguided efforts terminated in dead-ends. Over the years, these evolutionary forces distilled into undiluted form, the pure essence of what a programming language should be. The result was C++, and no other language holds a more important place in the history programming.

There are many reasons for the success of C++. Its syntax is terse, yet elegant, its object-model is streamlined and conceptually clean, and its libraries are carefully crafted and interlocking. These features by themselves, however, are not what earned C++ a place in history. Instead, it is these things *coupled with the power* that C++ puts into the hands of the programmer. No language before or since has given the programmer more direct control over the computer. With C++, the programmer is master of the machine—and this is the way that all programmers want it.

No boundaries, no limits, no constraints. That's C++.

What's Inside

This book is different from most other books on C++. Whereas other books teach the basics of the language, this book shows how to apply it to a wide range of interesting, useful, and, at times, mysterious programming tasks. In the process, it displays the power and elegance of the C++ language. Thus, it is through the *art* of C++ that the *artistry* of C++'s design is displayed.

In general, the book contains two types of applications. The first type I call "pure code" because they focus on expanding the C++ programming environment, itself. The garbage collector in Chapter 2, the thread control panel in Chapter 3, and the custom STL container in Chapter 8 are examples. The second type shows how C++ can be applied to a variety of computing tasks. For example, Chapter 5 develops a restartable Internet downloader, Chapter 6 shows how to create financial applications, and Chapter 8 applies C++ to Artificial Intelligence.

The book ends with a unique and interesting piece of code: the Mini C++ interpreter, which interprets a small subset of C++. Mini C++ gives insight into how the keywords and syntax of C++ work together to create the grammar of the language. Moreover, it lets you get "inside the language," showing some of the reasons behind C++'s design. Although Mini C++ is fun to use as-is, it can also serve as a starting point for your own language development, or be adapted to work as an interpreter for any other language.

Each chapter develops code that you can use as-is, without changes. For example, the garbage collector in Chapter 2 is applicable to many programming tasks. However, the real benefits result when you use the applications as starting points for your own development. For example, the Internet file downloader in Chapter 8 could be enhanced to start a download at a specific time, or to watch a download site, waiting to download until an updated file is posted. In general, think of the various programs and subsystems as launching pads for your own projects.

Knowledge of C++ Is Assumed

This book assumes that you have a solid grounding in the fundamentals of the C++ language. You should be able to create, compile, and run C++ programs. You should be able to use pointers, templates, and exceptions, understand copy constructors, and be familiar with the most common parts of the standard library. Thus, this book assumes that you have the skills that one would acquire in a course on C++.

If you need to refresh or enhance your basic knowledge, I recommend the following books.

> *C++ From the Ground Up*
>
> *C++: A Beginner's Guide*
>
> *C++: The Complete Reference*

All are published by McGraw-Hill/Osborne.

Don't Forget: Code on the Web

Remember, the source code for all of the examples and projects in this book is available free-of-charge on the Web at **www.osborne.com**.

More From Herb Schildt

The *Art of C++* is just one in the Herb Schildt series of programming books. Here are some others that you will find of interest.

To learn more about C++, we recommend the following.

C++: The Complete Reference

C++: A Beginner's Guide

Teach Yourself C++

C++ From the Ground Up

STL Programming From the Ground Up

To learn about Java programming, you will find these books especially helpful.

Java 2: The Complete Reference

The Art of Java (Co-authored with James Holmes)

Java 2: A Beginner's Guide

Java 2: Programmer's Reference

To learn about C# we suggest the following books:

C#: A Beginner's Guide

C#: The Complete Reference

If you want to learn about the C language, the foundation of all modern programming, then the following titles will be of interest.

C: The Complete Reference

Teach Yourself C

The Power of C++

THE ART

OF C++

C++ is all about power: the power to control the machine at its lowest level, the power to produce highly optimized code, the power to interact directly with the operating system. This power runs deep and wide. With C++ you have detailed control over objects, including their creation, destruction, and inheritance; access to pointers; and support for low-level I/O. You can add new features by defining classes and overloading operators. You can construct your own libraries and hand-optimize code. You can even "break the rules" when necessary. C++ is not a language for the timid. It is for the programmer who demands and deserves the world's most powerful programming language.

Of course, C++ is not just raw power. It is power channeled, focused, and directed. Its careful design, rich libraries, and subtle syntax yield a programming environment that is both flexible and agile. Although C++ excels in the creation of high-performance system code, it is suitable for any type of programming task. For example, its string handling is second to none, its math and numeric capabilities make it excellent for scientific programming, and its ability to produce fast object code makes it perfect for any CPU-intensive task.

The purpose of this book is to demonstrate the power, scope, and agility of C++. It does so by applying it to a varied cross section of applications. Some of the applications demonstrate the capabilities of the language itself. These are called "pure code" examples because they show the expressiveness of the C++ syntax and the elegance of its design. The garbage collector in Chapter 2 and the C++ interpreter in Chapter 9 are examples. Other applications illustrate the ease with which C++ can be applied to common programming tasks. For example, the download manager in Chapter 5 illustrates the ability of C++ to create high-performance networked code. Chapter 6 applies C++ to various financial computations. Collectively, the applications show the wide ranging versatility of C++.

Before moving on to the applications, however, it is good to reflect for a moment on the things that make C++ such a great language. To this end, this chapter takes some time to point out several of the features that define the "power of C++."

A Terse yet Rich Syntax

If there is one fundamental defining characteristic of C++, it is the terseness of its syntax. C++ defines only 63 keywords. In a seeming contradiction, much of the power of C++ is derived from *not* building into the language more features than are necessary. Instead, C++ defines a rich but compact syntax that provides the control statements, operators, data types, and object-oriented features necessary for any modern language—but not more! Thus, the C++ syntax is clean, consistent, and uncluttered.

This lean philosophy has two important benefits. First, the keywords and syntax of C++ apply to all environments in which C++ can be used. That is, the core features of C++ are universally available to all applications, independent of the execution environment. Features that are sensitive to the execution environment, such as multithreading, are left to the operating system, which is best able to handle them efficiently. Thus, C++ does not attempt a "one size fits all" solution, which can lead to degraded runtime performance.

Second, a streamlined, logically consistent syntax allows complex constructs to be expressed with clarity. This is an important advantage in a world in which programs have grown to truly enormous sizes. While it is, of course, true that a poor programmer will write poor C++ code, a good programmer can create amazingly clear and concise code. This ability to transparently represent complicated logic is one of the reasons that the C++ syntax has become the near universal language of programming.

Powerful Libraries

Of course, the modern programming environment requires many features beyond those supported by the C++ keywords and syntax. C++ provides access to those features in a truly elegant way: through its standard library. C++ defines what is arguably the most well-designed library available in any mainstream language. Its function library, which is a carryover from C, contains a wide-ranging array of non-object-oriented functions, such as **char** * string handling, character manipulation, and conversion functions, which are used by programmers everywhere. The C++ class library provides object-oriented support for I/O, strings, and the STL, among others.

Because of its reliance on library routines rather than keywords, new functionality can be added to C++ by simply expanding its library rather than by inventing new keywords. This makes it possible for C++ to adapt to changes in programming environments without requiring changes to the core language. Thus, C++ combines two seemingly conflicting traits: stability and flexibility.

Even in its function and class libraries, C++ takes a lean, "less is more" approach, which avoids the "one-size-fits-all" trap. The libraries offer only those features that can be reasonably implemented for a wide range of programming environments. For features unique to a specific environment, C++ enables access to the operating system. Thus, the C++ programmer has access to all features of the execution platform. This approach lets you write highly efficient code that best utilizes the attributes and capabilities of the execution environment.

The STL

There is one part of the standard class library that is so important that it deserves separate attention: the Standard Template Library (STL). The creation of the STL was a pivotal event that changed the way that programmers think about and use a language's library. Its impact was so profound that it has influenced the design of subsequent languages. For example, the Collections frameworks of both Java and C# are directly patterned after the STL.

At its core, the STL is a sophisticated set of template classes and functions that implement many popular and commonly used data structures, which the STL refers to as *containers*. For example, it includes containers that support vectors, lists, queues, and stacks. Because the STL is constructed from template classes and functions, its containers can be applied to nearly any type of data. Thus, the STL provides off-the-shelf solutions to a wide variety of programming problems.

Although its practical importance to the C++ programmer is not to be underestimated, there is a larger reason that the STL is important. It was in the vanguard of the *software component* revolution. From the beginning, programmers have sought ways to reuse their code. Because development and debugging is a costly process, code reuse is highly desirable.

In the early days, code reuse was achieved by cutting and pasting source code from one program to another. (Of course, this approach is still used today.) Next, programmers created reusable function libraries, such as those provided by C++. This was soon followed by standardized class libraries.

Building on the foundation of a class library, the STL took the concept one important step further: it modularized the library into generic components that are applicable to a wide range of data. Furthermore, because the STL is extensible, you can define your own containers, add your own algorithms, and even adapt the built-in containers. The ability to *extend*, *adapt*, and *reuse* functionality is the essence of the software component.

Today, as the component software revolution is nearing completion, it is easy to forget that it was the STL that laid much of the groundwork, including modularized functionality, standardized interfaces, and extensibility through inheritance. The history of computing will chronicle the STL as one of the major milestones in language design.

The Programmer Is in Control

There are two competing philosophies of programming languages. One says that the language should prevent a programmer from causing problems by avoiding features that can cause problems in the first place. Although this sounds good, it usually results in certain powerful yet potentially risky features being restricted, diluted, or left out entirely. Two examples of such features are pointers and explicit memory allocation. Pointers are considered risky because they are often misused by beginning programmers and can (in some cases) be used to breach security barriers. Explicit memory allocation (such as through **new** and **delete**) is considered risky because a programmer might unwisely allocate large blocks of memory, or forget to release memory that is no longer needed, resulting in a memory leak. Although both features come with risks, they also give you, the programmer, detailed control and the ability to create highly efficient code. Fortunately, C++ does not subscribe to this philosophy.

The second philosophy, and the one to which C++ adheres, is that "the programmer is king." This means that the programmer is in control. It is not the job of the language to prevent you from being a bad programmer. Rather, the primary goal of the language is to give the programmer an agile, unobtrusive environment in which to work. If you are a good programmer, your work will reflect it. If you program poorly, your work will reflect that, too. In essence, C++ gives you the power and then gets out of the way. A C++ programmer never has to "fight the language."

Obviously, most programmers prefer the philosophy of C++!

Detailed Control

C++ does more than just put you, the programmer, in control, it gives you *detailed control*. For example, consider the increment operator: ++. As you know, C++ defines both a prefix and a postfix version. The prefix version increments the operand before obtaining its value. The postfix version increments the operand after obtaining its value. This allows you to gain precise control over how expressions involving the ++ are executed. Another example of detailed control is the **register** specifier. By modifying a variable declaration with **register**, you are telling the compiler to optimize access to that variable. Thus, you can control which variables receive the highest priority for optimization. The fine-grained control that C++ gives the programmer is one reason C++ has effectively replaced assembler as the language of choice for programming system code.

Operator Overloading

One of the most important features in C++ is operator overloading because it supports *type extensibility*. Type extensibility is the attribute that enables you to add and fully integrate new data types into the C++ programming environment. Type extensibility is built on two features. The first is the class, which lets you define a new data type. The second is operator overloading, which lets you define what the various operators mean relative to a class type. Through operator overloading and classes, you can create a new data type and then operate on that type in the same way that you operate on built-in types: through operators.

Type extensibility is very powerful because it makes C++ an open system rather than a closed one. For example, imagine that you need to manage three-dimensional coordinates. You can do this by creating a new data type called **ThreeD** and then defining various operations on objects of that type. For example, you could use + to add two **ThreeD** coordinates, or = = to determine if two sets of coordinates are equal. Thus, you can write code that operates on **ThreeD** just as you would any of the built-in types, as shown here:

```
ThreeD a(0, 0, 0), b(1, 2, 3), c(5, 6, 7);

a = b + c;
// ...
if(a == c) // ...
```

Without operator overloading, operations on **ThreeD** objects would have to be handled by calls to functions, such as **addThreeD( )** or **isEqualThreeD( )**, which is a far less pleasing approach.

A Clean, Streamlined Object Model

The C++ object model is a masterpiece of brevity! In the ISO standard for C++, the object model is described in less than a page (six paragraphs, to be precise). Within those few paragraphs, the standard manages to explain the essence of an object, its lifetime, and polymorphism. For example, the standard gives this definition for an object, "An *object* is a region of storage." It is this sort of fundamental simplicity that makes the C++ object model so remarkable.

Of course, the syntax and semantics necessary to support objects, including their creation, destruction, inheritance, and so on, consume many, many pages in the standard. However, this is because of the depth of control that C++ gives you over objects, not because of quirks or inconsistencies of the object model. Moreover, because of the elegance of its design, the C++ object model is the pattern used by Java and C#.

The Legacy of C++

Invented by Dennis Ritchie in the 1970s, C marked the beginning of a radical transformation in programming. Although some earlier languages, most notably Pascal, had achieved significant success, it was C that established the paradigm that would influence a generation of computer languages. With C, the modern age of programming began.

Soon after the creation of C, a new factor emerged: object-oriented programming (OOP). Although we take OOP for granted today, at the time of its invention, it was a major step forward. The object-oriented philosophy quickly captured the imagination of programmers because it offered a powerful, new way to approach the job of programming. At that time, programs were becoming larger and their complexity was growing. Some way to handle this complexity was needed, and OOP offered a solution. OOP enabled large and complicated programs to be framed in terms of compartmentalized units of functionality (objects). This allowed a complex system to be reduced to more manageable parts. The problem was that C did not support objects.

Designed by Bjarne Stroustrup, C++ was built on the foundation of C. To C, Stroustrup added the keywords and syntax needed for object-oriented programming. By adding object-oriented features to the already popular C language, Stroustrup made it possible for thousands of programmers to move forward to OOP. With the creation of C++, the modern age of programming was fully realized. In one masterful stroke, Stroustrup created the world's most powerful computer language and charted the course for future language development.

Although the legacy of C++ is just beginning, it has already led to the creation of two important languages: Java and C#. Despite some minor differences, the syntax, object model, and overall "look and feel" of Java and C# are nearly identical to that of C++. Furthermore, the libraries of Java and C# reflect the design of those in C++, and the Collections frameworks of Java and C# are directly derived from the STL. The groundbreaking design of C++ reverberates loudly throughout computing.

The power that C++ puts in the hands of the programmer is why C++ became important. Its far-reaching influence is the reason it remains the preeminent language for programmers worldwide. Thus, the ultimate power of C++ is its legacy.

A Simple Garbage Collector for C++

Throughout the history of computing, there has been an ongoing debate concerning the best way to manage the use of dynamically allocated memory. Dynamically allocated memory is memory that is obtained during runtime from the *heap*, which is a region of free memory that is available for program use. The heap is also commonly referred to as *free store* or *dynamic memory*. Dynamic allocation is important because it enables a program to obtain, use, release, and then reuse memory during execution. Because nearly all real-world programs use dynamic allocation in some form, the way it is managed has a profound effect on the architecture and performance of programs.

In general, there are two ways that dynamic memory is handled. The first is the manual approach, in which the programmer must explicitly release unused memory in order to make it available for reuse. The second relies on an automated approach, commonly referred to as *garbage collection*, in which memory is automatically recycled when it is no longer needed. There are advantages and disadvantages to both approaches, and the favored strategy has shifted between the two over time.

C++ uses the manual approach to managing dynamic memory. Garbage collection is the mechanism employed by Java and C#. Given that Java and C# are newer languages, the current trend in computer language design seems to be toward garbage collection. This does not mean, however, that the C++ programmer is left on the "wrong side of history." Because of the power built into C++, it is possible—even easy—to create a garbage collector for C++. Thus, the C++ programmer can have the best of both worlds: manual control of dynamic allocation when needed and automatic garbage collection when desired.

This chapter develops a complete garbage collection subsystem for C++. At the outset, it is important to understand that the garbage collector does not replace C++'s built-in approach to dynamic allocation. Rather, it supplements it. Thus, both the manual and garbage collection systems can be used within the same program.

Aside from being a useful (and fascinating) piece of code in itself, a garbage collector was chosen for the first example in this book because it clearly shows the unsurpassed power of C++. Through the use of template classes, operator overloading, and C++'s inherent ability to handle the low-level elements upon which the computer operates, such as memory addresses, it is possible to transparently add a core feature to C++. For most other languages, changing the way that dynamic allocation is handled would require a change to the compiler itself. However, because of the unparalleled power that C++ gives the programmer, this task can be accomplished at the source code level.

The garbage collector also shows how a new type can be defined and fully integrated into the C++ programming environment. Such *type extensibility* is a key component of C++, and it's one that is often overlooked. Finally, the garbage collector testifies to C++'s ability to "get close to the machine" because it manipulates and manages pointers. Unlike some other languages which prevent access to the low-level details, C++ lets the programmer get as close to the hardware as necessary.

Comparing the Two Approaches to Memory Management

Before developing a garbage collector for C++, it is useful to compare garbage collection to the manual method that is built-in to C++. Normally, the use of dynamic memory in C++ requires a two-step process. First, memory is allocated from the heap via **new**. Second, when that memory is no longer needed, it is released by **delete**. Thus, each dynamic allocation follows this sequence:

p = new *some_object*;

// ...

delete p;

In general, each use of **new** must be balanced by a matching **delete**. If **delete** is not used, the memory is not released, even if that memory is no longer needed by your program.

Garbage collection differs from the manual approach in one key way: it automates the release of unused memory. Therefore, with garbage collection, dynamic allocation is a one-step operation. For example, in Java and C#, memory is allocated for use by **new**, but it is never explicitly freed by your program. Instead, the garbage collector runs periodically, looking for pieces of memory to which no other object points. When no other object points to a piece of dynamic memory, it means that there is no program element using that memory. When it finds a piece of unused memory, it frees it. Thus, in a garbage collection system, there is no **delete** operator, nor a need for one, either.

At first glance, the inherent simplicity of garbage collection makes it seem like the obvious choice for managing dynamic memory. In fact, one might question why the manual method is used at all, especially by a language as sophisticated as C++. However, in the case of dynamic allocation, first impressions prove deceptive because both approaches involve a set of trade-offs. Which approach is most appropriate is decided by the application. The following sections describe some of the issues involved.

The Pros and Cons of Manual Memory Management

The main benefit of manually managing dynamic memory is efficiency. Because there is no garbage collector, no time is spent keeping track of active objects or periodically looking for unused memory. Instead, when the programmer knows that the allocated object is no longer needed, the programmer explicitly frees it and no additional overhead is incurred. Because it has none of the overhead associated with garbage collection, the manual approach enables more efficient code to be written This is one reason why it was necessary for C++ to support manual memory management: it enabled the creation of high-performance code.

Another advantage to the manual approach is control. Although requiring the programmer to handle both the allocation and release of memory is a burden, the benefit is that the programmer gains complete control over both halves of the process. You know precisely when memory is being allocated and precisely when it is being released. Furthermore, when you release an object via **delete**, its destructor is executed at that point rather than at some later time, as can be the case with garbage collection. Thus, with the manual method you can control precisely when an allocated object is destroyed.

Although it is efficient, manual memory management is susceptible to a rather annoying type of error: the memory leak. Because memory must be freed manually, it is possible (even easy) to forget to do so. Failing to release unused memory means that the memory will remain allocated even if it is no longer needed. Memory leaks cannot occur in a garbage collection environment because the garbage collector ensures that unused objects are eventually freed. Memory leaks are a particularly troublesome problem in Windows programming, where the failure to release unused resources slowly degrades performance.

Other problems that can occur with C++'s manual approach include the premature releasing of memory that is still in use, and the accidental freeing of the same memory twice. Both of these errors can lead to serious trouble. Unfortunately, they may not show any immediate symptoms, making them hard to find.

The Pros and Cons of Garbage Collection

There are several different ways to implement garbage collection, each offering different performance characteristics. However, all garbage collection systems share a set of common attributes that can be compared against the manual approach. The main advantages to garbage collection are simplicity and safety. In a garbage collection environment, you explicitly allocate memory via **new**, but you never explicitly free it. Instead, unused memory is automatically recycled. Thus, it is not possible to forget to release an object or to release an object prematurely. This simplifies programming and prevents an entire class of problems. Furthermore, it is not possible to accidentally free dynamically allocated memory twice. Thus, garbage collection provides an easy-to-use, error-free, reliable solution to the memory management problem.

Unfortunately, the simplicity and safety of garbage collection come at a price. The first cost is the overhead incurred by the garbage collection mechanism. All garbage collection schemes consume some CPU cycles because the reclamation of unused memory is not a cost-free process. This overhead does not occur with the manual approach.

A second cost is loss of control over when an object is destroyed. Unlike the manual approach, in which an object is destroyed (and its destructor called) at a known point in time—when a **delete** statement is executed on that object—garbage collection does not have such a hard and fast rule. Instead, when garbage collection is used, an object is not destroyed until the collector runs and recycles the object, which may not occur until some arbitrary time in the future. For example, the collector might not run until the amount of free memory drops below a certain point. Furthermore, it is not always possible to know the order in which objects will be destroyed by the garbage collector. In some cases, the inability to know precisely when an object is destroyed can cause trouble because it also means that your program can't know precisely when the destructor for a dynamically allocated object is called.

For garbage collection systems that run as a background task, this loss of control can escalate into a potentially more serious problem for some types of applications because it introduces what is essentially nondeterministic behavior into a program. A garbage collector that executes in the background reclaims unused memory at times that are, for all practical purposes, unknowable. For example, the collector will usually run only when free CPU time is available. Because this might vary from one program run to the next, from one computer to next, or from one operating system to the next, the precise point in program execution at which the garbage collector executes is effectively nondeterministic. This is not a problem for many programs, but it can cause havoc with real-time applications in which the unexpected allocation of CPU cycles to the garbage collector could cause an event to be missed.

You Can Have It Both Ways

As the preceding discussions explained, both manual management and garbage collection maximize one feature at the expense of another. The manual approach maximizes efficiency and control at the expense of safety and ease of use. Garbage collection maximizes simplicity and safety but pays for it with a loss of runtime performance and control. Thus, garbage collection and manual memory management are essentially opposites, each maximizing the traits that the other sacrifices. This is why neither approach to dynamic memory management can be optimal for all programming situations.

Although opposites, the two approaches are not mutually exclusive. They can coexist. Thus, it is possible for the C++ programmer to have access to both approaches, choosing the proper method for the task at hand. All one needs to do is create a garbage collector for C++, and this is the subject of the rest of this chapter.

Creating a Garbage Collector in C++

Because C++ is a rich and powerful language, there are many different ways to implement a garbage collector. One obvious, but limited, approach is to create a garbage collector base class, which is then inherited by classes that want to use garbage collection. This would enable you to implement garbage collection on a class-by-class basis. This solution is, unfortunately, too narrow to be satisfying.

A better solution is one in which the garbage collector can be used with any type of dynamically allocated object. To provide such a solution, the garbage collector must:

1. Coexist with the built-in, manual method provided by C++.
2. Not break any preexisting code. Moreover, it must have no impact whatsoever on existing code.
3. Work transparently so that allocations that use garbage collection are operated on in the same way as those that don't.
4. Allocate memory using **new** in the same way that C++'s built-in approach does.
5. Work with all data types, including the built-in types such as **int** and **double**.
6. Be simple to use.

In short, the garbage collection system must be able to dynamically allocate memory using a mechanism and syntax that closely resemble that already used by C++ and not affect existing code. At first thought, this might seem to be a daunting task, but it isn't.

Understanding the Problem

The key challenge that one faces when creating a garbage collector is how to know when a piece of memory is unused. To understand the problem, consider the following sequence:

```
int *p;

p = new int(99);

p = new int(100);
```

Here, two **int** objects are dynamically allocated. The first contains the value 99 and a pointer to this value is stored in **p**. Next, an integer containing the value 100 is allocated, and its address is also stored in **p**, thus overwriting the first address. At this point, the memory for **int(99)** is not pointed to by **p** (or any other object) and can be freed. The question is, how does the garbage collector know that neither **p** nor any other object points to **int(99)**?

Here is a slight variation on the problem:

```
int *p, *q;

p = new int(99);

q = p; // now, q points to same memory as p

p = new int(100);
```

In this case, **q** points to the memory that was originally allocated for **p**. Even though **p** is then pointed to a different piece of memory, the memory that it originally pointed to can't be freed because it is still in use by **q**. The question: how does the garbage collector know this fact? The precise way that these questions are answered is determined by the garbage collection algorithm employed.

Choosing a Garbage Collection Algorithm

Before implementing a garbage collector for C++, it is necessary to decide what garbage collection algorithm to use. The topic of garbage collection is a large one, having been the focus of serious academic study for many years. Because it presents an intriguing problem for which there is a variety of solutions, a number of different garbage collection algorithms have been designed. It is far beyond the scope of this book to examine each in detail. However, there are three archetypal approaches: *reference counting*, *mark and sweep*, and *copying*. Before choosing an approach, it will be useful to review these three algorithms.

Reference Counting

In reference counting, each dynamically allocated piece of memory has associated with it a reference count. This count is incremented each time a reference to the memory is added and decremented each time a reference to the memory is removed. In C++ terms, this means that each time a pointer is set to point to a piece of allocated memory, the reference count associated with that memory is incremented. When the pointer is set to point elsewhere, the reference count is decremented. When the reference count drops to zero, the memory is unused and can be released.

The main advantage of reference counting is simplicity—it is easy to understand and implement. Furthermore, it places no restrictions on the organization of the heap because the reference count is independent of an object's physical location. Reference counting adds overhead to each pointer operation, but the collection phase is relatively low cost. The main disadvantage is that circular references prevent memory that is otherwise unused from being released. A circular reference occurs when two objects point to each other, either directly or indirectly. In this situation, neither object's reference count ever drops to zero. Some solutions to the circular reference problem have been devised, but all add complexity and/or overhead.

Mark and Sweep

Mark and sweep involves two phases. In the first phase, all objects in the heap are set to their unmarked state. Then, all objects directly or indirectly accessible from program variables are marked as "in-use." In phase two, all of allocated memory is scanned (that is, a *sweep* of memory is made), and all unmarked elements are released.

There are two main advantages of mark and sweep. First, it easily handles circular references. Second, it adds virtually no runtime overhead prior to collection. It has two main disadvantages. First, a considerable amount of time might be spent collecting garbage because the entire heap must be scanned during collection. Thus, garbage collection may cause unacceptable runtime characteristics for some programs. Second, although mark and sweep is simple conceptually, it can be tricky to implement efficiently.

Copying

The copying algorithm organizes free memory into two spaces. One is active (holding the current heap), and the other is idle. During garbage collection, in-use objects from the active space are identified and copied into the idle space. Then, the roles of the two spaces are reversed, with the idle space becoming active and the active space becoming idle. Copying offers the advantage of compacting the heap in the copy process. It has the disadvantage of allowing only half of free memory to be in use at any one time.

Which Algorithm?

Given that there are advantages and disadvantages to all of the three classical approaches to garbage collection, it might seem hard to choose one over the other. However, given the constraints enumerated earlier, there is a clear choice: reference counting. First and most importantly, reference counting can be easily "layered onto" the existing C++ dynamic allocation system. Second, it can be implemented in a straightforward manner and in a way that does not affect preexisting code. Third, it does not require any specific organization or structuring of the heap, thus the standard allocation system provided by C++ is unaffected.

The one drawback to using reference counting is its difficulty in handling circular references. This isn't an issue for many programs because intentional circular references are not all that common and can usually be avoided. (Even things that we call *circular*, such as a circular queue, don't necessarily involve a circular pointer reference.) Of course, there are cases in which circular references are needed. It is also possible to create a circular reference without knowing you have done so, especially when working with third-party libraries. Therefore, the garbage collector must provide some means to gracefully handle a circular reference, should one exist.

To handle the circular reference problem, the garbage collector developed in this chapter will release any remaining allocated memory when the program exits. This ensures that objects involved in a circular reference will be freed and their destructors called. It is important to understand that normally there will be no allocated objects remaining at program termination. This mechanism is explicitly for those objects that can't be released because of a circular reference. (You might want to experiment with other means of handling the circular reference problem. It presents an interesting challenge.)

Implementing the Garbage Collector

To implement a reference counting garbage collector, there must be some way to keep track of the number of pointers that point to each piece of dynamically allocated memory. The trouble is that C++ has no built-in mechanism that enables one object to know when another object is pointing to it. Fortunately, there is a solution: you can create a new pointer type that supports garbage collection. This is the approach used by the garbage collector in this chapter.

To support garbage collection, the new pointer type must do three things. First, it must maintain a list of reference counts for active dynamically allocated objects. Second, it must keep track of all pointer operations, increasing an object's reference count each time a pointer is pointed to that object and decreasing the count each time a pointer is redirected to another object. Third, it must recycle those objects whose reference counts drop to zero. Aside from supporting garbage collection, the new pointer type will look and feel just like a normal pointer. For example, all pointer operations, such as * and –>, are supported.

In addition to being a convenient way to implement a garbage collector, the creation of a garbage collection pointer type satisfies the constraint that the original C++ dynamic allocation system must be unaffected. When garbage collection is desired, garbage collection-enabled pointers are used. When garbage collection is not desired, normal C++ pointers are available. Thus, both types of pointers can be used within the same program.

To Multithread or Not?

Another consideration when designing a garbage collector for C++ is whether it should be single-threaded or multithreaded. That is, should the garbage collector be designed as a background process, running in its own thread and collecting garbage as CPU time permits? Or, should the garbage collector run in the same thread as the process that uses it, collecting garbage when certain program conditions occur? Both approaches have advantages and disadvantages.

The main advantage to creating a multithreaded garbage collector is efficiency. Garbage can be collected when idle CPU cycles are available. The disadvantage is, of course, that C++ does not provide any built-in support for multithreading. This means that any multithreaded approach will depend upon operating system facilities to support the multitasking. This makes the code nonportable.

The main advantage to using a single-threaded garbage collector is portability. It can be used in situations that do not support multithreading or in cases in which the price of multithreading is too high. The main disadvantage is that the rest of the program stops when garbage collection takes place.

In this chapter, the single-threaded approach is used because it works in all C++ environments. Thus, it can be used by all readers of this book. However, for those readers wanting a multithreaded solution, one is given in Chapter 3, which deals with the techniques needed to successfully multithread a C++ program in a Windows environment.

When to Collect Garbage?

One final question that needs to be answered before a garbage collector can be implemented: When is garbage collected? This is less of an issue for a multithreaded garbage collector, which can run continuously as a background task, collecting garbage whenever CPU cycles are available, than it is for a single-threaded garbage collector, such as that developed in this chapter, which must stop the rest of the program to collect garbage.

In the real world, garbage collection usually takes place only when there is sufficient reason to do so, such as the case of memory running low. This makes sense for two reasons. First, with some garbage collection algorithms, such as mark and sweep, there is no way to know that a piece of memory is unused without actually performing the collection. (That is, sometimes there is no way to know that there is garbage to be collected without actually collecting it!) Second, collecting garbage is a time-consuming process which should not be performed needlessly.

However, waiting for memory to run low before initiating garbage collection is not suitable for the purposes of this chapter because it makes it next to impossible to demonstrate the collector. Instead, the garbage collector developed in this chapter will collect garbage more frequently so that its actions can easily be observed. As the collector is coded, garbage is collected whenever a pointer goes out of scope. Of course, this behavior can easily be changed to fit your applications.

One last point: when using reference-count based garbage collection, it is technically possible to recycle unused memory as soon as its reference count drops to zero, rather than using a separate garbage collection phase. However, this approach adds overhead to every pointer operation. The method used by this chapter is to simply decrement the memory's reference count each time a pointer to that memory is redirected and let the collection process handle the actual recycling of memory at more convenient times. This reduces the runtime overhead associated with pointer operations, which one typically wants to be as fast as possible.

What About auto_ptr?

As many readers will know, C++ defines a library class called **auto_ptr**. Because an **auto_ptr** automatically frees the memory to which it points when it goes out of scope, you might think that it would be of use when developing a garbage collector, perhaps forming the foundation. This is not the case, however. The **auto_ptr** class is designed for a concept that the ISO C++ Standard calls "strict ownership," in which an **auto_ptr** "owns" the object to which it points. This ownership can be transferred to another **auto_ptr**, but in all cases some **auto_ptr** will own the object until it is destroyed. Furthermore, an **auto_ptr** is assigned an address of an object only when it is initialized. After that, you can't change the memory to which an **auto_ptr** points, except by assigning one **auto_ptr** to another. Because of **auto_ptr**'s "strict ownership" feature, it is not particularly useful when creating a garbage collector, and it is not used by the garbage collectors in this book.

A Simple C++ Garbage Collector

The entire garbage collector is shown here. As explained, the garbage collector works by creating a new pointer type that provides built-in support for garbage collection based on reference counting. The garbage collector is single-threaded, which means that it is quite portable and does not rely upon (or make assumptions about) the execution environment. This code should be stored in a file called **gc.h**.

There are two things to notice as you look through the code. First, most of the member functions are quite short and are defined inside their respective classes in the interest of efficiency. Recall that a function defined within its class is automatically in-lined, which eliminates the overhead of a function call. Only a few functions are long enough to require their definition to be outside their class.

Secondly, notice the comment near the top of the file. If you want to watch the action of the garbage collector, simply turn on the display option by defining the macro called **DISPLAY**. For normal use, leave **DISPLAY** undefined.

```cpp
// A single-threaded garbage collector.

#include <iostream>
#include <list>
#include <typeinfo>
#include <cstdlib>

using namespace std;

// To watch the action of the garbage collector, define DISPLAY.
// #define DISPLAY

// Exception thrown when an attempt is made to
// use an Iter that exceeds the range of the
// underlying object.
//
class OutOfRangeExc {
  // Add functionality if needed by your application.
};

// An iterator-like class for cycling through arrays
// that are pointed to by GCPtrs. Iter pointers
// ** do not ** participate in or affect garbage
// collection.  Thus, an Iter pointing to
// some object does not prevent that object
// from being recycled.
//
template <class T> class Iter {
  T *ptr;   // current pointer value
  T *end;   // points to element one past end
```

```cpp
    T *begin; // points to start of allocated array
    unsigned length; // length of sequence
public:

  Iter() {
    ptr = end = begin = NULL;
    length = 0;
  }

  Iter(T *p, T *first, T *last) {
    ptr =  p;
    end = last;
    begin = first;
    length = last - first;
  }

  // Return length of sequence to which this
  // Iter points.
  unsigned size() { return length; }

  // Return value pointed to by ptr.
  // Do not allow out-of-bounds access.
  T &operator*() {
    if( (ptr >= end) || (ptr < begin) )
      throw OutOfRangeExc();
    return *ptr;
  }

  // Return address contained in ptr.
  // Do not allow out-of-bounds access.
  T *operator->() {
    if( (ptr >= end) || (ptr < begin) )
      throw OutOfRangeExc();
    return ptr;
  }

  // Prefix ++.
  Iter operator++() {
    ptr++;
    return *this;
  }

  // Prefix --.
  Iter operator--() {
    ptr--;
    return *this;
```

```
  }

  // Postfix ++.
  Iter operator++(int notused) {
    T *tmp = ptr;

    ptr++;
    return Iter<T>(tmp, begin, end);
  }

  // Postfix --.
  Iter operator--(int notused) {
    T *tmp = ptr;

    ptr--;
    return Iter<T>(tmp, begin, end);
  }

  // Return a reference to the object at the
  // specified index. Do not allow out-of-bounds
  // access.
  T &operator[](int i) {
    if( (i < 0) || (i >= (end-begin)) )
      throw OutOfRangeExc();
    return ptr[i];
  }

  // Define the relational operators.
  bool operator==(Iter op2) {
    return ptr == op2.ptr;
  }

  bool operator!=(Iter op2) {
    return ptr != op2.ptr;
  }

  bool operator<(Iter op2) {
    return ptr < op2.ptr;
  }

  bool operator<=(Iter op2) {
    return ptr <= op2.ptr;
  }

  bool operator>(Iter op2) {
    return ptr > op2.ptr;
```

```
  }

  bool operator>=(Iter op2) {
    return ptr >= op2.ptr;
  }

  // Subtract an integer from an Iter.
  Iter operator-(int n) {
    ptr -= n;
    return *this;
  }

  // Add an integer to an Iter.
  Iter operator+(int n) {
    ptr += n;
    return *this;
  }

  // Return number of elements between two Iters.
  int operator-(Iter<T> &itr2) {
    return ptr - itr2.ptr;
  }

};


// This class defines an element that is stored
// in the garbage collection information list.
//
template <class T> class GCInfo {
public:
  unsigned refcount; // current reference count

  T *memPtr; // pointer to allocated memory

  /* isArray is true if memPtr points
     to an allocated array. It is false
     otherwise. */
  bool isArray; // true if pointing to array

  /* If memPtr is pointing to an allocated
     array, then arraySize contains its size */
  unsigned arraySize; // size of array

  // Here, mPtr points to the allocated memory.
  // If this is an array, then size specifies
```

```
    // the size of the array.
    GCInfo(T *mPtr, unsigned size=0) {
      refcount = 1;
      memPtr = mPtr;
      if(size != 0)
        isArray = true;
      else
        isArray = false;

      arraySize = size;
    }
};

// Overloading operator== allows GCInfos to be compared.
// This is needed by the STL list class.
template <class T> bool operator==(const GCInfo<T> &ob1,
               const GCInfo<T> &ob2) {
  return (ob1.memPtr == ob2.memPtr);
}



// GCPtr implements a pointer type that uses
// garbage collection to release unused memory.
// A GCPtr must only be used to point to memory
// that was dynamically allocated using new.
// When used to refer to an allocated array,
// specify the array size.
//
template <class T, int size=0> class GCPtr {

  // gclist maintains the garbage collection list.
  static list<GCInfo<T> > gclist;

  // addr points to the allocated memory to which
  // this GCPtr pointer currently points.
  T *addr;

  /* isArray is true if this GCPtr points
     to an allocated array. It is false
     otherwise. */
  bool isArray; // true if pointing to array

  // If this GCPtr is pointing to an allocated
  // array, then arraySize contains its size.
  unsigned arraySize; // size of the array
```

```cpp
  static bool first; // true when first GCPtr is created

  // Return an iterator to pointer info in gclist.
  typename list<GCInfo<T> >::iterator findPtrInfo(T *ptr);

public:

  // Define an iterator type for GCPtr<T>.
  typedef Iter<T> GCiterator;

  // Construct both initialized and uninitialized objects.
  GCPtr(T *t=NULL) {

    // Register shutdown() as an exit function.
    if(first) atexit(shutdown);
    first = false;

    list<GCInfo<T> >::iterator p;

    p = findPtrInfo(t);

    // If t is already in gclist, then
    // increment its reference count.
    // Otherwise, add it to the list.
    if(p != gclist.end())
      p->refcount++; // increment ref count
    else {
      // Create and store this entry.
      GCInfo<T> gcObj(t, size);
      gclist.push_front(gcObj);
    }

    addr = t;
    arraySize = size;
    if(size > 0) isArray = true;
    else isArray = false;
#ifdef DISPLAY
      cout << "Constructing GCPtr. ";
      if(isArray)
        cout << " Size is " << arraySize << endl;
      else
        cout << endl;
#endif
  }
```

```cpp
// Copy constructor.
GCPtr(const GCPtr &ob) {
  list<GCInfo<T> >::iterator p;

  p = findPtrInfo(ob.addr);
  p->refcount++; // increment ref count

  addr = ob.addr;
  arraySize = ob.arraySize;
  if(arraySize > 0) isArray = true;
  else isArray = false;
  #ifdef DISPLAY
    cout << "Constructing copy.";
    if(isArray)
      cout << " Size is " << arraySize << endl;
    else
      cout << endl;
  #endif
}

// Destructor for GCPTr.
~GCPtr();

// Collect garbage.  Returns true if at least
// one object was freed.
static bool collect();

// Overload assignment of pointer to GCPtr.
T *operator=(T *t);

// Overload assignment of GCPtr to GCPtr.
GCPtr &operator=(GCPtr &rv);

// Return a reference to the object pointed
// to by this GCPtr.
T &operator*() {
  return *addr;
}

// Return the address being pointed to.
T *operator->() { return addr; }

// Return a reference to the object at the
// index specified by i.
T &operator[](int i) {
```

```
    return addr[i];
  }

  // Conversion function to T *.
  operator T *() { return addr; }

  // Return an Iter to the start of the allocated memory.
  Iter<T> begin() {
    int size;

    if(isArray) size = arraySize;
    else size = 1;

    return Iter<T>(addr, addr, addr + size);
  }

  // Return an Iter to one past the end of an allocated array.
  Iter<T> end() {
    int size;

    if(isArray) size = arraySize;
    else size = 1;

    return Iter<T>(addr + size, addr, addr + size);
  }

  // Return the size of gclist for this type
  // of GCPtr.
  static int gclistSize() { return gclist.size(); }

  // A utility function that displays gclist.
  static void showlist();

  // Clear gclist when program exits.
  static void shutdown();
};

// Creates storage for the static variables
template <class T, int size>
  list<GCInfo<T> > GCPtr<T, size>::gclist;

template <class T, int size>
  bool GCPtr<T, size>::first = true;

// Destructor for GCPtr.
```

```
template <class T, int size>
GCPtr<T, size>::~GCPtr() {
  list<GCInfo<T> >::iterator p;

  p = findPtrInfo(addr);
  if(p->refcount) p->refcount--; // decrement ref count

  #ifdef DISPLAY
    cout << "GCPtr going out of scope.\n";
  #endif

  // Collect garbage when a pointer goes out of scope.
  collect();

  // For real use, you might want to collect
  // unused memory less frequently, such as after
  // gclist has reached a certain size, after a
  // certain number of GCPtrs have gone out of scope,
  // or when memory is low.
}

// Collect garbage. Returns true if at least
// one object was freed.
template <class T, int size>
bool GCPtr<T, size>::collect() {
  bool memfreed = false;

  #ifdef DISPLAY
    cout << "Before garbage collection for ";
    showlist();
  #endif

  list<GCInfo<T> >::iterator p;
  do {

    // Scan gclist looking for unreferenced pointers.
    for(p = gclist.begin(); p != gclist.end(); p++) {
      // If in-use, skip.
      if(p->refcount > 0) continue;

      memfreed = true;

      // Remove unused entry from gclist.
      gclist.remove(*p);
```

```cpp
        // Free memory unless the GCPtr is null.
        if(p->memPtr) {
          if(p->isArray) {
            #ifdef DISPLAY
              cout << "Deleting array of size "
                   << p->arraySize << endl;
            #endif
            delete[] p->memPtr; // delete array
          }
          else {
            #ifdef DISPLAY
              cout << "Deleting: "
                   << *(T *) p->memPtr << "\n";
            #endif
            delete p->memPtr; // delete single element
          }
        }

        // Restart the search.
        break;
      }

  } while(p != gclist.end());

  #ifdef DISPLAY
    cout << "After garbage collection for ";
    showlist();
  #endif

  return memfreed;
}

// Overload assignment of pointer to GCPtr.
template <class T, int size>
T * GCPtr<T, size>::operator=(T *t) {
  list<GCInfo<T> >::iterator p;

  // First, decrement the reference count
  // for the memory currently being pointed to.
  p = findPtrInfo(addr);
  p->refcount--;

  // Next, if the new address is already
  // existent in the system, increment its
  // count.  Otherwise, create a new entry
```

```
      // for gclist.
      p = findPtrInfo(t);
      if(p != gclist.end())
        p->refcount++;
      else {
        // Create and store this entry.
        GCInfo<T> gcObj(t, size);
        gclist.push_front(gcObj);
      }

      addr = t; // store the address.

      return t;
    }

    // Overload assignment of GCPtr to GCPtr.
    template <class T, int size>
    GCPtr<T, size> & GCPtr<T, size>::operator=(GCPtr &rv) {
      list<GCInfo<T> >::iterator p;

      // First, decrement the reference count
      // for the memory currently being pointed to.
      p = findPtrInfo(addr);
      p->refcount--;

      // Next, increment the reference count of
      // the new address.
      p = findPtrInfo(rv.addr);
      p->refcount++; // increment ref count

      addr = rv.addr;// store the address.

      return rv;
    }

    // A utility function that displays gclist.
    template <class T, int size>
    void GCPtr<T, size>::showlist() {
      list<GCInfo<T> >::iterator p;

      cout << "gclist<" << typeid(T).name() << ", "
           << size << ">:\n";
      cout << "memPtr      refcount      value\n";

      if(gclist.begin() == gclist.end()) {
```

```
    cout << "              -- Empty --\n\n";
    return;
  }

  for(p = gclist.begin(); p != gclist.end(); p++) {
    cout <<  "[" << (void *)p->memPtr << "]"
        << "        " << p->refcount << "        ";
    if(p->memPtr) cout << "    " << *p->memPtr;
    else cout << "    ---";
    cout << endl;
  }
  cout << endl;
}

// Find a pointer in gclist.
template <class T, int size>
typename list<GCInfo<T> >::iterator
  GCPtr<T, size>::findPtrInfo(T *ptr) {

  list<GCInfo<T> >::iterator p;

  // Find ptr in gclist.
  for(p = gclist.begin(); p != gclist.end(); p++)
    if(p->memPtr == ptr)
      return p;

  return p;
}

// Clear gclist when program exits.
template <class T, int size>
void GCPtr<T, size>::shutdown() {

  if(gclistSize() == 0) return; // list is empty

  list<GCInfo<T> >::iterator p;

  for(p = gclist.begin(); p != gclist.end(); p++) {
    // Set all reference counts to zero
    p->refcount = 0;
  }

  #ifdef DISPLAY
    cout << "Before collecting for shutdown() for "
         << typeid(T).name() << "\n";
```

```
   #endif

   collect();

   #ifdef DISPLAY
     cout << "After collecting for shutdown() for "
          << typeid(T).name() << "\n";
   #endif
}
```

An Overview of the Garbage Collector Classes

The garbage collector uses four classes: **GCPtr**, **GCInfo**, **Iter**, and **OutOfRangeExc**. Before examining the code in detail, it will be helpful to understand the role each class plays.

GCPtr

At the core of the garbage collector is the class **GCPtr**, which implements a garbage-collection pointer. **GCPtr** maintains a list that associates a reference count with each piece of memory allocated for use by a **GCPtr**. In general, here is how it works. Each time a **GCPtr** is pointed at a piece of memory, the reference count for that memory is incremented. If the **GCPtr** was previously pointing at a different piece of memory prior to the assignment, the reference count for that memory is decremented. Thus, adding a pointer to a piece of memory increases the memory's reference count. Removing a pointer decreases the memory's reference count. Each time a **GCPtr** goes out of scope, the reference count associated with the memory to which it currently points is decremented. When a reference count drops to zero, that piece of memory can be released.

    GCPtr is a template class that overloads the * and –> pointer operators and the array indexing operator [ ]. Thus, **GCPtr** creates a new pointer type and integrates it into the C++ programming environment. This allows a **GCPtr** to be used in much the same way that you use a normal C++ pointer. However, for reasons that will be made clear later in this chapter, **GCPtr** does not overload the ++, – –, or the other arithmetic operations defined for pointers. Thus, except through assignment, you cannot change the address to which a **GCPtr** object points. This may seems like a significant restriction, but it isn't because the **Iter** class provides these operations.

    For the sake of illustration, the garbage collector runs whenever a **GCPtr** object goes out of scope. At that time, the garbage collection list is scanned and all memory with a reference count of zero is released, even if it was not originally associated with the **GCPtr** that went out of scope. Your program can also explicitly request garbage collection if you need to recycle memory earlier.

GCInfo

As explained, **GCPtr** maintains a list that links reference counts with allocated memory. Each entry in this list is encapsulated in an object of type **GCInfo**. **GCInfo** stores the reference count in its **refcount** field and a pointer to the memory in its **memPtr** field. Thus, a **GCInfo** object binds a reference count to a piece of allocated memory.

GCInfo defines two other fields: **isArray** and **arraySize**. If **memPtr** points to an allocated array, then its **isArray** member will be **true** and the length of the array will be stored in its **arraySize** field.

The Iter Class

As explained, a **GCPtr** object allows you to access the memory to which it points by using the normal pointer operators * and –>, but it does not support pointer arithmetic. To handle situations in which you need to perform pointer arithmetic, you will use an object of type **Iter**. Iter is a template class similar in function to an STL iterator, and it defines all pointer operations, including pointer arithmetic. The main use of **Iter** is to enable you to cycle through the elements of a dynamically allocated array. It also provides bounds checking. You obtain an **Iter** from **GCPtr** by calling either **begin( )** or **end( )**, which work much like their equivalents in the STL.

It is important to understand that although **Iter** and the STL **iterator** type are similar, they are not the same, and you cannot use one in place of the other.

OutOfRangeExc

If an **Iter** encounters an attempt to access memory outside the range of the allocated memory, an **OutOfRangeExc** exception is thrown. For the purposes of this chapter, **OutOfRangeExc** contains no members. It is simply a type that can be thrown. However, you are free to add functionality to this class as your own applications dictate.

GCPtr In Detail

GCPtr is the heart of the garbage collector. It implements a new pointer type that keeps a reference count for objects allocated on the heap. It also provides the garbage collection functionality that recycles unused memory.

GCptr is a template class with this declaration:

```
template <class T, int size=0> class GCPtr {
```

GCPtr requires that you specify the type of the data that will be pointed to, which will be substituted for the generic type **T**. If an array is being allocated, you must specify the size of the array in the **size** parameter. Otherwise, **size** defaults to zero, which indicates that a single object is being pointed to. Here are two examples.

```
GCPtr<int> p; // declare a pointer to a single integer
GCPtr<int, 5> ap; // declare a pointer to an array of 5 integers
```

Here, **p** can point to single objects of type **int**, and **ap** can point to an array of 5 **int**s.

In the preceding examples, notice that you do not use the * operator when specifying the name of the **GCPtr** object. That is, to create a **GCPtr** to **int**, you *do not* use a statement like this:

```
GCPtr<int> *p; // this creates a pointer to a GCPtr<int> object
```

This declaration creates a normal C++ pointer called **p** that can point to a **GCPtr<int>** object. It does not create a **GCPtr** object that can point to **int**. Remember, **GCPtr** defines a pointer type by itself.

Be careful when specifying the type parameter to **GCPtr**. It specifies the type of the object to which the **GCPtr** object can point. Therefore, if you write a declaration like this:

```
GCPtr<int *> p; // this creates a GCPtr to pointers to ints
```

you are creating a **GCPtr** object that points to **int *** pointers, not a **GCPtr** to **int**s.

Because of its importance, each member of **GCPtr** is examined in detail in the following sections.

GCPtr Data Members

GCPtr declares the following data members:

```
// gclist maintains the garbage collection list.
static list<GCInfo<T> > gclist;

// addr points to the allocated memory to which
// this GCPtr pointer currently points.
T *addr;

/* isArray is true if this GCPtr points
   to an allocated array. It is false
   otherwise. */
bool isArray; // true if pointing to array

// If this GCPtr is pointing to an allocated
// array, then arraySize contains its size.
unsigned arraySize; // size of the array

static bool first; // true when first GCPtr is created
```

The **gclist** field contains a list of **GCInfo** objects. (Recall that **GCInfo** links a reference count with a piece of allocated memory.) This list is used by the garbage collector to determine when allocated memory is unused. Notice that **gclist** is a **static** member of **GCPtr**. This means that for each specific pointer type, there is only one **gclist**. For example, all pointers of type **GCPtr<int>** share one list, and all pointers of type **GCPtr<double>** share a different list. **gclist** is an instance of the STL **list** class. Using the STL substantially simplifies the code for **GCPtr** because there is no need for it to create its own set of list-handling functions.

GCPtr stores the address of the memory to which it points in **addr**. If **addr** points to an allocated array, then **isArray** will be **true**, and the length of the array will be stored in **arraySize**.

The **first** field is a **static** variable that is initially set to **true**. It is a flag that the **GCPtr** constructor uses to know when the first **GCPtr** object is created. After the first **GCPtr** object is constructed, **first** is set to false. It is used to register a termination function that will be called to shut down the garbage collector when the program ends.

The findPtrInfo( ) Function

GCPtr declares one private function: **findPtrInfo( )**. This function searches **gclist** for a specified address and returns an iterator to its entry. If the address is not found, an iterator to the end of **gclist** is returned. This function is used internally by **GCPtr** to update the reference counts of the objects in **gclist**. It is implemented as shown here:

```
// Find a pointer in gclist.
template <class T, int size>
typename list<GCInfo<T> >::iterator
  GCPtr<T, size>::findPtrInfo(T *ptr) {

  list<GCInfo<T> >::iterator p;

  // Find ptr in gclist.
  for(p = gclist.begin(); p != gclist.end(); p++)
    if(p->memPtr == ptr)
      return p;

  return p;
}
```

The GCIterator typedef

At the start of the public section of **GCPtr** is the **typedef** of **Iter<T>** to **GCiterator**. This **typedef** is bound to each instance of **GCPtr**, thus eliminating the need to specify the type parameter each time an **Iter** is needed for a specific version of **GCPtr**. This simplifies the declaration of an iterator. For example, to obtain an iterator to the memory pointed to by a specific **GCPtr**, you can use a statement like this:

```
GCPtr<int>::GCiterator itr;
```

The GCPtr Constructor

The constructor for **GCPtr** is shown here:

```
// Construct both initialized and uninitialized objects.
GCPtr(T *t=NULL) {

  // Register shutdown() as an exit function.
  if(first) atexit(shutdown);
  first = false;
```

```
   list<GCInfo<T> >::iterator p;

   p = findPtrInfo(t);

   // If t is already in gclist, then
   // increment its reference count.
   // Otherwise, add it to the list.
   if(p != gclist.end())
     p->refcount++; // increment ref count
   else {
     // Create and store this entry.
     GCInfo<T> gcObj(t, size);
     gclist.push_front(gcObj);
   }

   addr = t;
   arraySize = size;
   if(size > 0) isArray = true;
   else isArray = false;
#ifdef DISPLAY
     cout << "Constructing GCPtr. ";
     if(isArray)
       cout << " Size is " << arraySize << endl;
     else
       cout << endl;
#endif
}
```

GCPtr( ) allows both initialized and uninitialized instances to be created. If an initialized instance is declared, then the memory to which this **GCPtr** will point is passed through **t**. Otherwise, **t** will be null. Let's examine the operation of **GCPtr( )** in detail.

First, if **first** is true, it means that this is the first **GCPtr** object to be created. If this is the case, then **shutdown( )** is registered as a termination function by calling **atexit( )**. The **atexit( )** function is part of the standard C++ function library, and it registers a function that will be called when a program terminates. In this case, **shutdown( )** releases any memory that was prevented from being released because of a circular reference.

Next, a search of **gclist** is made, looking for any preexisting entry that matches the address in **t**. If one is found, then its reference count is incremented. If no preexising entry matches **t**, a new **GCInfo** object is created that contains this address, and this object is added to **gclist**.

GCPtr( ) then sets **addr** to the address specified by **t** and sets the values of **isArray** and **arraySize** appropriately. Remember, if you are allocating an array, you must explicitly specify the size of the array when you declare the **GCPtr** pointer that will point to it. If you don't, the memory won't be released correctly, and, in the case of an array of class objects, the destructors won't be called properly.

The GCPtr Destructor

The destructor for **GCPtr** is shown here:

```
// Destructor for GCPtr.
template <class T, int size>
GCPtr<T, size>::~GCPtr() {
  list<GCInfo<T> >::iterator p;

  p = findPtrInfo(addr);
  if(p->refcount) p->refcount--; // decrement ref count

  #ifdef DISPLAY
    cout << "GCPtr going out of scope.\n";
  #endif

  // Collect garbage when a pointer goes out of scope.
  collect();

  // For real use, you might want to collect
  // unused memory less frequently, such as after
  // gclist has reached a certain size, after a
  // certain number of GCPtrs have gone out of scope,
  // or when memory is low.
}
```

Garbage collection takes place each time a **GCPtr** goes out of scope. This is handled by ~**GCPtr( )**. First, a search of **gclist** is made, looking for the entry that corresponds to the address pointed to by the **GCPtr** being destroyed. Once found, its **refcount** field is decremented. Next, ~**GCptr( )** calls **collect( )** to release any unused memory (that is, memory whose reference count is zero).

As the comment at the end of ~**GCPtr( )** states, for real applications, it is probably better to collect garbage less often than each time a single **GCPtr** goes out of scope. Collecting less frequently will usually be more efficient. As explained earlier, collecting each time a **GCPtr** is destroyed is useful for demonstrating the garbage collector because it clearly illustrates the garbage collector's operation.

Collect Garbage with collect( )

The **collect( )** function is where garbage collection takes place. It is shown here:

```
// Collect garbage.  Returns true if at least
// one object was freed.
template <class T, int size>
bool GCPtr<T, size>::collect() {
```

```
    bool memfreed = false;

#ifdef DISPLAY
    cout << "Before garbage collection for ";
    showlist();
#endif

    list<GCInfo<T> >::iterator p;
    do {

        // Scan gclist looking for unreferenced pointers.
        for(p = gclist.begin(); p != gclist.end(); p++) {
            // If in-use, skip.
            if(p->refcount > 0) continue;

            memfreed = true;

            // Remove unused entry from gclist.
            gclist.remove(*p);

            // Free memory unless the GCPtr is null.
            if(p->memPtr) {
                if(p->isArray) {
                    #ifdef DISPLAY
                        cout << "Deleting array of size "
                             << p->arraySize << endl;
                    #endif
                    delete[] p->memPtr; // delete array
                }
                else {
                    #ifdef DISPLAY
                        cout << "Deleting: "
                             << *(T *) p->memPtr << "\n";
                    #endif
                    delete p->memPtr; // delete single element
                }
            }

            // Restart the search.
            break;
        }

    } while(p != gclist.end());

#ifdef DISPLAY
```

```
   cout << "After garbage collection for ";
   showlist();
#endif

  return memfreed;
}
```

The **collect( )** function works by scanning the contents of **gclist**, looking for entries that have a **refcount** of zero. When such an entry is found, it is removed from **gclist** by calling the **remove( )** function, which is a member of the STL **list** class. Then the memory associated with that entry is freed.

Recall that in C++, single objects are freed by **delete**, but arrays of objects are freed via **delete[ ]**. Thus, the value of the entry's **isArray** field determines whether **delete** or **delete[ ]** is used to free the memory. This is one reason you must specify the size of an allocated array for any **GCPtr** that will point to one: it causes **isArray** to be set to **true**. If **isArray** is not set correctly, it is impossible to properly release the allocated memory.

Although the point of garbage collection is to recycle unused memory automatically, you can take a measure of manual control if necessary. The **collect( )** function can be called directly by user code to request that garbage collection take place. Notice that it is declared as a **static** function within **GCPtr**. This means that it can be invoked without reference to any object. For example:

```
GCPtr<int>::collect(); // collect all unused int pointers
```

This causes **gclist<int>** to be collected. Because there is a different **gclist** for each type of pointer, you will need to call **collect( )** for each list that you want to collect. Frankly, if you need to closely manage the release of dynamically allocated objects, you are better off using the manual allocation system provided by C++. Directly calling **collect( )** is best reserved for specialized situations, such as when free memory is running unexpectedly low.

The Overloaded Assignment Operators

GCPtr overloads **operator=( )** twice: once for the assignment of a new address to a **GCPtr** pointer, and once for the assignment of one **GCPtr** pointer to another. Both versions are shown here:

```
// Overload assignment of pointer to GCPtr.
template <class T, int size>
T * GCPtr<T, size>::operator=(T *t) {
  list<GCInfo<T> >::iterator p;

  // First, decrement the reference count
  // for the memory currently being pointed to.
  p = findPtrInfo(addr);
  p->refcount--;
```

```
      // Next, if the new address is already
      // existent in the system, increment its
      // count.  Otherwise, create a new entry
      // for gclist.
      p = findPtrInfo(t);
      if(p != gclist.end())
        p->refcount++;
      else {
        // Create and store this entry.
        GCInfo<T> gcObj(t, size);
        gclist.push_front(gcObj);
      }

      addr = t; // store the address.

      return t;
}


// Overload assignment of GCPtr to GCPtr.
template <class T, int size>
GCPtr<T, size> & GCPtr<T, size>::operator=(GCPtr &rv) {
    list<GCInfo<T> >::iterator p;

    // First, decrement the reference count
    // for the memory currently being pointed to.
    p = findPtrInfo(addr);
    p->refcount--;

    // Next, increment the reference count of
    // the new address.
    p = findPtrInfo(rv.addr);
    p->refcount++; // increment ref count

    addr = rv.addr;// store the address.

    return rv;
}
```

The first overload of **operator=( )** handles assignments in which a **GCPtr** pointer is on the left and an address is on the right. For example, it handles cases like the one shown here:

```
GCPtr<int> p;
// ...
p = new int(18);
```

Here, the address returned by **new** is assigned to **p**. When this happens, **operator=(T *t)** is called with the new address passed to **t**. First, the entry in **gclist** for the memory that is currently being pointed to is found, and its reference count is decremented. Next, a search of **gclist** is made for the new address. If it is found, its reference count is incremented. Otherwise, a new **GCInfo** object is created for the new address, and this object is added to **gclist**. Finally, the new address is stored in the invoking object's **addr**, and this address is returned.

The second overload of the assignment operator, **operator=(GCPtr &rv)**, handles the following type of assignment:

```
GCPtr<int> p;
GCPtr<int> q;
// ...
p = new int(88);
q = p;
```

Here, both **p** and **q** are **GCPtr** pointers, and **p** is assigned to **q**. This version of the assignment operator works much like the other. First, the entry in **gclist** for the memory that is currently being pointed to is found, and its reference count is decremented. Next, a search of **gclist** is made for the new address, which is contained in **rv.addr**, and its reference count is incremented. Then the invoking object's **addr** field is set to the address contained in **rv.addr**. Finally, the right-hand object is returned. This allows a chain of assignments to take place, such as:

```
p = q = w = z;
```

There is one other important point to make about the way that the assignment operators work. As mentioned earlier in this chapter, it is technically possible to recycle memory as soon as its reference count drops to zero, but doing so puts an extra overhead on each pointer operation. This is why, in the overloaded assignment operators, the reference count for the memory previously pointed to by the left-hand operand is simply decremented, and no further action is taken. Thus, the management overhead associated with actually releasing memory and performing maintenance on **gclist** is avoided. These actions are deferred to later, when the garbage collector runs. This approach makes for faster runtimes for the code that uses a **GCPtr**. It also lets garbage collection take place at times that are (potentially) more convenient in terms of runtime performance.

The GCPtr Copy Constructor

Because of the need to keep track of each pointer to allocated memory, the default copy constructor (which makes a bitwise identical copy) cannot be used. Instead, **GCPtr** must define is own copy constructor, which is shown here:

```
// Copy constructor.
GCPtr(const GCPtr &ob) {
  list<GCInfo<T> >::iterator p;

  p = findPtrInfo(ob.addr);
```

```
      p->refcount++; // increment ref count

  addr = ob.addr;
  arraySize = ob.arraySize;
  if(arraySize > 0) isArray = true;
  else isArray = false;
  #ifdef DISPLAY
    cout << "Constructing copy.";
    if(isArray)
      cout << " Size is " << arraySize << endl;
    else
      cout << endl;
  #endif
}
```

Recall that a class' copy constructor is invoked when a copy of an object is required, such as when an object is passed as an argument to a function, when an object is returned from a function, or when one object is used to initialize another. **GCPtr**'s copy constructor duplicates the information contained in the original object. It also increments the reference count associated with the memory pointed to by the original object. When the copy goes out of scope, this reference count will be decremented.

Actually, the extra work performed by the copy constructor is not usually necessary because the overloaded assignment operators properly maintain the garbage collection list in most cases. However, there are a small number of cases in which the copy constructor is needed, such as when memory is allocated inside a function and a **GCPtr** to that memory is returned.

The Pointer Operators and Conversion Function

Because **GCPtr** is a pointer type, it must overload the pointer operators * and –>, plus the indexing operator [ ]. This is done by the functions shown here. Given that it is the ability to overload these operators that makes it possible to create a new pointer type, it is amazing how simple they are.

```
// Return a reference to the object pointed
// to by this GCPtr.
T &operator*() {
  return *addr;
}


// Return the address being pointed to.
T *operator->() { return addr; }


// Return a reference to the object at the
// index specified by i.
T &operator[](int i) {
  return addr[i];
}
```

The **operator*( )** function returns a reference to the object pointed to by the **addr** field of the invoking **GCPtr, operator–>( )** returns the address contained in **addr**, and **operator[ ]** returns a reference to the element specified by the index. **operator[ ]** should be used only on **GCPtrs** that point to allocated arrays.

As mentioned earlier, no pointer arithmetic is supported. For example, neither the **++** nor the **– –** operator is overloaded for **GCPtr**. The reason is that the garbage collection mechanism assumes that a **GCPtr** is pointing to *the start of* allocated memory. If a **GCPtr** could be incremented, for example, then when that pointer was garbage collected, the address used with **delete** would be invalid.

You have two options if you need to perform operations that involve pointer arithmetic. First, if the **GCPtr** is pointing to an allocated array, you can create an **Iter** that will let you cycle through that array. This approach is described later. Second, you can convert a **GCPtr** into a normal pointer by use of the **T *** conversion function defined by **GCPtr**. This function is shown here:

```
// Conversion function to T *.
operator T*() { return addr; }
```

This function returns a normal pointer that points to the address stored in **addr**. It can be used like this.

```
GCPtr<double> gcp = new double(99.2);
double *p;


p = gcp; // now, p points to same memory as gcp
p++; // because p is a normal pointer, it can be incremented
```

In the preceding example, because **p** is a normal pointer, it can be manipulated in any way that any other pointer can. Of course, whether such manipulations yield meaningful results is dependent upon your application.

The main advantage of the conversion to **T *** is that it lets you use **GCPtrs** in place of normal C++ pointers when working with preexisting code that requires such pointers. For example, consider this sequence:

```
GCPtr<char> str = new char[80];
strcpy(str, "this is a test");
cout << str << endl;
```

Here, **str** is a **GCPtr** pointer to **char** that is used in a call to **strcpy( )**. Because **strcpy( )** is expecting its arguments to be of type **char ***, the conversion to **T *** inside **GCPtr** is automatically invoked because, in this case, **T** is **char**. The same conversion is automatically invoked when **str** is used in the **cout** statement. Thus, the conversion function enables **GCPtrs** to seamlessly integrate with existing C++ functions and classes.

Keep in mind that the **T *** pointer returned by this conversion does not participate in or affect garbage collection. Thus, it is possible for the allocated memory to be freed even if a regular C++ pointer is still pointing to it. So, use the conversion to **T *** wisely—and infrequently.

The begin( ) and end( ) Functions

The **begin( )** and **end( )** functions, shown next, are similar to their counterparts in the STL:

```
// Return an Iter to the start of the allocated memory.
Iter<T> begin() {
  int size;

  if(isArray) size = arraySize;
  else size = 1;

  return Iter<T>(addr, addr, addr + size);
}

// Return an Iter to one past the end of an allocated array.
Iter<T> end() {
  int size;

  if(isArray) size = arraySize;
  else size = 1;

  return Iter<T>(addr + size, addr, addr + size);
}
```

The **begin( )** function returns an **Iter** to the start of the allocated array pointed to by **addr**. The **end( )** function returns an **Iter** to one past the end of the array. Although there is nothing that stops these functions from being called on a **GCPtr** that points to a single object, their purpose is to support operations on allocated arrays. (Obtaining an **Iter** to a single object is not harmful, just pointless.)

The shutdown( ) Function

If a program creates a circular reference of **GCPtr**s, then when the program ends there will still be dynamically allocated objects that need to be released. This is important because these objects might have destructors that need to be called. The **shutdown( )** function handles this task. This function is registered by **atexit( )** when the first **GCPtr** is created, as described earlier. This means that it will be called when the program terminates.

The **shutdown( )** function is shown here:

```
// Clear gclist when program exits.
template <class T, int size>
void GCPtr<T, size>::shutdown() {

  if(gclistSize() == 0) return; // list is empty

  list<GCInfo<T> >::iterator p;

  for(p = gclist.begin(); p != gclist.end(); p++) {
```

```
  // Set all reference counts to zero
  p->refcount = 0;
}

#ifdef DISPLAY
  cout << "Before collecting for shutdown() for "
       << typeid(T).name() << "\n";
#endif

collect();

#ifdef DISPLAY
  cout << "After collecting for shutdown() for "
       << typeid(T).name() << "\n";
#endif
}
```

First, if the list is empty, which it will normally be, then **shutdown( )** simply returns. Otherwise, it sets to zero the reference counts of the entries that still exist in **gclist**, and then it calls **collect( )**. Recall that **collect( )** releases any object that has a reference count of zero. Thus, setting the reference counts to zero ensures that all objects will be freed.

Two Utility Functions

GCPtr ends by defining two utility functions. The first is **gclistSize( )**, which returns the number of entries currently held in **gclist**. The second is **showlist( )**, which displays the contents of **gclist**. Neither of these are necessary for the implementation of a garbage collection pointer type, but they are useful when you want to watch the operation of the garbage collector.

GCInfo

The garbage collection list in **gclist** holds objects of type **GCInfo**. The **GCInfo** class is shown here:

```
// This class defines an element that is stored
// in the garbage collection information list.
//
template <class T> class GCInfo {
public:
  unsigned refcount; // current reference count

  T *memPtr; // pointer to allocated memory

  /* isArray is true if memPtr points
     to an allocated array. It is false
```

```
    otherwise. */
  bool isArray; // true if pointing to array

  /* If memPtr is pointing to an allocated
     array, then arraySize contains its size */
  unsigned arraySize; // size of array

  // Here, mPtr points to the allocated memory.
  // If this is an array, then size specifies
  // the size of the array.
  GCInfo(T *mPtr, unsigned size=0) {
    refcount = 1;
    memPtr = mPtr;
    if(size != 0)
      isArray = true;
    else
      isArray = false;

    arraySize = size;
  }
};
```

As mentioned earlier, each **GCInfo** object stores a pointer to allocated memory in **memPtr** and the reference count associated with that memory in **refcount**. If the memory pointed to by **memPtr** contains an array, then the length of that array must be specified when the **GCInfo** object is created. In this case, **isArray** is set to **true**, and the length of the array will be stored in **arraySize**.

GCInfo objects are stored in an STL **list**. To enable searches on this list, it is necessary to define **operator==( )**, as shown here:

```
// Overloading operator== allows GCInfos to be compared.
// This is needed by the STL list class.
template <class T> bool operator==(const GCInfo<T> &ob1,
               const GCInfo<T> &ob2) {
  return (ob1.memPtr == ob2.memPtr);
}
```

Two objects are equal only if both their **memPtr** fields are identical. Depending upon the compiler you are using, other operators may need to be overloaded to enable **GCInfos** to be stored in an STL **list**.

Iter

The **Iter** class implements an iterator-like object that can be used to cycle through the elements of an allocated array. **Iter** is not technically necessary because a **GCPtr** can be converted to a normal pointer of its base type, but **Iter** offers two advantages. First, it lets you cycle through an allocated array in a fashion similar to the way in which you cycle through the contents of an STL container. Thus, the syntax for using an **Iter** is familiar. Second, **Iter** will not allow out-of-range accesses. Thus, an **Iter** is a safe alternative to using a normal pointer. Understand, however, that **Iter** does not participate in garbage collection. Thus, if the underlying **GCPtr** on which an **Iter** is based goes out of scope, the memory to which it points will be freed whether or not it is still needed by that **Iter**.

Iter is a template class defined like this:

```
template <class T> class Iter {
```

The type of data to which the **Iter** points is passed through **T**.

Iter defines these instance variables:

```
T *ptr;    // current pointer value
T *end;    // points to element one past end
T *begin; // points to start of allocated array
unsigned length; // length of sequence
```

The address to which the **Iter** currently points is held in **ptr**. The address to the start of the array is stored in **begin**, and the address of an element one past the end of the array is stored in **end**. The length of the dynamic array is stored in **length**.

Iter defines the two constructors shown here. The first is the default constructor. The second constructs an **Iter**, given an initial value for **ptr**, and pointers to the beginning and end of the array.

```
Iter() {
ptr = end = begin = NULL;
  length = 0;
}

Iter(T *p, T *first, T *last) {
  ptr = p;
  end = last;
  begin = first;
  length = last - first;
}
```

For use by the garbage collector code shown in this chapter, the initial value of **ptr** will always equal **begin**. However, you are free to construct **Iter**s in which the initial value of **ptr** is a different value.

To enable **Iter**'s pointer-like nature, it overloads the ***** and **–>** pointer operators, and the array indexing operator **[ ]**, as shown here:

```
// Return value pointed to by ptr.
// Do not allow out-of-bounds access.
T &operator*() {
  if( (ptr >= end) || (ptr < begin) )
```

```
    throw OutOfRangeExc();
  return *ptr;
}


// Return address contained in ptr.
// Do not allow out-of-bounds access.
T *operator->() {
  if( (ptr >= end) || (ptr < begin) )
    throw OutOfRangeExc();
  return ptr;
}
// Return a reference to the object at the
// specified index. Do not allow out-of-bounds
// access.
T &operator[](int i) {
  if( (i < 0) || (i >= (end-begin)) )
    throw OutOfRangeExc();
  return ptr[i];
}
```

The * operator returns a reference to the element currently being pointed to in the dynamic array. The –> returns the address of the element currently being pointed to. The **[ ]** returns a reference to the element at the specified index. Notice that these operations do not allow an out-of-bounds access. If one is attempted, an **OutOfRangeExc** exception is thrown.

   Iter defines the various pointer arithmetic operators, such as ++, – –, and so on, which increment or decrement an **Iter**. These operators enable you to cycle through a dynamic array. In the interest of speed, none of the arithmetic operators perform range checks themselves. However, any attempt to access an out-of-bounds element will cause an exception, which prevents a boundary error. **Iter** also defines the relational operators. Both the pointer arithmetic and relational functions are straightforward and easy to understand.

   Iter also defines a utility function called **size( )**, which returns the length of the array to which the **Iter** points.

   As mentioned earlier, inside **GCPtr**, **Iter<T>** is **typedef**ed to **GCiterator** for each instance of **GCPtr**, which simplifies the declaration of an iterator. This means that you can use the type name **GCiterator** to obtain the **Iter** for any **GCPtr**.

How to Use GCPtr

Using a **GCPtr** is quite easy. First, include the file **gc.h**. Then, declare a **GCPtr** object, specifying the type of the data to which it will point. For example, to declare a **GCPtr** object called **p** that can point to an **int**, use this kind of declaration:

```
GCPtr<int> p; // p can point to int objects
```

Next, dynamically allocate the memory using **new** and assign the pointer returned by **new** to **p**, as shown here:

```
p = new int; // assign p the address of an int
```

You can assign a value to the allocated memory using an assignment operation like this:

```
*p = 88; // give that int a value
```

Of course, you can combine the three preceding statements like this:

```
GCPtr<int> p = new int(88); // declare and initialize
```

You can obtain the value of the memory at the location pointed to by **p**, as shown here:

```
int k = *p;
```

As these examples show, in general you use a **GCPtr** just like a normal C++ pointer. The only difference is that you don't need to delete the pointer when you are through with it. The memory allocated to that pointer will be automatically released when it is no longer needed.

Here is an entire program that assembles the pieces just shown:

```
#include <iostream>
#include <new>
#include "gc.h"

using namespace std;

int main() {
  GCPtr<int> p;

  try {
    p = new int;
  } catch(bad_alloc exc) {
    cout << "Allocation failure!\n";
    return 1;
  }

  *p = 88;

  cout << "Value at p is: " << *p << endl;

  int k = *p;

  cout << "k is " << k << endl;

  return 0;
}
```

The output from this program with the display option turned on is shown here. (Recall that you can watch the operation of the garbage collector by defining **DISPLAY** within **gc.h**.)

```
Constructing GCPtr.
Value at p is: 88
k is 88
GCPtr going out of scope.
Before garbage collection for gclist<int, 0>:
memPtr        refcount     value
[002F12C0]       0           88
[00000000]       0           ---

Deleting: 88
After garbage collection for gclist<int, 0>:
memPtr        refcount     value
          -- Empty --
```

When the program ends, **p** goes out of scope. This causes its destructor to be called, which causes the reference count for the memory pointed to by **p** to be decremented. Because **p** was the only pointer to this memory, this operation sets the reference count to zero. Next, **p**'s destructor calls **collect( )**, which scans **gclist**, looking for entries that have a reference count of zero. Because the entry previously associated with **p** has a reference count of zero, its memory is freed.

One other point: notice that prior to garbage collection, a null pointer entry is also in **gclist**. This null pointer was created when **p** was constructed. Recall that if a **GCPtr** is not given an initial address, the null address (which is zero) is used. Although it is not technically necessary to store a null pointer in **gclist** (because it is never freed), doing so simplifies other parts of **GCPtr** because it ensures that every **GCPtr** has a corresponding entry in **gclist**.

Handling Allocation Exceptions

As the preceding program shows, because the garbage collector does not change the way that memory is allocated via **new**, you handle allocation failures in the same way as usual, by catching the **bad_alloc** exception. (Recall that when **new** fails, it throws an exception of type **bad_alloc**.) Of course, the preceding program won't run out of memory, and the **try/catch** block isn't really needed, but a real-world program might exhaust the heap. Thus, you should always check for this possibility.

In general, the best way to respond to a **bad_alloc** exception when using garbage collection is to call **collect( )** to recycle any unused memory and then retry the allocation that failed. This technique is employed by the load-testing program shown later in this chapter. You can use the same basic technique in your own programs.

A More Interesting Example

Here is a more interesting example that shows the effect of a **GCPtr** going out of scope before the end of the program:

```
// Show a GCPtr going out of scope prior to the end
// of the program.
#include <iostream>
#include <new>
#include "gc.h"

using namespace std;

int main() {
  GCPtr<int> p;
  GCPtr<int> q;

  try {
    p = new int(10);
    q = new int(11);

    cout << "Value at p is: " << *p << endl;
    cout << "Value at q is: " << *q << endl;

    cout << "Before entering block.\n";

    // Now, create a local object.
    { // start a block
      GCPtr<int> r = new int(12);
      cout << "Value at r is: " << *r << endl;
    } // end the block, causing r to go out of scope

    cout << "After exiting block.\n";

  } catch(bad_alloc exc) {
    cout << "Allocation failure!\n";
    return 1;
  }

  cout << "Done\n";

  return 0;
}
```

This program produces the following output when the display option is turned on:

```
Constructing GCPtr.
Constructing GCPtr.
Value at p is: 10
Value at q is: 11
Before entering block.
```

```
Constructing GCPtr.
Value at r is: 12
GCPtr going out of scope.
Before garbage collection for gclist<int, 0>:
memPtr         refcount      value
[002F31D8]        0            12
[002F12F0]        1            11
[002F12C0]        1            10
[00000000]        0            ---

Deleting: 12
After garbage collection for gclist<int, 0>:
memPtr         refcount      value
[002F12F0]        1            11
[002F12C0]        1            10

After exiting block.
Done
GCPtr going out of scope.
Before garbage collection for gclist<int, 0>:
memPtr         refcount      value
[002F12F0]        0            11
[002F12C0]        1            10

Deleting: 11
After garbage collection for gclist<int, 0>:
memPtr         refcount      value
[002F12C0]        1            10

GCPtr going out of scope.
Before garbage collection for gclist<int, 0>:
memPtr         refcount      value
[002F12C0]        0            10

Deleting: 10
After garbage collection for gclist<int, 0>:
memPtr         refcount      value
             -- Empty --
```

Examine this program and its output closely. First, notice that **p** and **q** are created at the start of **main( )**, but **r** is not created until its block is entered. As you know, in C++, local variables are not created until their block is entered. When **r** is created, the memory to which it points is given an initial value of 12. This value is then displayed, and the block ends. This causes **r** to go out of scope, which means that its destructor is called. This causes **r**'s reference count in **gclist** to be decremented to zero. Then **collect( )** is called to collect garbage.

Because the display option is on, when **collect( )** begins, it displays the contents of **gclist**. Notice that it has four entries. The first is the one that was previously linked to **r**. Notice that its **refcount** field is zero, indicating that the memory pointed to by the **memPtr** field is no longer in use by any program element. The next two entries are still active, and they are linked to **p** and **q**. Because they are still in use, the memory they point to is not freed at this time. The final entry represents the null pointer to which **p** and **q** originally pointed when they were created. Because it is no longer in use, it will be removed from the list by **collect( )**. (Of course, no memory is freed when the null pointer is removed.)

Because no other **GCPtr** points to the same memory as **r**, its memory can be released, as the **Deleting: 12** line confirms. Once this is done, program execution continues after the block. Finally, **p** and **q** go out of scope when the program ends and their memory is released. In this case, **q**'s destructor is called first, meaning that it is collected first. Finally, **p** is destroyed and **gclist** is empty.

Allocating and Discarding Objects

It is important to understand that memory becomes subject to garbage collection as soon as its reference count drops to zero (which means that no **GCPtr** is pointing to it). It is not necessary for the **GCPtr** that originally pointed to that object to go out of scope. Thus, you can use a single **GCPtr** object to point to any number of allocated objects by simply assigning that **GCPtr** a new value. The discarded memory will eventually be collected. For example:

```
// Allocate and discard objects.
#include <iostream>
#include <new>
#include "gc.h"

using namespace std;

int main() {
  try {
    // Allocate and discard objects.
    GCPtr<int> p = new int(1);
    p = new int(2);
    p = new int(3);
    p = new int(4);

    // Manually collect unused objects for
    // demonstration purposes.
    GCPtr<int>::collect();

    cout << "*p: " << *p << endl;
  } catch(bad_alloc exc) {
    cout << "Allocation failure!\n";
```

```
      return 1;
   }


   return 0;
}
```

The output from this program, with the display option turned on, is shown here:

```
Constructing GCPtr.
Before garbage collection for gclist<int, 0>:
memPtr        refcount      value
[002F1310]       1          4
[002F1300]       0          3
[002F12D0]       0          2
[002F12A0]       0          1

Deleting: 3
Deleting: 2
Deleting: 1
After garbage collection for gclist<int, 0>:
memPtr        refcount      value
[002F1310]       1          4

*p: 4
GCPtr going out of scope.
Before garbage collection for gclist<int, 0>:
memPtr        refcount      value
[002F1310]       0          4

Deleting: 4
After garbage collection for gclist<int, 0>:
memPtr        refcount      value
              -- Empty --
```

In the program, **p**, a **GCPtr** to **int**, is assigned a pointer to four separate chunks of dynamic memory, each being initialized with a different value. Next, a call is made to **collect( )**, which forces garbage collection to take place. Notice the contents of **gclist**: three of the entries are marked inactive, and only the entry that points to the memory that was allocated last is still in use. Next, the unused entries are deleted. Finally, the program ends, **p** goes out of scope, and the final entry is removed.

Notice that the first three chunks of dynamic memory to which **p** pointed have reference counts of zero. This is because of the way the overloaded assignment operator works. Recall that when a **GCPtr** is assigned a new address, the reference count for its original value is decremented. Thus, each time **p** is assigned the address of a new integer, the reference count for the old address is reduced.

One other point: because **p** was initialized when it was declared, no null-pointer entry was generated and put on **gclist**. Remember, a null-pointer entry is created only when a **GCPtr** is declared without an initial value.

Allocating Arrays

If you are allocating an array using **new**, then you must tell **GCPtr** this fact by specifying its size when the **GCPtr** pointer to that array is declared. For example, here is the way to allocate an array of five **double**s:

```
GCPtr<double, 5> pda = new double[5];
```

The size must be specified for two reasons. First, it tells the **GCPtr** constructor that this object will point to an allocated array, which causes the **isArray** field to be set to **true**. When **isArray** is **true**, the **collect( )** function frees memory by using **delete[ ]**, which releases a dynamically allocated array, rather than **delete**, which releases only a single object. Therefore, in this example, when **pda** goes out of scope, **delete[ ]** is used and all five elements of **pda** are freed. Ensuring that the correct number of objects are freed is especially important when arrays of class objects are allocated. Only by using **delete[ ]** can you know that the destructor for each object will be called.

The second reason that the size must be specified is to prevent an out-of-bounds element from being accessed when an **Iter** is used to cycle through an allocated array. Recall that the size of the array (stored in **arraySize**) is passed by **GCPtr** to **Iter**'s constructor whenever an **Iter** is needed.

Be aware that nothing enforces the rule that an allocated array be operated on only through a **GCPtr** that has been specified as pointing to an array. This is solely your responsibility.

Once you have allocated an array, there are two ways you can access its elements. First, you can index the **GCPtr** that points to it. Second, you can use an iterator. Both methods are shown here.

Using Array Indexing

The following program creates a **GCPtr** to a 10-element array of **int**s. It then allocates that array and initializes it to the values 0 through 9. Finally, it displays those values. It performs these actions by indexing the **GCPtr**.

```
// Demonstrate indexing a GCPtr.
#include <iostream>
#include <new>
#include "gc.h"

using namespace std;

int main() {

  try {
    // Create a GCPtr to an allocated array of 10 ints.
```

```
    GCPtr<int, 10> ap = new int[10];

    // Give the array some values using array indexing.
    for(int i=0; i < 10; i++)
      ap[i] = i;

    // Now, show the contents of the array.
    for(int i=0; i < 10; i++)
      cout << ap[i] << " ";

    cout << endl;

  } catch(bad_alloc exc) {
    cout << "Allocation failure!\n";
    return 1;
  }


  return 0;
}
```

The output, with the display option off, is shown here:

```
0 1 2 3 4 5 6 7 8 9
```

Because a **GCPtr** emulates a normal C++ pointer, no array bounds checking is performed, and it is possible to overrun or under run the dynamically allocated array. So, use the same care when accessing an array through a **GCPtr** as you do when accessing an array through a normal C++ pointer.

Using Iterators

Although array indexing is certainly a convenient method of cycling through an allocated array, it is not the only method at your disposal. For many applications, the use of an iterator will be a better choice because it has the advantage of preventing boundary errors. Recall that for **GCPtr**, iterators are objects of type **Iter**. **Iter** supports the full complement of pointer operations, such as **++**. It also allows an iterator to be indexed like an array.

Here is the previous program reworked to use an iterator. Recall that the easiest way to obtain an iterator to a **GCPtr** is to use **GCiterator**, which is a **typedef** inside **GCPtr** that is automatically bound to the generic type **T**.

```
// Demonstrate an iterator.
#include <iostream>
#include <new>
#include "gc.h"

using namespace std;
```

```
int main() {

  try {
    // Create a GCPtr to an allocated array of 10 ints.
    GCPtr<int, 10> ap = new int[10];

    // Declare an int iterator.
    GCPtr<int>::GCiterator itr;

    // Assign itr a pointer to the start of the array.
    itr = ap.begin();

    // Give the array some values using array indexing.
    for(unsigned i=0; i < itr.size(); i++)
      itr[i] = i;

    // Now, cycle through array using the iterator.
    for(itr = ap.begin(); itr != ap.end(); itr++)
      cout << *itr << " ";

    cout << endl;

  } catch(bad_alloc exc) {
    cout << "Allocation failure!\n";
    return 1;
  } catch(OutOfRangeExc exc) {
    cout << "Out of range access!\n";
    return 1;
  }


  return 0;
}
```

On your own, you might want to try incrementing **itr** so that it points beyond the boundary of the allocated array. Then try accessing the value at that location. As you will see, an **OutOfRangeExc** is thrown. In general, you can increment or decrement an iterator any way you like without causing an exception. However, if it is not pointing within the underlying array, attempting to obtain or set the value at that location will cause a boundary error.

Using GCPtr with Class Types

GCPtr is used with class types in just the same way it is used with built-in types. For example, here is a short program that allocates objects of **MyClass**:

```
// Use GCPtr with a class type.
#include <iostream>
```

```cpp
#include <new>
#include "gc.h"

using namespace std;

class MyClass {
  int a, b;
public:
  double val;

  MyClass() { a = b = 0; }

  MyClass(int x, int y) {
    a = x;
    b = y;
    val = 0.0;
  }

  ~MyClass() {
    cout << "Destructing MyClass(" <<
            a << ", " << b << ")\n";
  }

  int sum() {
    return a + b;
  }

  friend ostream &operator<<(ostream &strm, MyClass &obj);
};

// An overloaded inserter to display MyClass.
ostream &operator<<(ostream &strm, MyClass &obj) {
  strm << "(" << obj.a << " " << obj.b << ")";
  return strm;
}

int main() {
  try {
    GCPtr<MyClass> ob = new MyClass(10, 20);

    // Show value via overloaded inserter.
    cout << *ob << endl;

    // Change object pointed to by ob.
    ob = new MyClass(11, 21);
```

```
    cout << *ob << endl;

    // Call a member function through a GCPtr.
    cout << "Sum is : " << ob->sum() << endl;

    // Assign a value to a class member through a GCPtr.
    ob->val = 98.6;
    cout << "ob->val: " << ob->val << endl;

    cout << "ob is now " << *ob << endl;
  } catch(bad_alloc exc) {
    cout << "Allocation error!\n";
    return 1;
  }

  return 0;
}
```

Notice how the members of **MyClass** are accessed through the use of the –> operator.
Remember, **GCPtr** defines a pointer type. Thus, operations through a **GCPtr** are performed
in exactly the same fashion that they are with any other pointer.

The output from the program, with the display option turned off, is shown here:

```
(10 20)
(11 21)
Sum is : 32
ob->val: 98.6
ob is now (11 21)
Destructing MyClass(11, 21)
Destructing MyClass(10, 20)
```

Pay special attention to the last two lines. These are output by ~**MyClass( )** when garbage
is collected. Even though only one **GCPtr** pointer was created, two **MyClass** objects were
allocated. Both of these objects are represented by entries in the garbage collection list. When
ob is destroyed, **gclist** is scanned for entries having a reference count of zero. In this case, two
such entries are found, and the memory to which they point is deleted.

A Larger Demonstration Program

The following program shows a larger example that exercises all of the features of **GCPtr**:

```
// Demonstrating GCPtr.
#include <iostream>
#include <new>
#include "gc.h"
```

```cpp
using namespace std;

// A simple class for testing GCPtr with class types.
class MyClass {
  int a, b;
public:
  double val;

  MyClass() { a = b = 0; }

  MyClass(int x, int y) {
    a = x;
    b = y;
    val = 0.0;
  }

  ~MyClass() {
    cout << "Destructing MyClass(" <<
        a << ", " << b << ")\n";
  }

  int sum() {
    return a + b;
  }

  friend ostream &operator<<(ostream &strm, MyClass &obj);
};

// Create an inserter for MyClass.
ostream &operator<<(ostream &strm, MyClass &obj) {
  strm << "(" << obj.a << " " << obj.b << ")";
  return strm;
}

// Pass a normal pointer to a function.
void passPtr(int *p) {
  cout << "Inside passPtr(): "
       << *p << endl;
}

// Pass a GCPtr to a function.
void passGCPtr(GCPtr<int, 0> p) {
  cout << "Inside passGCPtr(): "
       << *p << endl;
}
```

```
int main() {

  try {
    // Declare an int GCPtr.
    GCPtr<int> ip;

    // Allocate an int and assign its address to ip.
    ip = new int(22);

    // Display its value.
    cout << "Value at *ip: " << *ip << "\n\n";

    // Pass ip to a function
    passGCPtr(ip);

    // ip2 is created and then goes out of scope
    {
      GCPtr<int> ip2 = ip;
    }

    int *p = ip; // convert to int * pointer'

    passPtr(p); // pass int * to passPtr()

    *ip = 100; // Assign new value to ip

    // Now, use implicit conversion to int *
    passPtr(ip);
    cout << endl;

    // Create a GCPtr to an array of ints
    GCPtr<int, 5> iap = new int[5];

    // Initialize dynamic array.
    for(int i=0; i < 5; i++)
      iap[i] = i;

    // Display contents of array.
    cout << "Contents of iap via array indexing.\n";
    for(int i=0; i < 5; i++)
      cout << iap[i] << " ";
    cout << "\n\n";

    // Create an int GCiterator.
    GCPtr<int>::GCiterator itr;
```

```cpp
    // Now, use iterator to access dynamic array.
    cout << "Contents of iap via iterator.\n";
    for(itr = iap.begin(); itr != iap.end(); itr++)
      cout << *itr << " ";
    cout << "\n\n";

    // Generate and discard many objects
    for(int i=0; i < 10; i++)
      ip = new int(i+10);

    // Now, manually garbage collect GCPtr<int> list.
    // Keep in mind that GCPtr<int, 5> pointers
    // will not be collected by this call.
    cout << "Requesting collection on GCPtr<int> list.\n";
    GCPtr<int>::collect();

    // Now, use GCPtr with class type.
    GCPtr<MyClass> ob = new MyClass(10, 20);

    // Show value via overloaded insertor.
    cout << "ob points to " << *ob << endl;

    // Change object pointed to by ob.
    ob = new MyClass(11, 21);
    cout << "ob now points to " << *ob << endl;

    // Call a member function through a GCPtr.
    cout << "Sum is : " << ob->sum() << endl;

    // Assign a value to a class member through a GCPtr.
    ob->val = 19.21;
    cout << "ob->val: " << ob->val << "\n\n";

    cout << "Now work with pointers to class objects.\n";

    // Declare a GCPtr to a 5-element array
    // of MyClass objects.
    GCPtr<MyClass, 5> v;

    // Allocate the array.
    v = new MyClass[5];

    // Get a MyClass GCiterator.
    GCPtr<MyClass>::GCiterator mcItr;
```

```cpp
  // Initialize the MyClass array.
  for(int i=0; i<5; i++) {
    v[i] = MyClass(i, 2*i);
  }

  // Display contents of MyClass array using indexing.
  cout << "Cycle through array via array indexing.\n";
  for(int i=0; i<5; i++) {
    cout << v[i] << " ";
  }
  cout << "\n\n";

  // Display contents of MyClass array using iterator.
  cout << "Cycle through array through an iterator.\n";
  for(mcItr = v.begin(); mcItr != v.end(); mcItr++) {
    cout << *mcItr << " ";
  }
  cout << "\n\n";

  // Here is another way to write the preceding loop.
  cout << "Cycle through array using a while loop.\n";
  mcItr = v.begin();
  while(mcItr != v.end()) {
    cout << *mcItr << " ";
    mcItr++;
  }
  cout << "\n\n";

  cout << "mcItr points to an array that is "
       <<  mcItr.size() << " objects long.\n";

  // Find number of elements between two iterators.
  GCPtr<MyClass>::GCiterator mcItr2 = v.end()-2;
  mcItr = v.begin();
  cout << "The difference between mcItr2 and mcItr is "
       << mcItr2 - mcItr;
  cout << "\n\n";

  // Can also cycle through loop like this.
  cout << "Dynamically compute length of array.\n";
  mcItr = v.begin();
  mcItr2 = v.end();
  for(int i=0; i < mcItr2 - mcItr; i++) {
    cout << v[i] << " ";
  }
```

```cpp
      cout << "\n\n";


      // Now, display the array backwards.
      cout << "Cycle through array backwards.\n";
      for(mcItr = v.end()-1; mcItr >= v.begin(); mcItr--)
        cout << *mcItr << " ";
      cout << "\n\n";

      // Of course, can use "normal" pointer to
      // cycle through array.
      cout << "Cycle through array using 'normal' pointer\n";
      MyClass *ptr = v;
      for(int i=0; i < 5; i++)
        cout << *ptr++ << " ";
      cout << "\n\n";

      // Can access members through a GCiterator.
      cout << "Access class members through an iterator.\n";
      for(mcItr = v.begin(); mcItr != v.end(); mcItr++) {
        cout << mcItr->sum() << " ";
      }
      cout << "\n\n";

      // Can allocate and delete a pointer to a GCPtr
      // normally, just like any other pointer.
      cout << "Use a pointer to a GCPtr.\n";
      GCPtr<int> *pp = new GCPtr<int>();
      *pp = new int(100);
      cout << "Value at **pp is: " << **pp;
      cout << "\n\n";

      // Because pp is not a garbage collected pointer,
      // it must be deleted manually.
      delete pp;
  } catch(bad_alloc exc) {
      // A real application could attempt to free
      // memory by collect() when an allocation
      // error occurs.
      cout << "Allocation error.\n";
  }

  return 0;
}
```

Here is the output with the display option turned off:

```
Value at *ip: 22

Inside passGCPtr(): 22
Inside passPtr(): 22
Inside passPtr(): 100

Contents of iap via array indexing.
0 1 2 3 4

Contents of iap via iterator.
0 1 2 3 4

Requesting collection on GCPtr<int> list.
ob points to (10 20)
ob now points to (11 21)
Sum is : 32
ob->val: 19.21

Now work with pointers to class objects.
Destructing MyClass(0, 0)
Destructing MyClass(1, 2)
Destructing MyClass(2, 4)
Destructing MyClass(3, 6)
Destructing MyClass(4, 8)
Cycle through array via array indexing.
(0 0) (1 2) (2 4) (3 6) (4 8)

Cycle through array through an iterator.
(0 0) (1 2) (2 4) (3 6) (4 8)

Cycle through array using a while loop.
(0 0) (1 2) (2 4) (3 6) (4 8)

mcItr points to an array that is 5 objects long.
The difference between mcItr2 and mcItr is 3

Dynamically compute length of array.
(0 0) (1 2) (2 4) (3 6) (4 8)

Cycle through array backwards.
(4 8) (3 6) (2 4) (1 2) (0 0)

Cycle through array using 'normal' pointer
(0 0) (1 2) (2 4) (3 6) (4 8)
```

```
Access class members through an iterator.
0 3 6 9 12

Use a pointer to a GCPtr.
Value at **pp is: 100

Destructing MyClass(4, 8)
Destructing MyClass(3, 6)
Destructing MyClass(2, 4)
Destructing MyClass(1, 2)
Destructing MyClass(0, 0)
Destructing MyClass(11, 21)
Destructing MyClass(10, 20)
```

On your own, try compiling and running this program with the display option turned on. (That is, define **DISPLAY** in **gc.h**.) Next, walk through the program, matching the output against each statement. This will give you a good feel for the way the garbage collector works. Remember, garbage collection occurs whenever a **GCPtr** goes out of scope. This happens at various points in the program, such as when a function that receives a copy of a **GCPtr** returns. In this case, the copy goes out of scope and garbage collection takes place. Also remember that each type of **GCPtr** maintains its own **gclist**. Thus, collecting garbage from one list does not cause it to be collected from other types of lists.

Load Testing

The following program load tests **GCPtr** by repeatedly allocating and discarding objects until free memory is exhausted. When this occurs, a **bad_alloc** exception is thrown by **new**. Inside the exception handler, **collect( )** is explicitly called to reclaim the unused memory, and the process continues. You can use this same technique in your own programs.

```cpp
// Load test GCPtr by creating and discarding
// thousands of objects.
#include <iostream>
#include <new>
#include <limits>
#include "gc.h"

using namespace std;

// A simple class for load testing GCPtr.
class LoadTest {
  int a, b;
public:
  double n[100000]; // just to take up memory
  double val;
```

```
  LoadTest() { a = b = 0; }

  LoadTest(int x, int y) {
    a = x;
    b = y;
    val = 0.0;
  }

  friend ostream &operator<<(ostream &strm, LoadTest &obj);
};

// Create an inserter for LoadTest.
ostream &operator<<(ostream &strm, LoadTest &obj) {
  strm << "(" << obj.a << " " << obj.b << ")";
  return strm;
}

int main() {
  GCPtr<LoadTest> mp;
  int i;

  for(i = 1; i < 20000; i++) {
    try {
      mp = new LoadTest(i, i);
    } catch(bad_alloc xa) {
      // When an allocation error occurs, recycle
      // garbage by calling collect().
      cout << "Last object: " << *mp << endl;
      cout << "Length of gclist before calling collect(): "
           << mp.gclistSize() << endl;
      GCPtr<LoadTest>::collect();
      cout << "Length after calling collect(): "
           << mp.gclistSize() << endl;
    }
  }

  return 0;
}
```

A portion of the output from the program (with the display option off) is shown here. Of course, the precise output you see may differ because of the amount of memory available in your system and the compiler that you are using.

```
Last object: (518 518)
Length of gclist before calling collect(): 518
```

```
Length after calling collect(): 1
Last object: (1036 1036)
Length of gclist before calling collect(): 518
Length after calling collect(): 1
Last object: (1554 1554)
Length of gclist before calling collect(): 518
Length after calling collect(): 1
Last object: (2072 2072)
Length of gclist before calling collect(): 518
Length after calling collect(): 1
Last object: (2590 2590)
Length of gclist before calling collect(): 518
Length after calling collect(): 1
Last object: (3108 3108)
Length of gclist before calling collect(): 518
Length after calling collect(): 1
Last object: (3626 3626)
Length of gclist before calling collect(): 518
Length after calling collect(): 1
```

Some Restrictions

There are a few restrictions to using **GCPtr**:

1. You cannot create global **GCPtr**s. Recall that a global object goes out of scope after the rest of the program ends. When a global **GCPtr** goes out of scope, the **GCPtr** destructor calls **collect( )** to try to release the unused memory. The trouble is that, depending on how your C++ compiler is implemented, **gclist** may have already been destroyed. In this case, executing **collect( )** will cause a runtime error. Therefore, **GCPtr** should be used only when creating local objects.

2. When using dynamically allocated arrays, you must specify the size of the array when you declare a **GCPtr** that will point to it. There is no mechanism that enforces this, however, so be careful.

3. You must not attempt to release the memory pointed to by a **GCPtr** by explicitly using **delete**. If you need to immediately release an object, call **collect( )**.

4. A **GCPtr** object must point only to memory that is dynamically allocated via **new**. Assigning to a **GCPtr** object a pointer to any other memory will cause an error when the **GCPtr** object goes out of scope because an attempt will be made to free memory that was never allocated.

5. It is best to avoid circular pointer references for reasons described earlier in this chapter. Although all allocated memory is eventually released, objects containing circular references remain allocated until the program ends, rather than being released when they are no longer used by another program element.

Some Things to Try

It is easy to tailor **GCPtr** to the needs of your applications. As explained earlier, one of the changes that you might want to try is collecting garbage only after some metric has been reached, such as **gclist** reaching a certain size, or after a certain number of **GCPtr**s have gone out of scope.

An interesting enhancement to **GCPtr** is to overload **new** so that it automatically collects garbage when an allocation failure occurs. It is also possible to bypass the use of **new** when allocating memory for a **GCPtr** and use factory functions defined by **GCPtr** instead. Doing this lets you carefully control the dynamic allocation of memory, but it makes the allocation process fundamentally different than it is for C++'s built-in approach.

You might want to experiment with other solutions to the circular reference problem. One way is to implement the concept of a *weak reference*, which does not prevent garbage collection from occurring. You would then use a weak reference whenever a circular reference was needed.

Perhaps the most interesting variation on **GCPtr** is found in Chapter 3. There, a multithreaded version is created in which garbage collection takes place automatically, when free CPU time exists.

Multithreading in C++

THE ART
OF C++

Multithreading is becoming an increasingly important part of modern programming. One reason for this is that multithreading enables a program to make the best use of available CPU cycles, thus allowing very efficient programs to be written. Another reason is that multithreading is a natural choice for handling event-driven code, which is so common in today's highly distributed, networked, GUI-based environments. Of course, the fact that the most widely used operating system, Windows, supports multithreading is also a factor. Whatever the reasons, the increased use of multithreading is changing the way that programmers think about the fundamental architecture of a program. Although C++ does not contain built-in support for multithreaded programs, it is right at home in this arena.

Because of its growing importance, this chapter explores using C++ to create multithreaded programs. It does so by developing two multithreaded applications. The first is a thread control panel, which you can use to control the execution of threads within a program. This is both an interesting demonstration of multithreading and a practical tool that you can use when developing multithreaded applications. The second example shows how to apply multithreading to a practical example by creating a modified version of the garbage collector from Chapter 2 that runs in a background thread.

This chapter also serves another purpose: it shows how adept C++ is at interfacing directly to the operating system. In some other languages, such as Java, there is a layer of processing between your program and the OS. This layer adds overhead that can be unacceptable for some types of programs, such as those used in a real-time environment. In sharp contrast, C++ has direct access to low-level functionality provided by the operating system. This is one of the reasons C++ can produce higher performance code.

What Is Multithreading?

Before beginning, it is necessary to define precisely what is meant by the term *multithreading*. Multithreading is a specialized form of multitasking. In general, there are two types of multitasking: process-based and thread-based. A *process* is, in essence, a program that is executing. Thus, *process-based multitasking* is the feature that allows your computer to run two or more programs concurrently. For example, it is process-based multitasking that allows you to run a word processor at the same time you are using a spreadsheet or browsing the Internet. In process-based multitasking, a program is the smallest unit of code that can be dispatched by the scheduler.

A *thread* is a dispatchable unit of executable code. The name comes from the concept of a "thread of execution." In a *thread-based* multitasking environment, all processes have at least one thread, but they can have more. This means that a single program can perform two or more tasks concurrently. For instance, a text editor can be formatting text at the same time that it is printing, as long as these two actions are being performed by two separate threads. The differences between process-based and thread-based multitasking can be summarized like this: Process-based multitasking handles the concurrent execution of programs. Thread-based multitasking deals with the concurrent execution of pieces of the same program.

In the preceding discussions, it is important to clarify that true concurrent execution is possible only in a multiple-CPU system in which each process or thread has unrestricted access to a CPU. For single CPU systems, which constitute the vast majority of systems in use today, only the appearance of simultaneous execution is achieved. In a single CPU system, each process or thread receives a portion of the CPU's time, with the amount of time determined by several factors, including the priority of the process or thread. Although truly concurrent execution does not exist on most computers, when writing multithreaded programs, you should assume that it does. This is because you can't know the precise order in which separate threads will be executed, or if they will execute in the same sequence twice. Thus, it's best to program as if true concurrent execution is the case.

Multithreading Changes the Architecture of a Program

Multithreading changes the fundamental architecture of a program. Unlike a single-threaded program that executes in a strictly linear fashion, a multithreaded program executes portions of itself concurrently. Thus, all multithreaded programs include an element of parallelism. Consequently, a major issue in multithreaded programs is managing the interaction of the threads.

As explained earlier, all processes have at least one thread of execution, which is called the *main thread*. The main thread is created when your program begins. In a multithreaded program, the main thread creates one or more child threads. Thus, each multithreaded process starts with one thread of execution and then creates one or more additional threads. In a properly designed program, each thread represents a single logical unit of activity.

The principal advantage of multithreading is that it enables you to write very efficient programs because it lets you utilize the idle time that is present in most programs. Most I/O devices, whether they are network ports, disk drives, or the keyboard, are much slower than the CPU. Often, a program will spend a majority of its execution time waiting to send or receive data. With the careful use of multithreading, your program can execute another task during this idle time. For example, while one part of your program is sending a file over the Internet, another part can be reading keyboard input, and still another can be buffering the next block of data to send.

Why Doesn't C++ Contain Built-In Support for Multithreading?

C++ does not contain any built-in support for multithreaded applications. Instead, it relies entirely upon the operating system to provide this feature. Given that both Java and C# provide built-in support for multithreading, it is natural to ask why this isn't also the case for C++. The answers are efficiency, control, and the range of applications to which C++ is applied. Let's examine each.

By not building in support for multithreading, C++ does not attempt to define a "one size fits all" solution. Instead, C++ allows you to directly utilize the multithreading features provided by the operating system. This approach means that your programs can be multithreaded in the most efficient way supported by the execution environment. Because many multitasking environments offer rich support for multithreading, being able to access that support is crucial to the creation of high-performance, multithreaded programs.

Using operating system functions to support multithreading gives you access to the full range of control offered by the execution environment. Consider Windows. It defines a rich set of thread-related functions that enable finely grained control over the creation and management of a thread. For example, Windows has several ways to control access to a shared resource, including semaphores, mutexes, event objects, waitable timers, and critical sections. This level of flexibility cannot be easily designed into a language because the capabilities of operating systems differ. Thus, language-level support for multithreading usually means offering only a "lowest common denominator" of features. With C++, you gain access to all the features that the operating system provides. This is a major advantage when writing high-performance code.

C++ was designed for all types of programming, from embedded systems in which there is no operating system in the execution environment to highly distributed, GUI-based end-user applications and everything in between. Therefore, C++ cannot place significant constraints on its execution environment. Building in support for multithreading would have inherently limited C++ to only those environments that supported it and thus prevented C++ from being used to create software for nonthreaded environments.

In the final analysis, not building in support for multithreading is a major advantage for C++ because it enables programs to be written in the most efficient way possible for the target execution environment. Remember, C++ is all about power. In the case of multithreading, it is definitely a situation in which "less is more."

What Operating System and Compiler?

Because C++ relies on the operating system to provide support for multithreaded programming, it is necessary to choose an operating system as the target for the multithreaded applications in this chapter. Because Windows is the most widely used operating system in the world, it is the operating system used in this chapter. However, much of the information can be generalized to any OS that supports multithreading.

Because Visual C++ is arguably the most widely used compiler for producing Windows programs, it is the compiler required by the examples in this chapter. The importance of this is made apparent in the following section. However, if you are using another compiler, the code can be easily adapted to accommodate it.

NOTE

The examples in this chapter assume a basic, working knowledge of Windows programming.

An Overview of the Windows Thread Functions

Windows offers a wide array of Application Programming Interface (API) functions that support multithreading. Many readers will be at least somewhat familiar with the multithreading functions offered by Windows, but for those who are not, an overview of those used in this chapter is presented here. Keep in mind that Windows provides many other multithreading-based functions that you might want to explore on your own.

To use Windows' multithreading functions, you must include **<windows.h>** in your program.

Creating and Terminating a Thread

To create a thread, the Windows API supplies the **CreateThread( )** function. Its prototype is shown here:

> HANDLE CreateThread(LPSECURITY_ATTRIBUTES *secAttr*,
> SIZE_T *stackSize*,
> LPTHREAD_START_ROUTINE *threadFunc*,
> LPVOID *param*,
> DWORD *flags*,
> LPDWORD *threadID*);

Here, *secAttr* is a pointer to a set of security attributes pertaining to the thread. However, if *secAttr* is **NULL**, then the default security descriptor is used.

Each thread has its own stack. You can specify the size of the new thread's stack in bytes using the *stackSize* parameter. If this integer value is zero, then the thread will be given a stack that is the same size as the creating thread. In this case, the stack will be expanded, if necessary. (Specifying zero is the common approach taken to thread stack size.)

Each thread of execution begins with a call to a function, called the *thread function*, within the creating process. Execution of the thread continues until the thread function returns. The address of this function (that is, the entry point to the thread) is specified in *threadFunc*. All thread functions must have this prototype:

> DWORD WINAPI threadfunc(LPVOID *param*);

Any argument that you need to pass to the new thread is specified in **CreateThread( )**'s *param*. This 32-bit value is received by the thread function in its parameter. This parameter may be used for any purpose. The function returns its exit status.

The *flags* parameter determines the execution state of the thread. If it is zero, the thread begins execution immediately. If it is **CREATE_SUSPEND**, the thread is created in a suspended state, awaiting execution. (It may be started using a call to **ResumeThread( )**, discussed later.)

The identifier associated with a thread is returned in the long integer pointed to by *threadID*.

The function returns a handle to the thread if successful or **NULL** if a failure occurs. The thread handle can be explicitly destroyed by calling **CloseHandle( )**. Otherwise, it will be destroyed automatically when the parent process ends.

As just explained, a thread of execution terminates when its entry function returns. The process may also terminate the thread manually, using either **TerminateThread( )** or **ExitThread( )**, whose prototypes are shown here:

> BOOL TerminateThread(HANDLE *thread*, DWORD *status*);

> VOID ExitThread(DWORD *status*);

For **TerminateThread( )**, *thread* is the handle of the thread to be terminated. **ExitThread( )** can only be used to terminate the thread that calls **ExitThread( )**. For both functions, *status* is the termination status. **TerminateThread( )** returns nonzero if successful and zero otherwise.

Calling **ExitThread( )** is functionally equivalent to allowing a thread function to return normally. This means that the stack is properly reset. When a thread is terminated using **TerminateThread( )**, it is stopped immediately and does not perform any special cleanup activities. Also, **TerminateThread( )** may stop a thread during an important operation. For these reasons, it is usually best (and easiest) to let a thread terminate normally when its entry function returns.

The Visual C++ Alternatives to CreateThread( ) and ExitThread( )

Although **CreateThread( )** and **ExitThread( )** are the Windows API functions used to create and terminate a thread, we won't be using them in this chapter! The reason is that when these functions are used with Visual C++ (and possibly other Windows-compatible compilers), they can result in memory leaks, the loss of a small amount of memory. For Visual C++, if a multithreaded program utilizes C/C++ standard library functions and uses **CreateThread( )** and **ExitThread( )**, then small amounts of memory are lost. (If your program does not use the C/C++ standard library, then no such losses will occur.) To eliminate this problem, you must use functions defined by the Visual C++ runtime library to start and stop threads rather than those specified by the Win32 API. These functions parallel **CreateThread( )** and **ExitThread( )**, but do not generate a memory leak.

NOTE

*If you are using a compiler other than Visual C++, check its documentation to determine if you need to bypass **CreateThread( )** and **ExitThread( )** and how to do so, if necessary.*

The Visual C++ alternatives to **CreateThread( )** and **ExitThread( )** are **_beginthreadex( )** and **_endthreadex( )**. Both require the header file **<process.h>**. Here is the prototype for **_beginthreadex( )**:

```
uintptr_t _beginthreadex(void *secAttr, unsigned stackSize,
                         unsigned (__stdcall *threadFunc)(void *),
                         void *param, unsigned flags,
                         unsigned *threadID);
```

As you can see, the parameters to **_beginthreadex( )** parallel those to **CreateThread( )**. Furthermore, they have the same meaning as those specified by **CreateThread( )**. *secAttr* is a pointer to a set of security attributes pertaining to the thread. However, if *secAttr* is **NULL**, then the default security descriptor is used. The size of the new thread's stack, in bytes, is passed in *stackSize* parameter. If this value is zero, then the thread will be given a stack that is the same size as the main thread of the process that creates it.

The address of the thread function (that is, the entry point to the thread) is specified in *threadFunc*. For **_beginthreadex( )**, a thread function must have this prototype:

```
unsigned __stdcall threadfunc(void * param);
```

This prototype is functionally equivalent to the one for **CreateThread( )**, but it uses different type names. Any argument that you need to pass to the new thread is specified in the *param* parameter.

The *flags* parameter determines the execution state of the thread. If it is zero, the thread begins execution immediately. If it is **CREATE_SUSPEND**, the thread is created in a suspended state, awaiting execution. (It may be started using a call to **ResumeThread( )**.) The identifier associated with a thread is returned in the double word pointed to by *threadID*.

The function returns a handle to the thread if successful or zero if a failure occurs. The type **uintptr_t** specifies a Visual C++ type capable of holding a pointer or handle.

The prototype for **_endthreadex( )** is shown here:

```
void _endthreadex(unsigned status);
```

It functions just like **ExitThread( )** by stopping the thread and returning the exit code specified in *status*.

Because the most widely used compiler for Windows is Visual C++, the examples in this chapter will use **_beginthreadex( )** and **_endthreadex( )** rather than their equivalent API functions. If you are using a compiler other than Visual C++, simply substitute **CreateThread( )** and **EndThread( )**.

When using **_beginthreadex( )** and **_endthreadex( )**, you must remember to link in the multithreaded library. This will vary from compiler to compiler. Here are some examples. When using the Visual C++ command-line compiler, include the –MT option. To use the multithreaded library from the Visual C++ 6 IDE, first activate the Project | Settings property sheet. Then, select the C/C++ tab. Next, select Code Generation from the Category list box and then choose Multithreaded in the Use Runtime Library list box. For Visual C++ 7 .NET IDE, select Project | Properties. Next, select the C/C++ entry and highlight Code Generation. Finally, choose Multithreaded as the runtime library.

Suspending and Resuming a Thread

A thread of execution can be suspended by calling **SuspendThread( )**. It can be resumed by calling **ResumeThread( )**. The prototypes for these functions are shown here:

```
DWORD SuspendThread(HANDLE hThread);

DWORD ResumeThread(HANDLE hThread);
```

For both functions, the handle to the thread is passed in *hThread*.

Each thread of execution has associated with it a *suspend count*. If this count is zero, then the thread is not suspended. If it is nonzero, the thread is in a suspended state. Each call to **SuspendThread( )** increments the suspend count. Each call to **ResumeThread( )** decrements the suspend count. A suspended thread will resume only when its suspend count has reached zero. Therefore, to resume a suspended thread implies that there must be the same number of calls to **ResumeThread( )** as there have been calls to **SuspendThread( )**.

Both functions return the thread's previous suspend count or –1 if an error occurs.

Changing the Priority of a Thread

In Windows, each thread has associated with it a priority setting. A thread's priority determines how much CPU time a thread receives. Low priority threads receive little time. High priority threads receive a lot. Of course, how much CPU time a thread receives has a profound impact on its execution characteristics and its interaction with other threads currently executing in the system.

In Windows, a thread's priority setting is the combination of two values: the overall priority class of the process and the priority setting of the individual thread relative to that priority class. That is, a thread's actual priority is determined by combining the process' priority class with the thread's individual priority level. Each is examined next.

Priority Classes

By default, a process is given a priority class of normal, and most programs remain in the normal priority class throughout their execution lifetime. Although neither of the examples in this chapter changes the priority class, a brief overview of the thread priority classes is given here in the interest of completeness.

Windows defines six priority classes, which correspond to the values shown here, in order of highest to lowest priority:

REALTIME_PRIORITY_CLASS

HIGH_PRIORITY_CLASS

ABOVE_NORMAL_PRIORITY_CLASS

NORMAL_PRIORITY_CLASS

BELOW_NORMAL_PRIORITY_CLASS

IDLE_PRIORITY_CLASS

Programs are given the **NORMAL_PRIORITY_CLASS** by default. Usually, you won't need to alter the priority class of your program. In fact, changing a process' priority class can have negative consequences on the overall performance of the computer system. For example, if you increase a program's priority class to **REALTIME_PRIORITY_CLASS**, it will dominate the CPU. For some specialized applications, you may need to increase an application's priority class, but usually you won't. As mentioned, neither of the applications in this chapter changes the priority class.

In the event that you do want to change the priority class of a program, you can do so by calling **SetPriorityClass( )**. You can obtain the current priority class by calling **GetPriorityClass( )**. The prototypes for these functions are shown here:

DWORD GetPriorityClass(HANDLE *hApp*);

BOOL SetPriorityClass(HANDLE *hApp*, DWORD *priority*);

Here, *hApp* is the handle of the process. **GetPriorityClass( )** returns the priority class of the application or zero on failure. For **SetPriorityClass( )**, *priority* specifies the process' new priority class.

Thread Priorities

For any given priority class, each individual thread's priority determines how much CPU time it receives within its process. When a thread is first created, it is given normal priority, but you can change a thread's priority—even while it is executing.

You can obtain a thread's priority setting by calling **GetThreadPriority( )**. You can increase or decrease a thread's priority using **SetThreadPriority( )**. The prototypes for these functions are shown here:

> BOOL SetThreadPriority(HANDLE *hThread*, int *priority*);

> int GetThreadPriority(HANDLE *hThread*);

For both functions, *hThread* is the handle of the thread. For **SetThreadPriority( )**, *priority* is the new priority setting. If an error occurs, **SetThreadPriority( )** returns zero. It returns nonzero otherwise. For **GetThreadPriority( )**, the current priority setting is returned. The priority settings are shown here, in order of highest to lowest:

Thread Priority	Value
THREAD_PRIORITY_TIME_CRITICAL	15
THREAD_PRIORITY_HIGHEST	2
THREAD_PRIORITY_ABOVE_NORMAL	1
THREAD_PRIORITY_NORMAL	0
THREAD_PRIORITY_BELOW_NORMAL	-1
THREAD_PRIORITY_LOWEST	-2
THREAD_PRIORITY_IDLE	-15

These values are increments or decrements that are applied relative to the priority class of the process. Through the combination of a process' priority class and thread priority, Windows supports 31 different priority settings for application programs.

GetThreadPriority( ) returns **THREAD_PRIORITY_ERROR_RETURN** if an error occurs.

For the most part, if a thread has the normal priority class, you can freely experiment with changing its priority setting without fear of catastrophically affecting overall system performance. As you will see, the thread control panel developed in the next section allows you to alter the priority setting of a thread within a process (but does not change its priority class).

Obtaining the Handle of the Main Thread

It is possible to control the execution of the main thread. To do so, you will need to acquire its handle. The easiest way to do this is to call **GetCurrentThread( )**, whose prototype is shown here:

> HANDLE GetCurrentThread(void);

This function returns a pseudohandle to the current thread. It is called a pseudohandle because it is a predefined value that always refers to the current thread rather than specifically to the calling thread. It can, however, be used any place that a normal thread handle can.

Synchronization

When using multiple threads or processes, it is sometimes necessary to coordinate the activities of two or more. This process is called *synchronization*. The most common use of synchronization occurs when two or more threads need access to a shared resource that must be used by only one thread at a time. For example, when one thread is writing to a file, a second thread must be prevented from doing so at the same time. Another reason for synchronization is when one thread is waiting for an event that is caused by another thread. In this case, there must be some means by which the first thread is held in a suspended state until the event has occurred. Then the waiting thread must resume execution.

There are two general states that a task may be in. First, it may be *executing* (or ready to execute as soon as it obtains its time slice). Second, a task may be *blocked*, awaiting some resource or event, in which case its execution is *suspended* until the needed resource is available or the event occurs.

If you are not familiar with the synchronization problem or its most common solution, the semaphore, the next section discusses it.

Understanding the Synchronization Problem

Windows must provide special services that allow access to a shared resource to be synchronized, because without help from the operating system, there is no way for one process or thread to know that it has sole access to a resource. To understand this, imagine that you are writing programs for a multitasking operating system that does not provide any synchronization support. Further imagine that you have two concurrently executing threads, A and B, both of which, from time to time, require access to some resource R (such as a disk file) that must be accessed by only one thread at a time. As a means of preventing one thread from accessing R while the other is using it, you try the following solution. First, you establish a variable called **flag** that is initialized to zero and can be accessed by both threads. Then, before using each piece of code that accesses R, you wait for **flag** to be cleared, then set **flag**, access R, and finally, clear **flag**. That is, before either thread accesses R, it executes this piece of code:

```
while(flag) ; // wait for flag to be cleared
flag = 1; // set flag

// ... access resource R ...

flag = 0; // clear the flag
```

The idea behind this code is that neither thread will access R if **flag** is set. Conceptually, this approach is in the spirit of the correct solution. However, in actual fact it leaves much to be desired for one simple reason: it won't always work! Let's see why.

Using the code just given, it is possible for both processes to access R at the same time. The **while** loop is, in essence, performing repeated load and compare instructions on **flag** or, in other words, it is testing **flag**'s value. When **flag** is cleared, the next line of code sets **flag**'s value. The trouble is that it is possible for these two operations to be performed in two different time slices. Between the two time slices, the value of **flag** might have been accessed by the other thread, thus allowing R to be used by both threads at the same time. To understand this, imagine that thread A enters the **while** loop and finds that **flag** is zero, which is the green light to access R. However, before it can set **flag** to 1, its time slice expires and thread B resumes execution. If B executes its **while**, it too will find that **flag** is not set and assume that it is safe to access R. However, when A resumes it will also begin accessing R. The crucial aspect of the problem is that the testing and setting of **flag** do not comprise one uninterruptible operation. Rather, as just illustrated, they can be separated by a time slice. No matter how you try, there is no way, using only application-level code, that you can absolutely guarantee that one and only one thread will access R at one time.

The solution to the synchronization problem is as elegant as it is simple. The operating system (in this case Windows) provides a routine that in one uninterrupted operation, tests and, if possible, sets a flag. In the language of operating systems engineers, this is called a *test and set* operation. For historical reasons, the flags used to control access to a shared resource and provide synchronization between threads (and processes) are called *semaphores*. The semaphore is at the core of the Windows synchronization system.

The Windows Synchronization Objects

Windows supports several types of synchronization objects. The first type is the classic semaphore. When using a semaphore, a resource can be completely synchronized, in which case one and only one thread or process can access it at any one time, or the semaphore can allow no more than a small number of processes or threads access at any one time. Semaphores are implemented using a counter that is decremented when a task is granted the semaphore and incremented when the task releases it.

The second synchronization object is the mutex semaphore, or just *mutex*, for short. A mutex synchronizes a resource such that one and only one thread or process can access it at any one time. In essence, a mutex is a special case version of a standard semaphore.

The third synchronization object is the *event object*. It can be used to block access to a resource until some other thread or process signals that it can be used. (That is, an event object signals that a specified event has occurred.)

The fourth synchronization object is the *waitable timer*. A waitable timer blocks a thread's execution until a specific time. You can also create *timer queues*, which are lists of timers.

You can prevent a section of code from being used by more than one thread at a time by making it into a *critical section* using a critical section object. Once a critical section is entered by one thread, no other thread may use it until the first thread has left the critical section.

The only synchronization object used in this chapter is the mutex, which is described in the following section. However, all synchronization objects defined by Windows are available to the C++ programmer. As explained, this is one of the major advantages that results from C++'s reliance on the operating system to handle multithreading: all multithreading features are at your command.

Using a Mutex to Synchronize Threads

As explained, a mutex is a special-case semaphore that allows only one thread to access a resource at any given time. Before you can use a mutex, you must create one using **CreateMutex( )**, whose prototype is shown here:

```
HANDLE CreateMutex(LPSECURITY_ATTRIBUTES secAttr,
                   BOOL acquire,
                   LPCSTR name);
```

Here, *secAttr* is a pointer to the security attributes. If *secAttr* is **NULL**, the default security descriptor is used.

If the creating thread desires control of the mutex, then *acquire* must be **true**. Otherwise, pass **false**.

The *name* parameter points to a string that becomes the name of the mutex object. Mutexes are global objects, which may be used by other processes. As such, when two processes each open a mutex using the same name, both are referring to the same mutex. In this way, two processes can be synchronized. The name may also be **NULL**, in which case the semaphore is localized to one process.

The **CreateMutex( )** function returns a handle to the semaphore if successful or **NULL** on failure. A mutex handle is automatically closed when the main process ends. You can explicitly close a mutex handle when it is no longer needed by calling **CloseHandle( )**.

Once you have created a semaphore, you use it by calling two related functions: **WaitForSingleObject( )** and **ReleaseMutex( )**. The prototypes for these functions are shown here:

```
DWORD WaitForSingleObject(HANDLE hObject, DWORD howLong);

BOOL ReleaseMutex(HANDLE hMutex);
```

WaitForSingleObject( ) waits on a synchronization object. It does not return until the object becomes available or a time-out occurs. For use with mutexes, *hObject* will be the handle of a mutex. The *howLong* parameter specifies, in milliseconds, how long the calling routine will wait. Once that time has elapsed, a time-out error will be returned. To wait indefinitely, use the value **INFINITE**. The function returns **WAIT_OBJECT_0** when successful (that is, when access is granted). It returns **WAIT_TIMEOUT** when time-out is reached.

ReleaseMutex( ) releases the mutex and allows another thread to acquire it. Here, *hMutex* is the handle to the mutex. The function returns nonzero if successful and zero on failure.

To use a mutex to control access to a shared resource, wrap the code that accesses that resource between a call to **WaitForSingleObject( )** and **ReleaseMutex( )**, as shown in this skeleton. (Of course, the time-out period will differ from application to application.)

```
if(WaitForSingleObject(hMutex, 10000)==WAIT_TIMEOUT) {
   // handle time-out error
}

 // access the resource

ReleaseMutex(hMutex);
```

Generally, you will want to choose a time-out period that will be more than enough to accommodate the actions of your program. If you get repeated time-out errors when developing a multithreaded application, it usually means that you have created a *deadlock* condition. Deadlock occurs when one thread is waiting on a mutex that another thread never releases.

Creating a Thread Control Panel

When developing multithreaded programs, it is often useful to experiment with various priority settings. It is also useful to be able to dynamically suspend and resume a thread, or even terminate a thread. As you will see, it is quite easy, using the thread functions just described, to create a thread control panel that allows you to accomplish these things. Further, you can use the control panel while your multithreaded program is running. The dynamic nature of the thread control panel allows you to easily change the execution profile of a thread and observe the results.

The thread control panel developed in this section is capable of controlling one thread. However, you can create as many panels as needed, with each controlling a different thread. For the sake of simplicity, the control panel is implemented as a modeless dialog box that is owned by the desktop, not the application whose thread it controls.

The thread control panel is capable of performing the following actions:

►   Setting a thread's priority

►   Suspending a thread

►   Resuming a thread

►   Terminating a thread

It also displays the current priority setting of the thread. The thread control dialog box is shown in Figure 3-1.

As stated, the control panel is a modeless dialog box. As you know, when a modeless dialog box is activated, the rest of the application is still active. Thus, the control panel runs independently of the application for which it is being used.

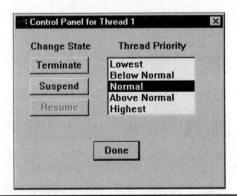

Figure 3-1   *The Thread Control dialog box*

The Thread Control Panel

The code for the thread control panel is shown here. This file is called **tcp.cpp**.

```cpp
// A thread control panel.

#include <map>
#include <windows.h>
#include "panel.h"
using namespace std;

const int NUMPRIORITIES = 5;
const int OFFSET = 2;

// Array of strings for priority list box.
char priorities[NUMPRIORITIES][80] = {
  "Lowest",
  "Below Normal",
  "Normal",
  "Above Normal",
  "Highest"
};

// A Thread Control Panel Class.
class ThrdCtrlPanel {
  // Information about the thread under control.
  struct ThreadInfo {
    HANDLE hThread; // handle of thread
    int priority;    // current priority
    bool suspended; // true if suspended
    ThreadInfo(HANDLE ht, int p, bool s) {
      hThread = ht;
      priority = p;
      suspended = s;
    }
  };

  // This map holds a ThreadInfo for each
  // active thread control panel.
  static map<HWND, ThreadInfo> dialogmap;

public:

  // Construct a control panel.
  ThrdCtrlPanel(HINSTANCE hInst, HANDLE hThrd);
```

```
    // The control panel's callback function.
    static LRESULT CALLBACK ThreadPanel(HWND hwnd, UINT message,
                        WPARAM wParam, LPARAM lParam);
};

// Define static member dialogmap.
map<HWND, ThrdCtrlPanel::ThreadInfo>
    ThrdCtrlPanel::dialogmap;

// Create a thread control panel.
ThrdCtrlPanel::ThrdCtrlPanel(HINSTANCE hInst,
                        HANDLE hThrd)
{
    ThreadInfo ti(hThrd,
                GetThreadPriority(hThrd)+OFFSET,
                false);

    // Owner window is desktop.
    HWND hDialog = CreateDialog(hInst, "ThreadPanelDB",
                    NULL,
                    (DLGPROC) ThreadPanel);

    // Put info about this dialog box in the map.
    dialogmap.insert(pair<HWND, ThreadInfo>(hDialog, ti));

    // Set the control panel's title.
    char str[80] = "Control Panel for Thread ";
    char str2[4];
    _itoa(dialogmap.size(), str2, 10);
    strcat(str, str2);
    SetWindowText(hDialog, str);

    // Offset each dialog box instance.
    MoveWindow(hDialog, 30*dialogmap.size(),
            30*dialogmap.size(),
            300, 250, 1);

    // Update priority setting in the list box.
    SendDlgItemMessage(hDialog, IDD_LB, LB_SETCURSEL,
                        (WPARAM) ti.priority, 0);

// Increase priority to ensure control.  You can
// change or remove this statement based on your
// execution environment.
SetThreadPriority(GetCurrentThread(),
```

```
                         THREAD_PRIORITY_ABOVE_NORMAL);
}


// Thread control panel dialog box callback function.
LRESULT CALLBACK ThrdCtrlPanel::ThreadPanel(HWND hwnd,
                                   UINT message,
                                   WPARAM wParam,
                                   LPARAM lParam)
{
  int i;
  HWND hpbRes, hpbSus, hpbTerm;

  switch(message) {
    case WM_INITDIALOG:
      // Initialize priority list box.
      for(i=0; i<NUMPRIORITIES; i++) {
        SendDlgItemMessage(hwnd, IDD_LB,
           LB_ADDSTRING, 0, (LPARAM) priorities[i]);
        }

        // Set suspend and resume buttons for thread.
        hpbSus = GetDlgItem(hwnd, IDD_SUSPEND);
        hpbRes = GetDlgItem(hwnd, IDD_RESUME);
        EnableWindow(hpbSus, true);  // enable Suspend
        EnableWindow(hpbRes, false); // disable Resume
        return 1;
    case WM_COMMAND:
      map<HWND, ThreadInfo>::iterator p = dialogmap.find(hwnd);

     switch(LOWORD(wParam)) {
       case IDD_TERMINATE:
         TerminateThread(p->second.hThread, 0);

         // Disable Terminate button.
         hpbTerm = GetDlgItem(hwnd, IDD_TERMINATE); }
         EnableWindow(hpbTerm, false); // disable

         // Disable Suspend and Resume buttons.
         hpbSus = GetDlgItem(hwnd, IDD_SUSPEND);
         hpbRes = GetDlgItem(hwnd, IDD_RESUME);
         EnableWindow(hpbSus, false); // disable Suspend
         EnableWindow(hpbRes, false); // disable Resume

         return 1;
       case IDD_SUSPEND:
```

```
SuspendThread(p->second.hThread);

  // Set state of the Suspend and Resume buttons.
  hpbSus = GetDlgItem(hwnd, IDD_SUSPEND);
  hpbRes = GetDlgItem(hwnd, IDD_RESUME);
  EnableWindow(hpbSus, false); // disable Suspend
  EnableWindow(hpbRes, true);  // enable Resume

  p->second.suspended = true;
  return 1;
case IDD_RESUME:
  ResumeThread(p->second.hThread);

  // Set state of the Suspend and Resume buttons.
  hpbSus = GetDlgItem(hwnd, IDD_SUSPEND);
  hpbRes = GetDlgItem(hwnd, IDD_RESUME);
  EnableWindow(hpbSus, true);  // enable Suspend
  EnableWindow(hpbRes, false); // disable Resume

  p->second.suspended = false;
  return 1;
case IDD_LB:
  // If a list box entry was clicked,
  // then change the priority.
   if(HIWORD(wParam)==LBN_DBLCLK) {
    p->second.priority = SendDlgItemMessage(hwnd,
                    IDD_LB, LB_GETCURSEL,
                    0, 0);
    SetThreadPriority(p->second.hThread,
                    p->second.priority-OFFSET);
   }
   return 1;
 case IDCANCEL:
   // If thread is suspended when panel is closed,
   // then resume thread to prevent deadlock.
   if(p->second.suspended) {
     ResumeThread(p->second.hThread);
    p->second.suspended = false;
   }

   // Remove this thread from the list.
   dialogmap.erase(hwnd);

   // Close the panel.
   DestroyWindow(hwnd);
   return 1;
```

```
      }
    }
    return 0;
}
```

The control panel requires the following resource file, called **tcp.rc**:

```
#include <windows.h>
#include "panel.h"

ThreadPanelDB DIALOGEX 20, 20, 140, 110
CAPTION "Thread Control Panel"
STYLE WS_BORDER | WS_VISIBLE | WS_POPUP | WS_CAPTION | WS_SYSMENU
{
  DEFPUSHBUTTON "Done", IDCANCEL, 55, 80, 33, 14
  PUSHBUTTON "Terminate", IDD_TERMINATE, 10, 20, 42, 12
  PUSHBUTTON "Suspend", IDD_SUSPEND, 10, 35, 42, 12
  PUSHBUTTON "Resume", IDD_RESUME, 10, 50, 42, 12
  LISTBOX IDD_LB, 65, 20, 63, 42, LBS_NOTIFY | WS_VISIBLE |
          WS_BORDER | WS_VSCROLL | WS_TABSTOP
  CTEXT "Thread Priority", IDD_TEXT1, 65, 8, 64, 10
  CTEXT "Change State", IDD_TEXT2, 0, 8, 64, 10
}
```

The control panel uses the following header file called **panel.h**:

```
#define IDD_LB          200
#define IDD_TERMINATE   202
#define IDD_SUSPEND     204
#define IDD_RESUME      206
#define IDD_TEXT1       208
#define IDD_TEXT2       209
```

To use the thread control panel, follow these steps:

1. Include **tcp.cpp** in your program.
2. Include **tcp.rc** in your program's resource file.
3. Create the thread or threads that you want to control.
4. Instantiate a **ThrdCtrlPanel** object for each thread.

Each **ThrdCtrlPanel** object links a thread with a dialog box that controls it.

For large projects in which multiple files need access to **ThrdCtrlPanel**, you will need to use a header file called **tcp.h** that contains the declaration for **ThrdCtrlPanel**. Here is **tcp.h**:

```
// A header file for the ThrdCtrlPanel class.

class ThrdCtrlPanel {
```

```
public:

  // Construct a control panel.
  ThrdCtrlPanel(HINSTANCE hInst, HANDLE hThrd);

  // The control panel's callback function.
  static LRESULT CALLBACK ThreadPanel(HWND hwnd, UINT message,
                          WPARAM wParam, LPARAM lParam);
};
```

A Closer Look at the Thread Control Panel

Let's take a closer look at the thread control panel. It begins by defining the following global definitions:

```
const int NUMPRIORITIES = 5;
const int OFFSET = 2;

// Array of strings for priority list box.
char priorities[NUMPRIORITIES][80] = {
  "Lowest",
  "Below Normal",
  "Normal",
  "Above Normal",
  "Highest"
};
```

The **priorities** array holds strings that correspond to a thread's priority setting. It initializes the list box inside the control panel that displays the current thread priority. The number of priorities is specified by **NUMPRIORITIES**, which is 5 for Windows. Thus, **NUMPRIORITIES** defines the number of different priorities that a thread may have. (If you adapt the code for use with another operating system, a different value might be required.) Using the control panel, you can set a thread to one of the following priorities:

> THREAD_PRIORITY_HIGHEST
>
> THREAD_PRIORITY_ABOVE_NORMAL
>
> THREAD_PRIORITY_NORMAL
>
> THREAD_PRIORITY_BELOW_NORMAL
>
> THREAD_PRIORITY_LOWEST

The other two thread priority settings:

> THREAD_PRIORITY_TIME_CRITICAL
>
> THREAD_PRIORITY_IDLE

are not supported because, relative to the control panel, they are of little practical value. For example, if you want to create a time-critical application, you are better off making its priority class time-critical.

OFFSET defines an offset that will be used to translate between list box indexes and thread priorities. You should recall that normal priority has the value zero. In this example, the highest priority is **THREAD_PRIORITY_HIGHEST**, which is 2. The lowest priority is **THREAD_PRIORITY_LOWEST**, which is –2. Because list box indexes begin at zero, the offset is used to convert between indexes and priority settings.

Next, the **ThrdCtrlPanel** class is declared. It begins as shown here:

```
// A Thread Control Panel Class.
class ThrdCtrlPanel {
  // Information about the thread under control.
  struct ThreadInfo {
    HANDLE hThread; // handle of thread
    int priority;   // current priority
    bool suspended; // true if suspended
    ThreadInfo(HANDLE ht, int p, bool s) {
      hThread = ht;
      priority = p;
      suspended = s;
    }
  };

  // This map holds a ThreadInfo for each
  // active thread control panel.
  static map<HWND, ThreadInfo> dialogmap;
```

Information about the thread under control is contained within a structure of type **ThreadInfo**. The handle of the thread is stored in **hThread**. Its priority is stored in **priority**. If the thread is suspended, then **suspended** will be **true**. Otherwise, **suspended** will be **false**.

The **static** member **dialogmap** is an STL map that links the thread information with the handle of the dialog box used to control that thread. Because there can be more than one thread control panel active at any given time, there must be some way to determine which thread is associated with which panel. It is **dialogmap** that provides this linkage.

The ThreadCtrlPanel Constructor

The **ThrdCtrlPanel** constructor is shown here. The constructor is passed the instance handle of the application and the handle of the thread being controlled. The instance handle is needed to create the control panel dialog box.

```
// Create a thread control panel.
ThrdCtrlPanel::ThrdCtrlPanel(HINSTANCE hInst,
                            HANDLE hThrd)
{
  ThreadInfo ti(hThrd,
```

```
                    GetThreadPriority(hThrd)+OFFSET,
                    false);


  // Owner window is desktop.
  HWND hDialog = CreateDialog(hInst, "ThreadPanelDB",
                    NULL,
                    (DLGPROC) ThreadPanel);


  // Put info about this dialog box in the map.
  dialogmap.insert(pair<HWND, ThreadInfo>(hDialog, ti));


  // Set the control panel's title.
  char str[80] = "Control Panel for Thread ";
  char str2[4];
  _itoa(dialogmap.size(), str2, 10);
  strcat(str, str2);
  SetWindowText(hDialog, str);


  // Offset each dialog box instance.
  MoveWindow(hDialog, 30*dialogmap.size(),
            30*dialogmap.size(),
            300, 250, 1);


  // Update priority setting in the list box.
  SendDlgItemMessage(hDialog, IDD_LB, LB_SETCURSEL,
                    (WPARAM) ti.priority, 0);


  // Increase priority to ensure control.  You can
  // change or remove this statement based on your
  // execution environment.
  SetThreadPriority(GetCurrentThread(),
                    THREAD_PRIORITY_ABOVE_NORMAL);
}
```

The constructor begins by creating a **ThreadInfo** instance called **ti** that contains the initial settings for the thread. Notice that the priority is obtained by calling **GetThreadPriority( )** for the thread being controlled. Next, the control panel dialog box is created by calling **CreateDialog( )**. **CreateDialog( )** is a Windows API function that creates a modeless dialog box, which makes it independent of the application that creates it. The handle of this dialog box is returned and stored in **hDialog**. Next, **hDialog** and the thread information contained in **ti** are stored in **dialogmap**. Thus, the thread is linked with the dialog box that controls it.

Next, the title of the dialog box is set to reflect the number of the thread. The number of the thread is obtained based on the number of entries in **dialogmap**. An alternative that you might want to try implementing is to explicitly pass a name for each thread to the **ThrdCtrlPanel** constructor. For the purposes of this chapter, simply numbering each thread is sufficient.

Next, the control panel's position on the screen is offset a bit by calling **MoveWindow( )**, another Windows API function. This enables multiple panels to be displayed without each one fully covering the one before it. The thread's priority setting is then displayed in the priority list box by calling the Windows API function **SendDlgItemMessage( )**.

Finally, the current thread has its priority increased to above normal. This ensures that the application receives enough CPU time to be responsive to user input no matter what is the priority level of the thread under control. This step may not be needed in all cases. You can experiment to find out.

The ThreadPanel( ) Function

ThreadPanel( ) is the Windows callback function that responds to user interaction with the thread control panel. Like all dialog box callback functions, it receives a message each time the user changes the state of a control. It is passed the handle of the dialog box in which the action occurred, the message, and any additional information required by the message. Its general mode of operation is the same as that for any other callback function used by a dialog box. The following discussion describes what happens for each message.

When the thread control panel dialog box is first created, it receives a **WM_INITDIALOG** message, which is handled by this **case** sequence:

```
case WM_INITDIALOG:
  // Initialize priority list box.
  for(i=0; i<NUMPRIORITIES; i++) {
    SendDlgItemMessage(hwnd, IDD_LB,
        LB_ADDSTRING, 0, (LPARAM) priorities[i]);
  }

  // Set Suspend and Resume buttons for thread.
  hpbSus = GetDlgItem(hwnd, IDD_SUSPEND);
  hpbRes = GetDlgItem(hwnd, IDD_RESUME);
  EnableWindow(hpbSus, true);  // enable Suspend
  EnableWindow(hpbRes, false); // disable Resume
  return 1;
```

This initializes the priority list box and sets the Suspend and Resume buttons to their initial states, which are Suspend enabled and Resume disabled.

Each user interaction generates a **WM_COMMAND** message. Each time this message is received, an iterator to this dialog box's entry in **dialogmap** is retrieved, as shown here:

```
case WM_COMMAND:
  map<HWND, ThreadInfo>::iterator p = dialogmap.find(hwnd);
```

The information pointed to by **p** will be used to properly process each action. Because **p** is an iterator for a map, it points to an object of type **pair**, which is a structure defined by the STL. This structure contains two fields: **first** and **second**. These fields correspond to the information that comprises the key and the value, respectively. In this case, the handle is the key and the thread information is the value.

A code indicating precisely what action has occurred is contained in the low-order word of **wParam**, which is used to control a **switch** statement that handles the remaining messages. Each is described next.

When the user presses the Terminate button, the thread under control is stopped. This is handled by this **case** sequence:

```
case IDD_TERMINATE:
  TerminateThread(p->second.hThread, 0);

  // Disable Terminate button.
  hpbTerm = GetDlgItem(hwnd, IDD_TERMINATE);
  EnableWindow(hpbTerm, false); // disable

  // Disable Suspend and Resume buttons.
  hpbSus = GetDlgItem(hwnd, IDD_SUSPEND);
  hpbRes = GetDlgItem(hwnd, IDD_RESUME);
  EnableWindow(hpbSus, false); // disable Suspend
  EnableWindow(hpbRes, false); // disable Resume

  return 1;
```

The thread is stopped with a call to **TerminateThread( )**. Notice how the handle for the thread is obtained. As explained, because **p** is an iterator for a map, it points to an object of type **pair** that contains the key in its **first** field and the value in its **second** field. This is why the thread handle is obtained by the expression **p->second.hThread**. After the thread is stopped, the Terminate button is disabled.

Once a thread has been terminated, it cannot be resumed. Notice that the control panel uses **TerminateThread( )** to halt execution of a thread. As mentioned earlier, this function must be used with care. If you use the control panel to experiment with threads of your own, you will want to make sure that no harmful side effects are possible.

When the user presses the Suspend button, the thread is suspended. This is accomplished by the following sequence:

```
case IDD_SUSPEND:
  SuspendThread(p->second.hThread);

  // Set state of the Suspend and Resume buttons.
  hpbSus = GetDlgItem(hwnd, IDD_SUSPEND);
  hpbRes = GetDlgItem(hwnd, IDD_RESUME);
  EnableWindow(hpbSus, false); // disable Suspend
  EnableWindow(hpbRes, true);  // enable Resume

  p->second.suspended = true;
  return 1;
```

The thread is suspended by a call to **SuspendThread( )**. Next, the state of the Suspend and Resume buttons are updated such that Resume is enabled and Suspend is disabled. This prevents the user from attempting to suspend a thread twice.

A suspended thread is resumed when the Resume button is pressed. It is handled by this code:

```
case IDD_RESUME:
  ResumeThread(p->second.hThread);

  // Set state of the Suspend and Resume buttons.
  hpbSus = GetDlgItem(hwnd, IDD_SUSPEND);
  hpbRes = GetDlgItem(hwnd, IDD_RESUME);
  EnableWindow(hpbSus, true);  // enable Suspend
  EnableWindow(hpbRes, false); // disable Resume

  p->second.suspended = false;
  return 1;
```

The thread is resumed by a call to **ResumeThread( )**, and the Suspend and Resume buttons are set appropriately.

To change a thread's priority, the user double-clicks an entry in the Priority list box. This event is handled as shown next:

```
case IDD_LB:
  // If a list box entry was double-clicked,
  // then change the priority.
  if(HIWORD(wParam)==LBN_DBLCLK) {
    p->second.priority = SendDlgItemMessage(hwnd,
                       IDD_LB, LB_GETCURSEL,
                       0, 0);
    SetThreadPriority(p->second.hThread,
                    p->second.priority-OFFSET);
  }
  return 1;
```

List boxes generate various types of notification messages that describe the precise type of event that occurred. Notification messages are contained in the high-order word of **wParam**. One of these messages is **LBN_DBLCLK**, which means that the user double-clicked an entry in the box. When this notification is received, the index of the entry is retrieved by calling the Windows API function **SendDlgItemMessage( )**, requesting the current selection. This value is then used to set the thread's priority. Notice that **OFFSET** is subtracted to normalize the value of the index.

Finally, when the user closes the thread control panel dialog box, the **IDCANCEL** message is sent. It is handled by the following sequence:

```
case IDCANCEL:
  // If thread is suspended when panel is closed,
  // then resume thread to prevent deadlock.
  if(p->second.suspended) {
```

```
    ResumeThread(p->second.hThread);
    p->second.suspended = false;
}

// Remove this thread from the list.
dialogmap.erase(hwnd);

// Close the panel.
DestroyWindow(hwnd);
return 1;
```

If the thread was suspended, it is restarted. This is necessary to avoid accidentally deadlocking the thread. Next, this dialog box's entry in **dialogmap** is removed. Finally, the dialog box is removed by calling the Windows API function **DestroyWindow( )**.

Demonstrating the Control Panel

Here is a program that includes the thread control panel and demonstrates its use. Sample output is shown in Figure 3-2. The program creates a main window and defines two child threads. When started, these threads simply count from 0 to 50,000, displaying the count in the main window. These threads can be controlled by activating a thread control panel.

To use the program, first begin execution of the threads by selecting Start Threads from the Threads menu (or by pressing F2) and then activate the thread control panels by selecting Control Panels from the Threads menu (or by pressing F3). Once the control panels are active, you can experiment with different priority settings and so on.

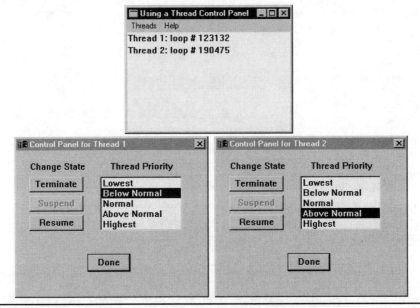

Figure 3-2   *Sample output from the thread control panel sample program*

NOTE

It is beyond the scope of this book to teach Windows programming. However, the operation of this sample program is straightforward and should be easily understood by all Windows programmers.

```
// Demonstrate the thread control panel.
#include <windows.h>
#include <process.h>
#include "thrdapp.h"
#include "tcp.cpp"

const int MAX = 500000;

LRESULT CALLBACK WindowFunc(HWND, UINT, WPARAM, LPARAM);

unsigned __stdcall MyThread1(void * param);
unsigned __stdcall MyThread2(void * param);

char str[255]; // holds output strings

unsigned tid1, tid2; // thread IDs
HANDLE hThread1, hThread2; // thread handles

HINSTANCE hInst; // instance handle

int WINAPI WinMain(HINSTANCE hThisInst, HINSTANCE hPrevInst,
                   LPSTR args, int winMode)
{
  HWND hwnd;
  MSG msg;
  WNDCLASSEX wcl;
  HACCEL hAccel;

  // Define a window class.
  wcl.cbSize = sizeof(WNDCLASSEX);

  wcl.hInstance = hThisInst;      // handle to this instance
  wcl.lpszClassName = "MyWin";    // window class name
  wcl.lpfnWndProc = WindowFunc;   // window function
  wcl.style = 0;                  // default style

  wcl.hIcon = LoadIcon(NULL, IDI_APPLICATION); // large icon
  wcl.hIconSm = NULL; // use small version of large icon
  wcl.hCursor = LoadCursor(NULL, IDC_ARROW);  // cursor style
```

```
wcl.lpszMenuName = "ThreadAppMenu"; // main menu

wcl.cbClsExtra = 0; // no extra memory needed
wcl.cbWndExtra = 0;

// Make the window background white.
wcl.hbrBackground = (HBRUSH) GetStockObject(WHITE_BRUSH);

// Register the window class.
if(!RegisterClassEx(&wcl)) return 0;

/* Now that a window class has been registered, a window
   can be created. */
hwnd = CreateWindow(
  wcl.lpszClassName, // name of window class
  "Using a Thread Control Panel", // title
  WS_OVERLAPPEDWINDOW, // window style - normal
  CW_USEDEFAULT, // X coordinate - let Windows decide
  CW_USEDEFAULT, // Y coordinate - let Windows decide
  260,            // width
  200,            // height
  NULL,           // no parent window
  NULL,           // no override of class menu
  hThisInst,      // instance handle
  NULL            // no additional arguments
);

hInst = hThisInst; // save instance handle

// Load the keyboard accelerators.
hAccel = LoadAccelerators(hThisInst, "ThreadAppMenu");

// Display the window.
ShowWindow(hwnd, winMode);
UpdateWindow(hwnd);

// Create the message loop.
while(GetMessage(&msg, NULL, 0, 0))
{
  if(!TranslateAccelerator(hwnd, hAccel, &msg)) {
    TranslateMessage(&msg); // translate keyboard messages
    DispatchMessage(&msg); // return control to Windows
  }
}
```

```
    return msg.wParam;
}


/* This function is called by Windows and is passed
   messages from the message queue.
*/
LRESULT CALLBACK WindowFunc(HWND hwnd, UINT message,
                            WPARAM wParam, LPARAM lParam)
{
  int response;

  switch(message) {
    case WM_COMMAND:
      switch(LOWORD(wParam)) {
        case IDM_THREAD: // create the threads
          hThread1 = (HANDLE) _beginthreadex(NULL, 0,
                                MyThread1, (void *) hwnd,
                                0, &tid1);
          hThread2 = (HANDLE) _beginthreadex(NULL, 0,
                                MyThread2, (void *) hwnd,
                                0, &tid2);
          break;
        case IDM_PANEL: // activate control panel
          ThrdCtrlPanel(hInst, hThread1);
          ThrdCtrlPanel(hInst, hThread2);
          break;
        case IDM_EXIT:
          response = MessageBox(hwnd, "Quit the Program?",
                                "Exit", MB_YESNO);
          if(response == IDYES) PostQuitMessage(0);
          break;
        case IDM_HELP:
          MessageBox(hwnd,
                  "F1: Help\nF2: Start Threads\nF3: Panel",
                  "Help", MB_OK);
          break;
      }
      break;
    case WM_DESTROY: // terminate the program
      PostQuitMessage(0);
      break;
    default:
     return DefWindowProc(hwnd, message, wParam, lParam);
  }
```

```
    return 0;
}


// First thread.
unsigned __stdcall MyThread1(void * param)
{
  int i;
  HDC hdc;

  for(i=0; i<MAX; i++) {
    wsprintf(str, "Thread 1: loop # %5d ", i);
    hdc = GetDC((HWND) param);
    TextOut(hdc, 1, 1, str, lstrlen(str));
    ReleaseDC((HWND) param, hdc);
  }

  return 0;
}


// Second thread.
unsigned __stdcall MyThread2(void * param)
{
  int i;
  HDC hdc;

  for(i=0; i<MAX; i++) {
    wsprintf(str, "Thread 2: loop # %5d ", i);
    hdc = GetDC((HWND) param);
    TextOut(hdc, 1, 20, str, lstrlen(str));
    ReleaseDC((HWND) param, hdc);
  }

  return 0;
}
```

This program requires the header file **thrdapp.h**, shown here:

```
#define IDM_THREAD    100
#define IDM_HELP      101
#define IDM_PANEL     102
#define IDM_EXIT      103
```

The resource file required by the program is shown here:

```
#include <windows.h>
#include "thrdapp.h"
```

```
#include "tcp.rc"

ThreadAppMenu MENU
{
  POPUP "&Threads" {
    MENUITEM "&Start Threads\tF2", IDM_THREAD
    MENUITEM "&Control Panels\tF3", IDM_PANEL
    MENUITEM "E&xit\tCtrl+X", IDM_EXIT
  }
  MENUITEM "&Help", IDM_HELP
}

ThreadAppMenu ACCELERATORS
{
  VK_F1, IDM_HELP, VIRTKEY
  VK_F2, IDM_THREAD, VIRTKEY
  VK_F3, IDM_PANEL, VIRTKEY
  "^X", IDM_EXIT
}
```

A Multithreaded Garbage Collector

Although controlling threads using the thread control panel is useful when developing multithreaded programs, ultimately it is using threads that makes them important. Toward this end, this chapter shows a multithreaded version of the **GCPtr** garbage collector class originally developed in Chapter 2. Recall that the version of **GCPtr** shown in Chapter 2 collected unused memory each time a **GCPtr** object went out of scope. Although this approach is fine for some applications, often a better alternative is to have the garbage collector run as a background task, recycling memory whenever free CPU cycles are available. The implementation developed here is designed for Windows, but the same basic techniques apply to other multithreaded environments.

To convert **GCPtr** into a background task is actually fairly easy, but it does involve a number of changes. Here are the main ones:

1. Member variables that support the thread must be added to **GCPtr**. These variables include the thread handle, the mutex handle, and an instance counter that keeps track of the number of **GCPtr** objects in existence.

2. The constructor for **GCPtr** must start the garbage collection thread. The constructor must also create the mutex that controls synchronization. This must happen only once, when the first **GCPtr** object is created.

3. Another exception must be defined that will be used to indicate a time-out condition.

4. The **GCPtr** destructor must no longer call **collect( )**. Garbage collection is handled by the garbage collection thread.

5. A function called **gc( )** that serves as the thread entry point for the garbage collector must be defined.

6. A function called **isRunning( )** must be defined. It returns true if the garbage collection is in use.

7. The member functions of **GCPtr** that access the garbage collection list contained in **gclist** must be synchronized so that only one thread at a time can access the list.

The following sections show the changes.

The Additional Member Variables

The multithreaded version of **GCPtr** requires that the following member variables be added:

```
// These support multithreading.
unsigned tid; // thread id
static HANDLE hThrd;  // thread handle
static HANDLE hMutex; // handle of mutex

static int instCount; // counter of GCPtr objects
```

The ID of the thread used by the garbage collector is stored in **tid**. This member is unused except in the call to **_beginthreadex( )**. The handle to the thread is stored in **hThrd**. The handle of the mutex used to synchronize access to **GCPtr** is stored in **hMutex**. A count of **GCPtr** objects in existence is maintained in **instCount**. The last three are **static** because they are shared by all instances of **GCPtr**. They are defined like this, outside of **GCPtr**:

```
template <class T, int size>
  int GCPtr<T, size>::instCount = 0;

template <class T, int size>
  HANDLE GCPtr<T, size>::hMutex = 0;

template <class T, int size>
  HANDLE GCPtr<T, size>::hThrd = 0;
```

The Multithreaded GCPtr Constructor

In addition to its original duties, the multithreaded **GCPtr( )** must create the mutex, start the garbage collector thread, and update the instance counter. Here is the updated version:

```
// Construct both initialized and uninitialized objects.
GCPtr(T *t=NULL) {

  // When first object is created, create the mutex
  // and register shutdown().
  if(hMutex==0) {
    hMutex = CreateMutex(NULL, 0, NULL);
```

```
    atexit(shutdown);
}

if(WaitForSingleObject(hMutex, 10000)==WAIT_TIMEOUT)
  throw TimeOutExc();

list<GCInfo<T> >::iterator p;

p = findPtrInfo(t);

// If t is already in gclist, then
// increment its reference count.
// Otherwise, add it to the list.
if(p != gclist.end())
  p->refcount++; // increment ref count
else {
  // Create and store this entry.
  GCInfo<T> gcObj(t, size);
  gclist.push_front(gcObj);
}

addr = t;
arraySize = size;
if(size > 0) isArray = true;
else isArray = false;

// Increment instance counter for each new object.
instCount++;

// If the garbage collection thread is not
// currently running, start it running.
if(hThrd==0) {
  hThrd = (HANDLE) _beginthreadex(NULL, 0, gc,
          (void *) 0, 0, (unsigned *) &tid);

  // For some applications, it will be better
  // to lower the priority of the garbage collector
  // as shown here:
  //
  // SetThreadPriority(hThrd,
  //                   THREAD_PRIORITY_BELOW_NORMAL);
}

ReleaseMutex(hMutex);
}
```

Let's examine this code closely. First, if **hMutex** is zero, it means that this is the first **GCPtr** object to be created and no mutex has yet been created for the garbage collector. If this is the case, the mutex is created and its handle is assigned to **hMutex**. At the same time, the function **shutdown( )** is registered as a termination function by calling **atexit( )**.

It is important to note that in the multithreaded garbage collector, **shutdown( )** serves two purposes. First, as in the original version of **GCPtr**, **shutdown( )** frees any unused memory that has not been released because of a circular reference. Second, when a program using the multithreaded garbage collector ends, it stops the garbage collection thread. This means that there might still be dynamically allocated objects that haven't been freed. This is important because these objects might have destructors that need to be called. Because **shutdown( )** releases all remaining objects, it also releases these objects.

Next, the mutex is acquired by calling **WaitForSingleObject( )**. This is necessary to prevent two threads from accessing **gclist** at the same time. Once the mutex has been acquired, a search of **gclist** is made, looking for any preexisting entry that matches the address in **t**. If one is found, its reference count is incremented. If no preexising entry matches **t**, a new **GCInfo** object is created that contains this address, and this object is added to **gclist**. Then, **addr**, **arraySize**, and **isArray** are set. These actions are the same as in the original version of **GCPtr**.

Next, **instCount** is incremented. Recall that **instCount** is initialized to zero. Incrementing it each time an object is created keeps track of how many **GCPtr** objects are in existence. As long as this count is above zero, the garbage collector will continue to execute.

Next, if **hThrd** is zero (as it is initially), then no thread has yet been created for the garbage collector. In this case, **_beginthreadex( )** is called to begin the thread. A handle to the thread is then assigned to **hThrd**. The thread entry function is called **gc( )**, and it is examined shortly.

Finally, the mutex is released and the constructor returns. It is important to point out that each call to **WaitForSingleObject( )** must be balanced by a call to **ReleaseMutex( )**, as shown in the **GCPtr** constructor. Failure to release the mutex will cause deadlock.

The TimeOutExc Exception

As you probably noticed in the code for **GCPtr( )** described in the preceding section, if the mutex cannot be acquired after 10 seconds, then a **TimeOutExc** is thrown. Frankly, 10 seconds is a very long time, so a time-out shouldn't ever happen unless something disrupts the task scheduler of the operating system. However, in the event it does occur, your application code may want to catch this exception. The **TimeOutExc** class is shown here:

```
// Exception thrown when a time-out occurs
// when waiting for access to hMutex.
//
class TimeOutExc {
  // Add functionality if needed by your application.
};
```

Notice that it contains no members. Its existence as a unique type is sufficient for the purposes of this chapter. Of course, you can add functionality if desired.

The Multithreaded GCPtr Destructor

Unlike the single-threaded version of the **GCPtr** destructor, the multithreaded version of **~GCPtr( )** does not call **collect( )**. Instead, it simply decrements the reference count of the memory pointed to by the **GCPtr** that is going out of scope. The actual collection of garbage (if any exists) is handled by the garbage collection thread. The destructor also decrements the instance counter, **instCount**.

The multithreaded version of **~GCPtr( )** is shown here:

```
// Destructor for GCPtr.
template <class T, int size>
GCPtr<T, size>::~GCPtr() {
  if(WaitForSingleObject(hMutex, 10000)==WAIT_TIMEOUT)
    throw TimeOutExc();

  list<GCInfo<T> >::iterator p;

  p = findPtrInfo(addr);
  if(p->refcount) p->refcount--; // decrement ref count

  // Decrement instance counter for each object
  // that is destroyed.
  instCount--;

  ReleaseMutex(hMutex);
}
```

The gc( ) Function

The entry function for the garbage collector is called **gc( )**, and it is shown here:

```
// Entry point for garbage collector thread.
template <class T, int size>
unsigned __stdcall GCPtr<T, size>::gc(void * param) {
  #ifdef DISPLAY
    cout << "Garbage collection started.\n";
  #endif

  while(isRunning()) {
    collect();
  }

  collect(); // collect garbage on way out

  // Release and reset the thread handle so
```

```
    // that the garbage collection thread can
    // be restarted if necessary.
    CloseHandle(hThrd);
    hThrd = 0;

  #ifdef DISPLAY
    cout << "Garbage collection terminated for "
          << typeid(T).name() << "\n";
  #endif

    return 0;
}
```

The **gc( )** function is quite simple: it runs as long as the garbage collector is in use. The **isRunning( )** function returns true if **instCount** is greater than zero (which means that the garbage collector is still needed) and false otherwise. Inside the loop, **collect( )** is called continuously. This approach is suitable for demonstrating the multithreaded garbage collector, but it is probably too inefficient for real-world use. You might want to experiment with calling **collect( )** less often, such as only when memory runs low. You could also experiment by calling the Windows API function **Sleep( )** after each call to **collect( )**. **Sleep( )** pauses the execution of the calling thread for a specified number of milliseconds. While sleeping, a thread does not consume CPU time.

When **isRunning( )** returns false, the loop ends, causing **gc( )** to eventually end, which stops the garbage collection thread. Because of the multithreading, it is possible that there will still be an entry on **gclist** that has not yet been freed even though **isRunning( )** returns false. To handle this case, a final call to **collect( )** is made before **gc( )** ends.

Finally, the thread handle is released via a call to the Windows API function **CloseHandle( )**, and its value is set to zero. Setting **hThrd** to zero enables the **GCPtr** constructor to restart the thread if later in the program new **GCPtr** objects are created.

The isRunning( ) Function

The **isRunning( )** function is shown here:

```
// Returns true if the collector is still in use.
static bool isRunning() { return instCount > 0; }
```

It simply compares **instCount** to zero. As long as **instCount** is greater than 0, at least one **GCPtr** pointer is still in existence and the garbage collector is still needed.

Synchronizing Access to gclist

Many of the functions in **GCPtr** access **gclist**, which holds the garbage collection list. Access to **gclist** must be synchronized to prevent two or more threads from attempting to use it at the same time. The reason for this is easy to understand. If access were not synchronized, then, for example, one thread might be obtaining an iterator to the end of the list at the same time that another thread is adding or deleting an element from the list. In this case, the iterator would be invalid. To prevent such problems, each sequence of code that accesses **gclist** must be guarded by a mutex. The copy constructor for **GCPtr** shown here is one example:

```
// Copy constructor.
GCPtr(const GCPtr &ob) {
  if(WaitForSingleObject(hMutex, 10000)==WAIT_TIMEOUT)
    throw TimeOutExc();

  list<GCInfo<T> >::iterator p;

  p = findPtrInfo(ob.addr);
  p->refcount++; // increment ref count

  addr = ob.addr;
  arraySize = ob.arraySize;
  if(arraySize > 0) isArray = true;
  else isArray = false;

  instCount++; // increase instance count for copy

  ReleaseMutex(hMutex);
}
```

Notice that the first thing that the copy constructor does is acquire the mutex. Then it creates a copy of the object and adjusts the reference count for the memory being pointed to. On its way out, the copy constructor releases the mutex. This same basic method is applied to all functions that access **gclist**.

Two Other Changes

There are two other changes that you must make to the original version of the garbage collector. First, recall that the original version of **GCPtr** defined a **static** variable called **first** that indicated when the first **GCPtr** was created. This variable is no longer needed because **hMutex** now performs this function. Thus, remove **first** from **GCPtr**. Because it is a **static** variable, you will also need to remove its definition outside of **GCPtr**.

In the original, single-threaded version of the garbage collector, if you defined the **DISPLAY** macro, you could watch the garbage collector in action. Most of that code has been removed in the multithreaded version because multithreading causes the output to be scrambled and unintelligible in most cases. For the multithreaded version, defining **DISPLAY** simply lets you know when the garbage collector has started and when it has stopped.

The Entire Multithreaded Garbage Collector

The entire multithreaded version of the garbage collector is shown here. Call this file **gcthrd.h**.

```cpp
// A garbage collector that runs as a background task.

#include <iostream>
#include <list>
#include <typeinfo>
#include <cstdlib>
#include <windows.h>
#include <process.h>

using namespace std;

// To watch the action of the garbage collector, define DISPLAY.
// #define DISPLAY

// Exception thrown when an attempt is made to
// use an Iter that exceeds the range of the
// underlying object.
//
class OutOfRangeExc {
  // Add functionality if needed by your application.
};

// Exception thrown when a time-out occurs
// when waiting for access to hMutex.
//
class TimeOutExc {
  // Add functionality if needed by your application.
};

// An iterator-like class for cycling through arrays
// that are pointed to by GCPtrs. Iter pointers
// ** do not ** participate in or affect garbage
// collection.  Thus, an Iter pointing to
// some object does not prevent that object
// from being recycled.
//
template <class T> class Iter {
  T *ptr;   // current pointer value
  T *end;   // points to element one past end
  T *begin; // points to start of allocated array
  unsigned length; // length of sequence
public:

  Iter() {
    ptr = end = begin = NULL;
```

```
      length = 0;
    }

    Iter(T *p, T *first, T *last) {
      ptr = p;
      end = last;
      begin = first;
      length = last - first;
    }


    // Return length of sequence to which this
    // Iter points.
    unsigned size() { return length; }

    // Return value pointed to by ptr.
    // Do not allow out-of-bounds access.
    T &operator*() {
      if( (ptr >= end) || (ptr < begin) )
        throw OutOfRangeExc();
      return *ptr;
    }


    // Return address contained in ptr.
    // Do not allow out-of-bounds access.
    T *operator->() {
      if( (ptr >= end) || (ptr < begin) )
        throw OutOfRangeExc();
      return ptr;
    }


    // Prefix ++.
    Iter operator++() {
      ptr++;
      return *this;
    }


    // Prefix --.
    Iter operator--() {
      ptr--;
      return *this;
    }


    // Postfix ++.
    Iter operator++(int notused) {
      T *tmp = ptr;
```

```
    ptr++;
    return Iter<T>(tmp, begin, end);
}


// Postfix --.
Iter operator--(int notused) {
  T *tmp = ptr;

  ptr--;
  return Iter<T>(tmp, begin, end);
}


// Return a reference to the object at the
// specified index. Do not allow out-of-bounds
// access.
T &operator[](int i) {
  if( (i < 0) || (i >= (end-begin)) )
    throw OutOfRangeExc();
  return ptr[i];
}


// Define the relational operators.
bool operator==(Iter op2) {
  return ptr == op2.ptr;
}


bool operator!=(Iter op2) {
  return ptr != op2.ptr;
}


bool operator<(Iter op2) {
  return ptr < op2.ptr;
}


bool operator<=(Iter op2) {
  return ptr <= op2.ptr;
}


bool operator>(Iter op2) {
  return ptr > op2.ptr;
}


bool operator>=(Iter op2) {
  return ptr >= op2.ptr;
}
```

```cpp
    // Subtract an integer from an Iter.
    Iter operator-(int n) {
      ptr -= n;
      return *this;
    }

    // Add an integer to an Iter.
    Iter operator+(int n) {
      ptr += n;
      return *this;
    }

    // Return number of elements between two Iters.
    int operator-(Iter<T> &itr2) {
      return ptr - itr2.ptr;
    }
};


// This class defines an element that is stored
// in the garbage collection information list.
//
template <class T> class GCInfo {
public:
  unsigned refcount; // current reference count

  T *memPtr; // pointer to allocated memory

  /* isArray is true if memPtr points
     to an allocated array. It is false
     otherwise. */
  bool isArray; // true if pointing to array

  /* If memPtr is pointing to an allocated
     array, then arraySize contains its size */
  unsigned arraySize; // size of array

  // Here, mPtr points to the allocated memory.
  // If this is an array, then size specifies
  // the size of the array.
  GCInfo(T *mPtr, unsigned size=0) {
    refcount = 1;
    memPtr = mPtr;
    if(size != 0)
      isArray = true;
```

```
      else
        isArray = false;

    arraySize = size;
  }
};


// Overloading operator== allows GCInfos to be compared.
// This is needed by the STL list class.
template <class T> bool operator==(const GCInfo<T> &ob1,
                const GCInfo<T> &ob2) {
  return (ob1.memPtr == ob2.memPtr);
}



// GCPtr implements a pointer type that uses
// garbage collection to release unused memory.
// A GCPtr must only be used to point to memory
// that was dynamically allocated using new.
// When used to refer to an allocated array,
// specify the array size.
//
template <class T, int size=0> class GCPtr {

  // gclist maintains the garbage collection list.
  static list<GCInfo<T> > gclist;

  // addr points to the allocated memory to which
  // this GCPtr pointer currently points.
  T *addr;

  /* isArray is true if this GCPtr points
     to an allocated array. It is false
     otherwise. */
  bool isArray; // true if pointing to array

  // If this GCPtr is pointing to an allocated
  // array, then arraySize contains its size.
  unsigned arraySize; // size of the array

  // These support multithreading.
  unsigned tid; // thread id
  static HANDLE hThrd;  // thread handle
  static HANDLE hMutex; // handle of mutex
```

```
    static int instCount; // counter of GCPtr objects

    // Return an iterator to pointer info in gclist.
    typename list<GCInfo<T> >::iterator findPtrInfo(T *ptr);

public:

    // Define an iterator type for GCPtr<T>.
    typedef Iter<T> GCiterator;

    // Construct both initialized and uninitialized objects.
    GCPtr(T *t=NULL) {

      // When first object is created, create the mutex
      // and register shutdown().
      if(hMutex==0) {
        hMutex = CreateMutex(NULL, 0, NULL);
        atexit(shutdown);
      }

      if(WaitForSingleObject(hMutex, 10000)==WAIT_TIMEOUT)
        throw TimeOutExc();

      list<GCInfo<T> >::iterator p;

      p = findPtrInfo(t);

      // If t is already in gclist, then
      // increment its reference count.
      // Otherwise, add it to the list.
      if(p != gclist.end())
        p->refcount++; // increment ref count
      else {
        // Create and store this entry.
        GCInfo<T> gcObj(t, size);
        gclist.push_front(gcObj);
      }

      addr = t;
      arraySize = size;
      if(size > 0) isArray = true;
      else isArray = false;

      // Increment instance counter for each new object.
      instCount++;
```

```cpp
    // If the garbage collection thread is not
    // currently running, start it running.
    if(hThrd==0) {
      hThrd = (HANDLE) _beginthreadex(NULL, 0, gc,
              (void *) 0, 0, (unsigned *) &tid);

      // For some applications, it will be better
      // to lower the priority of the garbage collector
      // as shown here:
      //
      // SetThreadPriority(hThrd,
      //                   THREAD_PRIORITY_BELOW_NORMAL);
    }

    ReleaseMutex(hMutex);
}

// Copy constructor.
GCPtr(const GCPtr &ob) {
    if(WaitForSingleObject(hMutex, 10000)==WAIT_TIMEOUT)
      throw TimeOutExc();

    list<GCInfo<T> >::iterator p;

    p = findPtrInfo(ob.addr);
    p->refcount++; // increment ref count

    addr = ob.addr;
    arraySize = ob.arraySize;
    if(arraySize > 0) isArray = true;
    else isArray = false;

    instCount++; // increase instance count for copy

    ReleaseMutex(hMutex);
}

// Destructor for GCPTr.
~GCPtr();

// Collect garbage.  Returns true if at least
// one object was freed.
static bool collect();

// Overload assignment of pointer to GCPtr.
```

```
T *operator=(T *t);

// Overload assignment of GCPtr to GCPtr.
GCPtr &operator=(GCPtr &rv);

// Return a reference to the object pointed
// to by this GCPtr.
T &operator*() {
  return *addr;
}

// Return the address being pointed to.
T *operator->() { return addr; }

// Return a reference to the object at the
// index specified by i.
T &operator[](int i) {
  return addr[i];
}

// Conversion function to T *.
operator T *() { return addr; }

// Return an Iter to the start of the allocated memory.
Iter<T> begin() {
  int size;

  if(isArray) size = arraySize;
  else size = 1;

  return Iter<T>(addr, addr, addr + size);
}

// Return an Iter to one past the end of an allocated array.
Iter<T> end() {
  int size;

  if(isArray) size = arraySize;
  else size = 1;

  return Iter<T>(addr + size, addr, addr + size);
}

// Return the size of gclist for this type
// of GCPtr.
```

```cpp
  static int gclistSize() {
    if(WaitForSingleObject(hMutex, 10000)==WAIT_TIMEOUT)
      throw TimeOutExc();

    unsigned sz = gclist.size();

    ReleaseMutex(hMutex);
    return sz;
  }

  // A utility function that displays gclist.
  static void showlist();

  // The following functions support multithreading.
  //
  // Returns true if the collector is still in use.
  static bool isRunning() { return instCount > 0; }

  // Clear gclist when program exits.
  static void shutdown();

  // Entry point for garbage collector thread.
  static unsigned __stdcall gc(void * param);
};

// Create storage for the static variables.
template <class T, int size>
  list<GCInfo<T> > GCPtr<T, size>::gclist;

template <class T, int size>
  int GCPtr<T, size>::instCount = 0;

template <class T, int size>
  HANDLE GCPtr<T, size>::hMutex = 0;

template <class T, int size>
  HANDLE GCPtr<T, size>::hThrd = 0;

// Destructor for GCPtr.
template <class T, int size>
GCPtr<T, size>::~GCPtr() {
  if(WaitForSingleObject(hMutex, 10000)==WAIT_TIMEOUT)
    throw TimeOutExc();

  list<GCInfo<T> >::iterator p;
```

```
    p = findPtrInfo(addr);
    if(p->refcount) p->refcount--; // decrement ref count

    // Decrement instance counter for each object
    // that is destroyed.
    instCount--;

    ReleaseMutex(hMutex);
}

// Collect garbage.  Returns true if at least
// one object was freed.
template <class T, int size>
bool GCPtr<T, size>::collect() {
  if(WaitForSingleObject(hMutex, 10000)==WAIT_TIMEOUT)
    throw TimeOutExc();

  bool memfreed = false;

  list<GCInfo<T> >::iterator p;
  do {

    // Scan gclist looking for unreferenced pointers.
    for(p = gclist.begin(); p != gclist.end(); p++) {
      // If in-use, skip.
      if(p->refcount > 0) continue;

      memfreed = true;

      // Remove unused entry from gclist.
      gclist.remove(*p);

      // Free memory unless the GCPtr is null.
      if(p->memPtr) {
        if(p->isArray) {
          delete[] p->memPtr; // delete array
        }
        else {
          delete p->memPtr; // delete single element
        }
      }

      // Restart the search.
      break;
    }
```

```
  } while(p != gclist.end());

  ReleaseMutex(hMutex);

  return memfreed;
}


// Overload assignment of pointer to GCPtr.
template <class T, int size>
T * GCPtr<T, size>::operator=(T *t) {
  if(WaitForSingleObject(hMutex, 10000)==WAIT_TIMEOUT)
    throw TimeOutExc();

  list<GCInfo<T> >::iterator p;

  // First, decrement the reference count
  // for the memory currently being pointed to.
  p = findPtrInfo(addr);
  p->refcount--;

  // Next, if the new address is already
  // existent in the system, increment its
  // count.  Otherwise, create a new entry
  // for gclist.
  p = findPtrInfo(t);
  if(p != gclist.end())
    p->refcount++;
  else {
    // Create and store this entry.
    GCInfo<T> gcObj(t, size);
    gclist.push_front(gcObj);
  }

  addr = t; // store the address.

  ReleaseMutex(hMutex);

  return t;
}


// Overload assignment of GCPtr to GCPtr.
template <class T, int size>
GCPtr<T, size> & GCPtr<T, size>::operator=(GCPtr &rv) {
  if(WaitForSingleObject(hMutex, 10000)==WAIT_TIMEOUT)
    throw TimeOutExc();
```

```
    list<GCInfo<T> >::iterator p;

  // First, decrement the reference count
  // for the memory currently being pointed to.
  p = findPtrInfo(addr);
  p->refcount--;

  // Next, increment the reference count
  // of the new object.
  p = findPtrInfo(rv.addr);
  p->refcount++; // increment ref count

  addr = rv.addr;// store the address.

  ReleaseMutex(hMutex);

  return rv;
}

// A utility function that displays gclist.
template <class T, int size>
void GCPtr<T, size>::showlist() {
  if(WaitForSingleObject(hMutex, 10000)==WAIT_TIMEOUT)
    throw TimeOutExc();

  list<GCInfo<T> >::iterator p;

  cout << "gclist<" << typeid(T).name() << ", "
       << size << ">:\n";
  cout << "memPtr       refcount     value\n";

  if(gclist.begin() == gclist.end()) {
    cout << "             -- Empty --\n\n";
    return;
  }

  for(p = gclist.begin(); p != gclist.end(); p++) {
    cout <<  "[" << (void *)p->memPtr << "]"
         << "         " << p->refcount << "        ";
    if(p->memPtr) cout << "    " << *p->memPtr;
    else cout << "    ---";
    cout << endl;
  }
  cout << endl;
```

```
    ReleaseMutex(hMutex);
}


// Find a pointer in gclist.
template <class T, int size>
typename list<GCInfo<T> >::iterator
  GCPtr<T, size>::findPtrInfo(T *ptr) {

    list<GCInfo<T> >::iterator p;

    // Find ptr in gclist.
    for(p = gclist.begin(); p != gclist.end(); p++)
      if(p->memPtr == ptr)
        return p;

    return p;
}

// Entry point for garbage collector thread.
template <class T, int size>
unsigned __stdcall GCPtr<T, size>::gc(void * param) {
    #ifdef DISPLAY
      cout << "Garbage collection started.\n";
    #endif

    while(isRunning()) {
        collect();
    }

    collect(); // collect garbage on way out

    // Release and reset the thread handle so
    // that the garbage collection thread can
    // be restarted if necessary.
    CloseHandle(hThrd);
    hThrd = 0;

    #ifdef DISPLAY
      cout << "Garbage collection terminated for "
           << typeid(T).name() << "\n";
    #endif

    return 0;
}
```

```
// Clear gclist when program exits.
template <class T, int size>
void GCPtr<T, size>::shutdown() {

  if(gclistSize() == 0) return; // list is empty

  list<GCInfo<T> >::iterator p;

#ifdef DISPLAY
    cout << "Before collecting for shutdown() for "
         << typeid(T).name() << "\n";
#endif

  for(p = gclist.begin(); p != gclist.end(); p++) {
    // Set all remaining reference counts to zero.
    p->refcount = 0;
  }

  collect();

#ifdef DISPLAY
    cout << "After collecting for shutdown() for "
         << typeid(T).name() << "\n";
#endif
}
```

Using the Multithreaded Garbage Collector

To use the multithreaded garbage collector, include **gcthrd.h** in your program. Then, use **GCPtr** in the same way as described in Chapter 2. When you compile the program, you must remember to link in the multithreaded libraries, as explained earlier in this chapter in the section describing **_beginthreadex( )** and **_endthreadex( )**.

To see the effects of the multithreaded garbage collector, try this version of the load test program originally shown in Chapter 2:

```
// Demonstrate the multithreaded garbage collector.
#include <iostream>
#include <new>
#include "gcthrd.h"

using namespace std;

// A simple class for load testing GCPtr.
class LoadTest {
```

```
    int a, b;
public:
  double n[100000]; // just to take-up memory
  double val;

  LoadTest() { a = b = 0; }

  LoadTest(int x, int y) {
    a = x;
    b = y;
    val = 0.0;
  }

  friend ostream &operator<<(ostream &strm, LoadTest &obj);
};

// Create an inserter for LoadTest.
ostream &operator<<(ostream &strm, LoadTest &obj) {
  strm << "(" << obj.a << " " << obj.b << ")";
  return strm;
}

int main() {
  GCPtr<LoadTest> mp;
  int i;

  for(i = 1; i < 2000; i++) {
    try {
      mp = new LoadTest(i, i);
      if(!(i%100))
        cout << "gclist contains " << mp.gclistSize()
             << " entries.\n";
    } catch(bad_alloc xa) {
      // For most users, this exception won't
      // ever occur.
      cout << "Last object: " << *mp << endl;
      cout << "Length of gclist: "
           << mp.gclistSize() << endl;
    }
  }

  return 0;
}
```

Here is a sample run. (Of course, your output may vary.) This output was produced with the display option turned on by defining **DISPLAY** within **gcthrd.h**.

```
Garbage collection started.
gclist contains 42 entries.
gclist contains 35 entries.
gclist contains 29 entries.
gclist contains 22 entries.
gclist contains 18 entries.
gclist contains 11 entries.
gclist contains 4 entries.
gclist contains 51 entries.
gclist contains 47 entries.
gclist contains 40 entries.
gclist contains 33 entries.
gclist contains 26 entries.
gclist contains 19 entries.
gclist contains 15 entries.
gclist contains 10 entries.
gclist contains 3 entries.
gclist contains 53 entries.
gclist contains 46 entries.
gclist contains 42 entries.
Before collecting for shutdown() for class LoadTest
After collecting for shutdown() for class LoadTest
```

As you can see, because **collect( )** is running in the background, **gclist** never gets very large, even though thousands of objects are being allocated and abandoned.

Some Things to Try

Creating successful multithreaded programs can be quite challenging. One reason for this is the fact that multithreading requires that you think of programs in parallel rather than linear terms. Furthermore, at runtime, threads interact in ways that are often difficult to anticipate. Thus, you might be surprised (or even bewildered) by the actions of a multithreaded program. The best way to get good at multithreading is to play with it. Toward this end, here are some ideas that you might want to try.

Try adding another list box to the thread control panel that lets the user adjust the priority class of the thread in addition to its priority value. Try adding various synchronization objects to the control panel that can be turned on or off under user control. This will let you experiment with different synchronization options.

For the multithreaded garbage collector, try collecting garbage less often, such as when **gclist** reaches a certain size or after free memory drops to a predetermined point. Alternatively, you could use a waitable timer to activate garbage collection on a regular basis. Finally, you might want to experiment with the garbage collector's priority class and settings to find which level is optimal for your use.

Extending C++

For the typical C++ programmer, programming is not just a job, it's a way of life. We programmers appreciate not only the raw power of the language, but also its nuances and subtleties. Much like a connoisseur savors a vintage wine, we enjoy the finer points of the language. Of course, our interest in C++ is not confined to simply using it to create programs. Instead, we find ourselves attracted to the language itself and to the issues surrounding the design and development of languages in general.

Because of the interest that most C++ programmers have in computer languages, it is a rare C++ programmer who has not daydreamed about adding a new feature to the language. (How often have you thought, "How great it would be if C++ had ...")? The trouble is that most programmers don't have access to the source code for a full-blown C++ compiler to which they can add their experimental constructs. Fortunately, there is an easy way to experiment with your own extensions to C++: by creating a translator that converts your experimental ideas into their equivalent C++ code. Such a translator is the topic of this chapter.

Why Use a Translator?

You might question why a translator is needed to experiment with a new language feature when there appears to be an obvious alternative: the standard C++ preprocessor. As all readers know, the preprocessor supports macro substitutions, in which one text sequence is substituted for another. For years, preprocessor macros have been used to add experimental features to C++. For example, one construct commonly implemented by macros is the **repeat/until** loop. A **repeat/until** loop is similar to C++'s **do/while** loop except that a **repeat/until** runs until some condition becomes true. (Thus, a **repeat/until** runs while its conditional expression is false.) This differs from the **do/while** loop, which runs until some condition becomes false. Because of the similarities between the **repeat/until** and the **do/while**, it is possible to use macros to implement a **repeat/until**, as the following fragment shows:

```
#define repeat do
#define until(exp) while(!(exp))
// ...
int i=0;
repeat {
  cout << "i: " << i << endl;
  i++;
} until(i==10);
```

The macros cause **do** to be substituted for **repeat**, and **while** to be substituted for **until**. Also, the conditional expression is reversed in the **while**. Thus, the **repeat/until** loop in the preceding fragment is converted by the preprocessor into this **do/while** loop:

```
do {
  cout << "i: " << i << endl;
  i++;
} while(!(i==10));
```

As this example shows, the use of macros to implement a **repeat/until** construct is both an easy and reasonable approach.

Given the long-standing tradition of using macros to implement experimental features, why would one want to build a translator? That is, why not just use macros like those used for the **repeat/until**? The answer is that macro substitutions cannot be used to add all types of experimental features. Furthermore, even in cases in which a macro substitution will work, not all are as elegant or conceptually pure as those used by the **repeat/until** example. Although programmers have managed some very impressive feats with macros, in many cases they have been achieved by use of complex and hard-to-understand **#define** directives. Such "macro tricks" often serve to destructure code, are hard to verify for correctness, and often lack resiliency. Frankly, many C++ programmers (including this author) avoid the use of complicated macros for just these reasons.

Fortunately, there is an alternative to complicated macros that can be used to experiment with a wide variety of new C++ features: you can build a translator that handles, under program control, the conversion of an experimental construct into its equivalent C++ code. Using such a "pre-preprocessor" enables you to add features to C++ that are either difficult or impossible to implement using preprocessor macros. Such a translator is also an interesting project in its own right, and the basic framework can be readily adapted for other purposes.

It is important to understand that although the translator developed in this chapter is capable of performing sophisticated text substitutions, it still has its limitations. Because the translator implements a single-pass algorithm that reads the source file only once, it can be used to experiment with only those constructs that can be handled by single-pass substitution. (You can change this behavior, if you want.) Aside from performing sophisticated text substitutions, the translator is completely ignorant about the contents of the program. That is, it knows nothing about the type of a variable, what an operator means, or even what the previously read token was. Thus, the translator is not a parser for the C++ language. It is simply an engine for specialized text substitutions; in essence, it is a specialized preprocessor. Despite these limitations, you can use it to experiment with a wide array of ideas.

NOTE

If you're interested in a parser for C++, see Chapter 9.

The Experimental Keywords

Before developing the translator, it is necessary to define what translations it performs. The translator developed in this chapter handles the following experimental extensions to C++:

- ► A **foreach** loop
- ► A **cases** statement
- ► A **typeof** operator
- ► A **repeat/until** loop

With the exception of the **repeat/until** loop, which is included simply for illustration, the other keywords use a syntax that would be difficult (or impossible) to translate using macro substitutions. Each of these experimental keywords is described here.

The foreach Loop

Contemporary language development has embraced the **foreach** loop. For example, **foreach** is part of C# and a "for each" style loop is being added to Java. Furthermore, the "for each" concept is already incorporated into one of the newest parts of C++ because the STL (Standard Template Library) defines the **for_each( )** algorithm, which applies a function to each element in a container. However, C++ does not currently define a general-purpose **foreach** loop.

The **foreach** was invented to handle a situation that occurs quite often in programming: the need to cycle through the elements of an array (or other type of collection of objects) in strictly sequential fashion, from beginning to end. For example, consider this fragment that computes the average of the values in an array:

```
int n[] = { 1, 7, 3, 11, 5 };
double avg=0.0;

for(int i=0; i < 5; i++)
  avg += n[i];

cout << "Average: " << avg/5 << endl;
```

To compute the average of the values in **n**, each element in the array is read in order, from start to finish. Of course, this is just one instance of a general concept. The same type of loop is used to find the minimum or maximum value in an array, to sum the array's values, to compute the least common denominator, or for a hundred other uses. Moreover, the same type of loop construct is used whenever the contents of an array need to be accessed. The **foreach** loop was created to simplify and streamline such loops.

The value of the **foreach** is that it eliminates the need to manually index the array. Instead, the **foreach** automatically cycles through the entire array, obtaining one element at a time, in sequence. For example, here is the preceding fragment rewritten using a **foreach**:

```
int n[] = { 1, 7, 3, 11, 5 };
double avg=0.0;

foreach(int x in n)
  avg += x;

cout << "Average: " << avg/5 << endl;
```

With each pass through the loop, **x** is automatically given a value equal to the next element in **n**. Thus, on the first iteration **x** contains 1, on the second iteration **x** contains 7, and so on. Not only is the syntax streamlined, it also prevents counting errors.

The syntax for the **foreach** loop is shown here:

foreach(*type varname* in *arrayname*)

Here, *type* is the type of the loop variable, its name is specified by *varname*, and the array being accessed is specified by *arrayname*. Furthermore, *varname* is local to the loop and not known outside of it. (This syntax is borrowed from C#.) Remember, with each iteration of the loop, *varname* will contain (in sequential order) the value of the next element of the specified array.

The translator converts a **foreach** loop into its equivalent C++ **for** loop.

The cases Statement

The **cases** statement allows you to specify a range of values that will be matched by a **switch** expression. Normally, when you want the same code sequence to be used by two or more **case** statements, you must use "stacked" **case** statements, as the following example shows:

```
switch(i) {
  case 1:
  case 2:
  case 3:
  case 4:
    // do something for cases 1 to 4
    break;
  case 5:
    // do something else
    break;
  // ...
}
```

Stacked **case** statements, such as those for 1 through 4 in the example, are common in programming. They can also be tedious to code. Wouldn't it be convenient to be able to specify a range of values within a single **case**? The translator enables you to do precisely that!

The translator implements a **cases** statement that lets you define a range of values that are all handled by a single code sequence. For example, the preceding code can be rewritten as shown here using the **cases** statement:

```
switch(i) {
  cases 1 to 4:
    // do something for cases 1 to 4
    break;
  case 5:
    // do something else
    break;
  // ...
}
```

Thus, when **i** is between 1 and 4 inclusive, that value will be matched by the **cases** statement.

The syntax for **cases** is shown here:

cases *start* to *end*:

Here, *start* is the first value to match, and *end* is the last value to match.

The translator converts a **cases** statement into series of stacked **case** statements.

The typeof Operator

Runtime type ID has become an important part of most modern programming. Although C++'s built-in support for it is superb, we programmers are a restless lot and sometimes try to improve on a good thing! The **typeof** experimental operator is a case in point. It simply provides an alternative syntax for an operation already supported by C++: the comparison of two types. Thus, **typeof** adds no new functionality, but it offers a different perspective on the process.

Normally, the **typeid** operator is used when a type comparison is required. For example, consider the following statement, which determines if the object pointed to by **ptr1** is of the same type as the object pointed to by **ptr2**:

```
if(typeid(*ptr1) == typeid(*ptr2))
  cout << "ptr1 points to same type as ptr2\n";
```

In this statement, the **typeid** operator obtains the type of the objects pointed to by **ptr1** and **ptr2**. If these two types are the same, the **if** statement succeeds. A statement such as this might be used when working with polymorphic classes, for example. In this case, the type of an object being pointed to by a base class pointer can't always be known at compile time, and a runtime check is needed.

Although there is nothing wrong with **typeid** or the preceding statement, the following approach offers an intriguing alternative syntax:

```
if(typeof *ptr1 same as *ptr2)
  cout << "ptr1 points to same type as ptr2\n";
```

In this statement, the **typeof** operator is used to compare two types. The result is true if the two types are the same and false otherwise. Although it performs the same operation as the first version, it changes the way in which the operation is expressed, which lets you see it from a different point of view. It also demonstrates the range of ideas that the translator lets you experiment with.

The syntax for **typeof** is shown here:

typeof *op1* same as *op2*

Here, *op1* and *op2* specify either a type identifier (such as **int** or **MyClass**) or an object. Thus, **typeof** can be used to compare the types of two objects, the type of an object to a known type, or two types.

The translator converts **typeof** into its corresponding **typeid** expression.

The repeat/until Loop

As explained earlier, it is quite easy to use preprocessor macros to experiment with a **repeat/until** loop. The translator implements **repeat/until** simply for illustration and because it serves as a model for any other type of loop with which you might want to experiment.

A Translator for Experimental C++ Features

The entire code for the translator is shown here. To follow along, call this file **trans.cpp**.

```cpp
// A translator for experimental C++ extensions.
#include <iostream>
#include <fstream>
#include <cctype>
#include <cstring>
#include <string>

using namespace std;

// Prototypes for the functions that handle
// the extended keywords.
void foreach();
void cases();
void repeat();
void until();
void typeof();

// Prototypes for tokenizing the input file.
bool gettoken(string &tok);
void skipspaces();

// Indentation padding string.
string indent = "";

// The input and output file streams.
ifstream fin;
ofstream fout;

// Exception class for syntax errors.
class SyntaxExc {
  string what;
public:
  SyntaxExc(char *e) { what = string(e); }
  string geterror() { return what; }
};
```

```cpp
int main(int argc, char *argv[]) {
  string token;

  if(argc != 3) {
    cout << "Usage: ep <input file> <output file>\n";
    return 1;
  }

  fin.open(argv[1]);

  if(!fin) {
    cout << "Cannot open " << argv[1] << endl;
    return 1;
  }

  fout.open(argv[2]);

  if(!fout) {
    cout << "Cannot open " << argv[2] << endl;
    return 1;
  }

  // Write header.
  fout << "// Translated from an .exp source file.\n";

  try {
    // Main translation loop.
    while(gettoken(token)) {

      // Skip over // comments.
      if(token == "//") {
        do {
          fout << token;
          gettoken(token);
        } while(token.find('\n') == string::npos);
        fout << token;
      }

      // Skip over /* comments.
      else if(token == "/*") {
        do {
          fout << token;
          gettoken(token);
```

```
      } while(token != "*/");
      fout << token;
    }

    // Skip over quoted string.
    else if(token == "\"") {
      do {
        fout << token;
        gettoken(token);
      } while(token != "\"");
      fout << token;
    }

    else if(token == "foreach") foreach();

    else if(token == "cases") cases();

    else if(token == "repeat") repeat();

    else if(token == "until") until();

    else if(token == "typeof") typeof();

    else fout << token;
  }
} catch(SyntaxExc exc) {
  cout << exc.geterror() << endl;
  return 1;
}

  return 0;
}

// Get the next token from the input stream.
bool gettoken(string &tok) {
  char ch;
  char ch2;
  static bool trackIndent = true;

  tok = "";

  ch = fin.get();

  // Check for EOF and return false if EOF
  // is found.
```

```cpp
    if(!fin) return false;

    // Read whitespace.
    if(isspace(ch)) {
      while(isspace(ch)) {
        tok += ch;

        // Reset indent counter with each new line.
        if(ch == '\n') {
          indent = "";
          trackIndent = true;
        }
        else if(trackIndent) indent += ch;

        ch = fin.get();
      }
      fin.putback(ch);
      return true;
    }

    // Stop tracking indentation after encountering
    // first non-whitespace character on a line.
    trackIndent = false;

    // Read an identifier or keyword.
    if(isalpha(ch) || ch=='_') {
      while(isalpha(ch) || isdigit(ch) || ch=='_') {
        tok += ch;
        ch = fin.get();
      }
      fin.putback(ch);
      return true;
    }

    // Read a number.
    if(isdigit(ch)) {
      while(isdigit(ch) || ch=='.' ||
            tolower(ch) == 'e' ||
            ch == '-' || ch =='+') {
        tok += ch;
        ch = fin.get();
      }
      fin.putback(ch);
      return true;
    }
```

```
// Check for \"
if(ch == '\\') {
  ch2 = fin.get();
  if(ch2 == '"') {
    tok += ch;
    tok += ch2;
    ch = fin.get();
  } else
    fin.putback(ch2);
}

// Check for '"'
if(ch == '\'') {
  ch2 = fin.get();
  if(ch2 == '"') {
    tok += ch;
    tok += ch2;
    return true;
  } else
    fin.putback(ch2);
}

// Check for begin comment symbols.
if(ch == '/') {
  tok += ch;
  ch = fin.get();
  if(ch == '/' || ch == '*') {
    tok += ch;
  }
  else fin.putback(ch);
  return true;
}

// Check for end comment symbols.
if(ch == '*') {
  tok += ch;
  ch = fin.get();
  if(ch == '/') {
    tok += ch;
  }
  else fin.putback(ch);
  return true;
}

tok += ch;
```

```
    return true;
}

// Translate a foreach loop.
void foreach() {
  string token;
  string varname;
  string arrayname;

  char forvarname[5] = "_i";
  static char counter[2] = "a";

  // Create loop control variable for generated
  // for loop.
  strcat(forvarname, counter);
  counter[0]++;

  // Only 26 foreach loops in a file because
  // generated loop control variables limited to
  // _ia to _iz. This can be changed if desired.
  if(counter[0] > 'z')
    throw SyntaxExc("Too many foreach loops.");

  fout << "int " << forvarname
       << " = 0;\n";

  // Write beginning of generated for loop.
  fout << indent << "for(";

  skipspaces();

  // Read the (
  gettoken(token);
  if(token[0] != '(')
    throw SyntaxExc("( expected in foreach.");

  skipspaces();

  // Get the type of the foreach variable.
  gettoken(token);
  fout << token << " ";

  skipspaces();

  // Read and save the foreach variable's name.
```

```
    gettoken(token);
    varname = token;

    skipspaces();

    // Read the "in"
    gettoken(token);
    if(token != "in")
      throw SyntaxExc("in expected in foreach.");

    skipspaces();

    // Read the array name.
    gettoken(token);
    arrayname = token;

    fout << varname << " = " << arrayname << "[0];\n";

    // Construct target value.
    fout << indent + "    " << forvarname << " < "
         << "((sizeof " << token << ")/"
         << "(sizeof " << token << "[0]));\n";

    fout << indent + "    " << forvarname << "++, "
         << varname << " = " << arrayname << "["
         << forvarname << "])";

    skipspaces();

    // Read the )
    gettoken(token);
    if(token[0] != ')')
      throw SyntaxExc(") expected in foreach.");
}

// Translate a cases statement.
void cases() {
    string token;
    int start, end;

    skipspaces();

    // Get starting value.
    gettoken(token);
```

```cpp
if(isdigit(token[0])) {
  // is an int constant
  start = atoi(token.c_str());
}
else if(token[0] == '\'') {
  // is char constant
  gettoken(token);

  start = (int) token[0];

  // discard closing '
  gettoken(token);
  if(token[0] != '\'')
    throw SyntaxExc("' expected in cases.");
}
else
 throw SyntaxExc("Constant expected in cases.");

skipspaces();

// Read and discard the "to".
gettoken(token);
if(token != "to")
  throw SyntaxExc("to expected in cases.");

skipspaces();

// Get ending value.
gettoken(token);

if(isdigit(token[0])) {
  // is an int constant
  end = atoi(token.c_str());
}
else if(token[0] == '\'') {
  // is char constant
  gettoken(token);

  end = (int) token[0];

  // discard closing '
  gettoken(token);
  if(token[0] != '\'')
    throw SyntaxExc("' expected in cases.");
}
```

```
    else
      throw SyntaxExc("Constant expected in cases.");

    skipspaces();

    // Read and discard the :
    gettoken(token);

    if(token != ":")
      throw SyntaxExc(": expected in cases.");

    // Generate stacked case statments.
    fout << "case " << start << ":\n";
    for(int i = start+1 ; i <= end; i++) {
      fout << indent << "case " << i << ":";
      if(i != end) fout << endl;
    }
}

// Translate a repeat loop.
void repeat() {
  fout << "do";
}

// Translate an until.
void until() {
  string token;
  int parencount = 1;

  fout << "while";

  skipspaces();

  // Read and store the (
  gettoken(token);
  if(token != "(")
    throw SyntaxExc("( expected in typeof.");
  fout << "(";

  // Begin while by reversing and
  // parenthesizing the condition.
  fout << "!(";

  // Now, read the expression.
  do {
```

```
      if(!gettoken(token))
        throw SyntaxExc("Unexpected EOF encountered.");

      if(token == "(") parencount++;
      if(token == ")") parencount--;

      fout << token;
    } while(parencount > 0);
    fout << ")";
}

// Translate a typeof expression.
void typeof() {
  string token;
  string temp;

  fout << "typeid(";

  skipspaces();

  gettoken(token);

  do {
    temp = token;

    if(!gettoken(token))
      throw SyntaxExc("Unexpected EOF encountered.");

    if(token != "same") fout << temp;
  } while(token != "same");

  skipspaces();

  gettoken(token);

  if(token != "as") throw SyntaxExc("as expected.");

  fout << ") == typeid(";

  skipspaces();

  do {
    if(!gettoken(token))
```

```
      throw SyntaxExc("Unexpected EOF encountered.");

    fout << token;
  } while(token != ")");
  fout << ")";
}


void skipspaces() {
  char ch;

  do {
    ch = fin.get();
  } while(isspace(ch));
  fin.putback(ch);
}
```

Using the Translator

To use the translator, first create a file containing a program that uses the experimental keywords. To keep things straight, use the **.exp** file extension for files that use the experimental constructs. Understand that an **exp** file will usually contain mostly standard C++ code. It's just that it also contains one or more experimental features that will be converted into C++ by the translator. For example, here is an **exp** file that demonstrates the **foreach** loop. Notice that most of the program consists of normal C++ code.

```
// Demonstrate the foreach loop.
#include <iostream>
using namespace std;

int main() {
  int nums[] = { 1, 6, 19, 4, -10, 88 };
  int min;

  // Find the minimum value.
  min = nums[0];
  foreach(int x in nums)
    if(min > x) min = x;

  cout << "Minimum is " << min << endl;

  return 0;
}
```

To convert an **exp** file into a standard **cpp** file, run it through the translator. For example, assuming that this file is called **foreach.exp**, the following command line will translate it into pure C++ code that can be compiled by a C++ compiler:

```
trans foreach.exp foreach.cpp
```

After **trans** runs, **foreach.cpp** will contain the following C++ program:

```cpp
// Translated from an .exp source file.
// Demonstrate the foreach loop.
#include <iostream>
using namespace std;

int main() {
  int nums[] = { 1, 6, 19, 4, -10, 88 };
  int min;

  // Find the minimum value.
  min = nums[0];
  int _ia = 0;
  for(int x = nums[0];
      _ia < ((sizeof nums)/(sizeof nums[0]));
      _ia++, x = nums[_ia])
    if(min > x) min = x;

  cout << "Minimum is " << min << endl;

  return 0;
}
```

The remainder of this chapter describes how the translation works.

How the Translator Works

The translator operates in a straightforward manner. It simply reads the input file and writes it to the output file. In the process, when it finds an experimental keyword, it substitutes the equivalent C++ code. This inherent simplicity is why the translator is useful for experimentation. It takes no great effort to implement an extension and then try it. The following sections describe the action of each part of the translator in detail.

The Global Declarations

The translator begins by defining the following global variables and class:

```cpp
// Indentation padding string.
string indent = "";
```

```
// The input and output file streams.
ifstream fin;
ofstream fout;

// Exception class for syntax errors.
class SyntaxExc {
  string what;
public:
  SyntaxExc(char *e) { what = string(e); }
  string geterror() { return what; }
};
```

The current whitespace sequence used to indent a line is stored in **indent**. This string is used to add the proper amount of indentation when multiple lines of code are substituted for an experimental construct.

The input file stream is stored in **fin**; the output file stream is held in **fout**. When the program begins, the filenames specified on the command line are linked to **fin** and **fout**.

Syntax errors encountered during the translation of an experimental construct are reported by throwing a **SyntaxExc** object. As it is written, **SyntaxExc** contains only a string that describes the error, but you can add functionality, if desired.

The main( ) Function

The **main( )** function performs two duties. First, it opens the input and output files specified on the command line. This will be familiar code to all C++ programmers. Second, it runs the main loop of the translator, which handles the translation of the experimental keywords. The main loop is shown here:

```
try {
  // Main translation loop.
  while(gettoken(token)) {

    // Skip over // comments.
    if(token == "//") {
      do {
        fout << token;
        gettoken(token);
      } while(token.find('\n') == string::npos);
      fout << token;
    }

    // Skip over /* comments.
    else if(token == "/*") {
      do {
        fout << token;
```

```
      gettoken(token);
    } while(token != "*/");
    fout << token;
  }

  // Skip over quoted string.
  else if(token == "\"") {
    do {
      fout << token;
      gettoken(token);
    } while(token != "\"");
    fout << token;
  }

  else if(token == "foreach") foreach();

  else if(token == "cases") cases();

  else if(token == "repeat") repeat();

  else if(token == "until") until();

  else if(token == "typeof") typeof();

  else fout << token;
  }
} catch(SyntaxExc exc) {
  cout << exc.geterror() << endl;
  return 1;
}
}
```

With each iteration of the loop, a token is read from the input file. If the token does not require translation, it is written to the output file. However, if the token contains one of the experimental keywords, then the proper function is called to translate that keyword into its corresponding C++ code. Notice that the loop skips over comments and quoted strings, copying them to the output file without testing their contents for the experimental keywords. This is necessary to prevent the translation of a keyword that is contained in a comment or quoted string.

If a syntax error is detected in the translation of an experimental feature, then a **SyntaxExc** object is thrown by the code doing the translating, and it is caught by the **catch** in **main( )**, which simply displays the error. You can enhance the error report to include a line number or other information if you desire.

The gettoken( ) and skipspaces( ) Functions

In order for the translator to convert an experimental keyword into its equivalent C++ code, it must be able to know when a keyword has been found. To enable this, the input file must be processed on a token by token basis. Here, the term *token* is used in a very loose sense. It simply means a piece of text. The translator does not require finely grained tokenization. It simply needs to recognize identifiers (including keywords), numbers, and whitespace. Most other characters can be processed as single characters.

The **gettoken( )** function is shown here:

```cpp
// Get the next token from the input stream.
bool gettoken(string &tok) {
  char ch;
  char ch2;
  static bool trackIndent = true;

  tok = "";

  ch = fin.get();

  // Check for EOF and return false if EOF
  // is found.
  if(!fin) return false;

  // Read whitespace.
  if(isspace(ch)) {
    while(isspace(ch)) {
      tok += ch;

      // Reset indent counter with each new line.
      if(ch == '\n') {
        indent = "";
        trackIndent = true;
      }
      else if(trackIndent) indent += ch;

      ch = fin.get();
    }
    fin.putback(ch);
    return true;
  }

  // Stop tracking indentation after encountering
  // first non-whitespace character on a line.
  trackIndent = false;
```

```cpp
// Read an identifier or keyword.
if(isalpha(ch) || ch=='_') {
  while(isalpha(ch) || isdigit(ch) || ch=='_') {
    tok += ch;
    ch = fin.get();
  }
  fin.putback(ch);
  return true;
}

// Read a number.
if(isdigit(ch)) {
  while(isdigit(ch) || ch=='.' ||
        tolower(ch) == 'e' ||
        ch == '-' || ch =='+') {
    tok += ch;
    ch = fin.get();
  }
  fin.putback(ch);
  return true;
}

// Check for \"
if(ch == '\\') {
  ch2 = fin.get();
  if(ch2 == '"') {
    tok += ch;
    tok += ch2;
    ch = fin.get();
  } else
    fin.putback(ch2);
}

// Check for '"'
if(ch == '\'') {
  ch2 = fin.get();
  if(ch2 == '"') {
    tok += ch;
    tok += ch2;
    return true;
  } else
    fin.putback(ch2);
}
```

```
// Check for begin comment symbols.
if(ch == '/') {
  tok += ch;
  ch = fin.get();
  if(ch == '/' || ch == '*') {
    tok += ch;
  }
  else fin.putback(ch);
  return true;
}

// Check for end comment symbols.
if(ch == '*') {
  tok += ch;
  ch = fin.get();
  if(ch == '/') {
    tok += ch;
  }
  else fin.putback(ch);
  return true;
}

tok += ch;

return true;
}
```

The **gettoken( )** function has one parameter, a string called **tok**, that is passed a reference to a **string** object. This object will contain the token when the function returns. The function returns true if a token was read and false if the end of the file is encountered.

The **gettoken( )** function begins by setting **tok** to the null string. It then reads the next character from **fin** and stores it in **ch**. If this read encounters the end of the file, then false is returned. Otherwise, **ch** is tested against a number of possibilities.

First, if **ch** is a whitespace, then a loop is entered that reads whitespace characters until the first nonwhitespace character is read. The whitespace characters are appended to **tok**. The nonwhitespace character is returned to the input stream with a call to **fin.putback( )**. At the end of the loop, **tok** contains all of the whitespace characters that were read, and this is the token returned to the calling routine.

There is one other thing to notice in the whitespace loop. If a newline is read, **indent** is set to the null string and the **trackIndent** variable is set to true. When **trackIndent** is true, whitespace will be stored in **indent**. After the whitespace loop, **trackIndent** is set to false. Thus, only the leading whitespace on a line is stored in **indent**.

If **ch** is not a whitespace character, other possibilities are tested. If the next token is an identifier or keyword, it begins with a letter or underscore and is read by the next loop in **gettoken( )**. Otherwise, if **ch** is a digit, then a number is read.

If **ch** is not a whitespace, letter, underscore, or digit, then five special conditions are checked for. The first is the \" sequence. As explained, the translator performs no translations of the text in quoted strings. When the translator finds an opening quote, it simply copies all text between it and the closing quote. However, it is necessary to prevent an embedded quote from being mistaken as the beginning or end of a quoted string. Thus, the backslash sequence \" must be handled as a pair. The same situation applies when a character constant specifies a quote. The comment symbols must also be handled as pairs of characters, so **gettoken( )** checks for //, /*, and */.

Occasionally during translation it is necessary to discard the spaces present in an experimental statement because they have no relationship to the C++ code being produced. The **skipspaces( )** function shown here accomplishes this. It simply reads and discards spaces.

```
void skipspaces() {
  char ch;

  do {
    ch = fin.get();
  } while(isspace(ch));
  fin.putback(ch);
}
```

Translating the foreach Loop

The most challenging translation is the **foreach** loop. The function that handles this is **foreach( )**, and it is shown here:

```
// Translate a foreach loop.
void foreach() {
  string token;
  string varname;
  string arrayname;

  char forvarname[5] = "_i";
  static char counter[2] = "a";

  // Create loop control variable for generated
  // for loop.
  strcat(forvarname, counter);
  counter[0]++;

  // Only 26 foreach loops in a file because
  // generated loop control variables limited to
```

```
  // _ia to _iz. This can be changed if desired.
  if(counter[0] > 'z')
    throw SyntaxExc("Too many foreach loops.");

  fout << "int " << forvarname
       << " = 0;\n";

  // Write beginning of generated for loop.
  fout << indent << "for(";

  skipspaces();

  // Read the (
  gettoken(token);
  if(token[0] != '(')
    throw SyntaxExc("( expected in foreach.");

  skipspaces();

  // Get the type of the foreach variable.
  gettoken(token);
  fout << token << " ";

  skipspaces();

  // Read and save the foreach variable's name.
  gettoken(token);
  varname = token;

  skipspaces();

  // Read the "in"
  gettoken(token);
  if(token != "in")
    throw SyntaxExc("in expected in foreach.");

  skipspaces();

  // Read the array name.
  gettoken(token);
  arrayname = token;

  fout << varname << " = " << arrayname << "[0];\n";

  // Construct target value.
```

```
fout << indent + "      " << forvarname << " < "
     << "((sizeof " << token << ")/"
     << "(sizeof " << token << "[0]));\n";

fout << indent + "      " << forvarname << "++, "
     << varname << " = " << arrayname << "["
     << forvarname << "])";

skipspaces();

// Read the )
gettoken(token);
if(token[0] != ')')
  throw SyntaxExc(") expected in foreach.");
}
```

The translator converts a **foreach** loop into its equivalent **for** loop. This involves handling two rather complicated issues. To understand them, consider the following example:

```
double nums[] = { 1.1, 2.2, 3.3 };
double sum = 0.0;

foreach(double v in nums)
  sum += v;
```

The **foreach** loop is translated into the following C++ code:

```
int _ia = 0;
for(double v = nums[0];
    _ia < ((sizeof nums)/(sizeof nums[0]));
    _ia++, v = nums[_ia])
  sum += v;
```

First, notice that the **for** loop requires a loop control variable, called **_ia** in this case, but no such variable is present in the **foreach** statement. Remember, the variable declared in the **foreach**, which is **v** in this case, receives the values of the elements of the array. It is not a loop counter. This means that a loop control variable must be created. This variable cannot be declared inside the **for** because this declaration needs to be reserved for the declaration of the **foreach** variable, **v**, which must be local to the loop. Thus, it is necessary to declare the loop control variable outside the **for** loop. This requires the generation of a unique integer variable name that won't conflict with any other variables used within its scope.

Second, the **for** must cycle through all elements in the array (**nums**, in this case), but the size of the array is not part of the **foreach** specification. This means that the number of elements in the array must be computed. Fortunately, this can be accomplished through the use of **sizeof**, as described shortly.

Now, let's go through each step in the translation process. The **foreach** translation begins by constructing a (hopefully) unique variable that will be used as the **for** loop control variable. This variable's name begins with **_i**, to which a letter between **a** and **z** is added. The first generated variable in a file is called **_ia**, the second **_ib**, and so on. Up to 26 such variables are allowed. This isn't the best way to generate nonconflicting variable names, but it has the advantage of simplicity and is sufficient for the purposes of experimenting with a **foreach** loop. This variable is given a type of **int** and its declaration is written to the output file.

Next, the **for** loop is begun by writing **for(** to the output file. Then the initialization portion of the **for** is constructed. First, the type and name of the **foreach** variable is read and copied to the output file. Next, the keyword **in** is read and discarded. The array name is then read and used to construct an initialization that sets the **foreach** variable to the value of the first element in the array.

Next, the conditional portion of the **for** is generated. In this section, the loop control variable is tested against a value that represents the number of elements in the array. This value is computed by dividing the size of the array by the size of an individual element in the array. This division is necessary because **sizeof** returns the size in bytes of an array, not the number of elements in the array.

Finally, the iteration portion of the **for** is created. It increments the loop control variable and sets the **foreach** variable to the value of the next element in the array. Before returning, **foreach( )** confirms that the **foreach** statement ends with a **)**.

One last point: In C#, the **foreach** can be used with arrays *and* collections (which are much like STL containers). For simplicity, this version will work only with arrays. However, you can try adapting it so that it can be used to cycle through STL containers.

Translating the cases Statement

As explained earlier, the **cases** statement provides a single-statement alternative to specifying a series of stacked **case** statements. It is translated by the **cases( )** function, shown here:

```
// Translate a cases statement.
void cases() {
  string token;
  int start, end;

  skipspaces();

  // Get starting value.
  gettoken(token);

  if(isdigit(token[0])) {
    // is an int constant
    start = atoi(token.c_str());
  }
  else if(token[0] == '\'') {
    // is char constant
```

```
    gettoken(token);

    start = (int) token[0];

    // discard closing '
    gettoken(token);
    if(token[0] != '\'')
      throw SyntaxExc("' expected in cases.");
  }
  else
   throw SyntaxExc("Constant expected in cases.");

  skipspaces();

  // Read and discard the "to".
  gettoken(token);
  if(token != "to")
    throw SyntaxExc("to expected in cases.");

  skipspaces();

  // Get ending value.
  gettoken(token);

  if(isdigit(token[0])) {
    // is an int constant
    end = atoi(token.c_str());
  }
  else if(token[0] == '\'') {
    // is char constant
    gettoken(token);

    end = (int) token[0];

    // discard closing '
    gettoken(token);
    if(token[0] != '\'')
      throw SyntaxExc("' expected in cases.");
  }
  else
   throw SyntaxExc("Constant expected in cases.");

  skipspaces();

  // Read and discard the :
```

```
  gettoken(token);

  if(token != ":")
    throw SyntaxExc(": expected in cases.");

  // Generate stacked case statements.
  fout << "case " << start << ":\n";
  for(int i = start+1 ; i <= end; i++) {
    fout << indent << "case " << i << ":";
    if(i != end) fout << endl;
  }
}
```

Although it looks like a lot of code, it's actually a simple translation. Recall that a **cases** statement lets you specify a range of values that will match a **switch** expression. The translator simply converts that range into a series of stacked **case** statements. For example, this **switch** statement:

```
switch(val) {
  cases 0 to 3:
    cout << "val is 0, 1, 2, or 3\n";
    break;
  case 4:
    cout << "val is 4\n";
}
```

is translated into this equivalent C++ code:

```
switch(val) {
  case 0:
  case 1:
  case 2:
  case 3:
    cout << "val is 0, 1, 2, or 3\n";
    break;
  case 4:
    cout << "val is 4\n";
}
```

As you can see, individual **case** statements representing the range of values specified by the **cases** statement have been produced.

The **cases( )** function works like this. First, the beginning value in the range is read. This value will be either an integer or character constant. If it is an integer constant, it will begin with a digit. If it is a character constant, it will begin with a single quote. Either way, this value is stored as an integer value in **start**. Next, the **to** is read and discarded. Then the ending value is read. It too might be either an integer or character constant. Its value is stored in the integer variable **end**. Finally, a series of stacked **case** statements are output, one for each value in the range.

Translating the typeof Operator

The **typeof** operator supports an alternative syntax for comparing two types. As explained earlier, its general form is

typeof *op1* same as *op2*

Here, *op1* and *op2* specify either a type identifier (such as **int** or **MyClass**) or an object. Thus, **typeof** can be used to compare the types of two objects, the type of an object to a known type, or two types. Its outcome is true if the types are the same and false otherwise. The **typeof** operator is converted into a C++ expression that compares the results of applying the **typeid** operator to each operand.

The translation of **typeof** is handled by the **typeof( )** function, shown here:

```
// Translate a typeof expression.
void typeof() {
  string token;
  string temp;

  fout << "typeid(";

  skipspaces();

  gettoken(token);

  do {
    temp = token;

    if(!gettoken(token))
      throw SyntaxExc("Unexpected EOF encountered.");

    if(token != "same") fout << temp;
  } while(token != "same");

  skipspaces();

  gettoken(token);

  if(token != "as") throw SyntaxExc("as expected.");

  fout << ") == typeid(";
```

```
  skipspaces();

  do {
    if(!gettoken(token))
      throw SyntaxExc("Unexpected EOF encountered.");

    fout << token;
  } while(token != ")");
  fout << ")";
}
```

The operation of **typeof( )** is easy to follow. It reads the first operand and outputs a **typeid** expression containing that type. It then reads and discards the **same** and **as** keywords. Then it reads the second operand and outputs the corresponding **typeid** expression. Thus, this **typeof** statement:

```
if(typeof obj same as Myclass)
  cout << "obj is a MyClass object.\n";
```

is translated into this C++ code:

```
if(typeid(obj) == typeid(Myclass))
  cout << "obj is a MyClass object.\n";
```

Translating a repeat/until Loop

As mentioned earlier, the translator handles a **repeat**/**until** loop mostly for the sake of illustration, since it is easier to use macros to handle this construct. However, having the translator perform this conversion does save you the effort of defining **repeat** and **until** macros in every program that uses them. It also serves as a model that can be adapted for other types of loops.

The **repeat** keyword is translated by the **repeat( )** method, shown here, which simply substitutes **do**:

```
// Translate a repeat loop.
void repeat() {
  fout << "do";
}
```

The **until** keyword is handled by **until( )**, which is shown next:

```
// Translate an until.
void until() {
  string token;
  int parencount = 1;

  fout << "while";
```

```
  skipspaces();

  // Read and store the (
  gettoken(token);
  if(token != "(")
    throw SyntaxExc("( expected in typeof.");
  fout << "(";

  // Begin while by reversing and
  // parenthesizing the condition.
  fout << "!(";

  // Now, read the expression.
  do {
    if(!gettoken(token))
      throw SyntaxExc("Unexpected EOF encountered.");

    if(token == "(") parencount++;
    if(token == ")") parencount--;

    fout << token;
  } while(parencount > 0);
  fout << ")";
}
```

The **until( )** function substitutes the keyword **while** for **until** and then reverses the conditional expression. (Remember, a **repeat/until** loop runs until something becomes true. A **do/while** loop runs until something becomes false.)

Although conceptually simple, reversing the conditional expression requires a bit of work on the part of the translator. The reason is that it can't simply add a **!** to the start of the expression. It must also parenthesize the expression that the **!** precedes. To understand why, consider this **repeat/until** loop:

```
int i=0;

repeat {
  cout << i << " ";
  i++;
} until (i==10);
```

It is translated into the following **do/while**:

```
int i=0;

do {
```

```
    cout << i << " ";
    i++;
} while(!(i==10));
```

The parentheses in the conditional expression of the **while** ensure that the loop will run as
long as **i** does not equal 10. However, if the parentheses were removed, as shown here:

```
} while(!i==10);
```

the loop would run while **!i** was equal to 10, which is a completely different condition!

To parenthesize the **until** expression, the translator must add an opening parenthesis to
the start of the expression and a closing parenthesis to the end of it. The question is, how
does the translator know when the conditional expression has ended? It determines this by
counting closing parentheses. Recall that the expression in the **until** is contained within a
pair of parentheses. The parenthesis count is stored in the **parencount** variable, which is
initialized to 1 (which corresponds to the opening parenthesis of the **until** expression). When
copying the conditional expression, the translator increments **parencount** each time an
opening parenthesis is found and decrements it each time a closing parenthesis is encountered.
Thus, when **parencount** drops to zero, the end of the expression has been reached, and the
final closing parenthesis can be added.

A Demonstration Program

The following program demonstrates the experimental features supported by the translator:

```
// Demonstrate all of the experimental features
// supported by the translator.
#include <iostream>
using namespace std;

// Create a polymorphic base class.
class A {
public:
  virtual void f() { };
};

// And a concrete subclass.
class B: public A {
public:
  void f() {}
};

int main() {
  int n[] = { 1, 2, 3, 4, 5, 6, 7, 8, 9, 10 };
  double dn[] = {1.1, 2.2, 3.3, 4.4 };
```

```
    cout << "Using a foreach loop.\n";

    /* Keywords, such as foreach or typeof
       are ignored when inside comments
       or quoted strings. */

    // A foreach loop.
    foreach(int x in n )
      cout << x << ' ';

    cout << "\n\n";

    cout << "Using nested foreach loops.\n";

    // A foreach loop with a block.
    foreach(double f in dn) {
      cout << f << ' ';
      cout << f*f << ' ';

      // A nested foreach loop.
      foreach(double f in dn)
        cout << f/3 << " ";

      cout << endl;
    }

    cout << endl;

    cout << "Demonstrate cases statement.\n";

    cout << "A cases statement that uses integer constants:\n";

    // Demonstrate cases statement that uses
    // integer constants.
    for(int i=0; i < 12; i++)
      switch(i) {
        case 0:
          cout << "case 0\n";
          break;
        cases 1 to 6:
          cout << "cases 1 to 6\n";
          break;
        case 7:
          cout << "case 7\n";
          break;
        cases 8 to 10:
```

```
          cout << "cases 8 to 10\n";
          break;
       default:
          cout << "case 11\n";
    }

cout << "\n";

cout << "A cases statement that uses character constants:\n";

// Demonstrate a cases statement that uses
// character constants.
for(char ch='a'; ch <= 'e'; ch++)
  switch(ch) {
    case 'a':
      cout << "case a\n";
      break;
    cases 'b' to 'd':
      cout << "cases b to d\n";
      break;
    case 'e':
      cout << "case e\n";
  }

cout << endl;

cout << "A repeat/until loop.\n";

// Demonstrate a repeat/until loop.
int k = 0;
repeat {
  k++;
  cout << "k: " << k << " ";
} until(k==10);

cout << "\n\n";

cout << "Use typeof.\n";

// Demonstrate typeof.
A *aPtr;
B *bPtr, bObj;

// Assign a base pointer to derived object.
aPtr = &bObj;
bPtr = &bObj;
```

```
    if(typeof *aPtr same as *bPtr)
      cout << "aPtr points to same type of object as bPtr\n";

    if(typeof *aPtr same as B)
     cout << "aPtr points to B object\n";

    return 0;
}
```

When this program is run through the translator, the following C++ code is produced:

```
// Translated from an .exp source file.
// Demonstrate all of the experimental features
// supported by the translator.
#include <iostream>
using namespace std;

// Create a polymorphic base class.
class A {
public:
  virtual void f() { };
};

// And a concrete subclass.
class B: public A {
public:
  void f() {}
};

int main() {
  int n[] = { 1, 2, 3, 4, 5, 6, 7, 8, 9, 10 };
  double dn[] = {1.1, 2.2, 3.3, 4.4 };

  cout << "Using a foreach loop.\n";

  /* Keywords, such as foreach or typeof
     are ignored when inside comments
     or quoted strings. */

  // A foreach loop.
  int _ia = 0;
  for(int x = n[0];
      _ia < ((sizeof n)/(sizeof n[0]));
      _ia++, x = n[_ia])
```

```
        cout << x << ' ';

cout << "\n\n";

cout << "Using nested foreach loops.\n";

// A foreach loop with a block.
int _ib = 0;
for(double f = dn[0];
    _ib < ((sizeof dn)/(sizeof dn[0]));
    _ib++, f = dn[_ib]) {
  cout << f << ' ';
  cout << f*f << ' ';

  // A nested foreach loop.
  int _ic = 0;
  for(double f = dn[0];
      _ic < ((sizeof dn)/(sizeof dn[0]));
      _ic++, f = dn[_ic])
    cout << f/3 << " ";

  cout << endl;
}

cout << endl;

cout << "Demonstrate cases statement.\n";

cout << "A cases statement that uses integer constants:\n";

// Demonstrate cases statement that uses
// integer constants.
for(int i=0; i < 12; i++)
  switch(i) {
    case 0:
      cout << "case 0\n";
      break;
    case 1:
    case 2:
    case 3:
    case 4:
    case 5:
    case 6:
      cout << "cases 1 to 6\n";
      break;
    case 7:
```

```
          cout << "case 7\n";
          break;
        case 8:
        case 9:
        case 10:
          cout << "cases 8 to 10\n";
          break;
        default:
          cout << "case 11\n";
    }

cout << "\n";

cout << "A cases statement that uses character constants:\n";

// Demonstrate a cases statement that uses
// character constants.
for(char ch='a'; ch <= 'e'; ch++)
  switch(ch) {
    case 'a':
      cout << "case a\n";
      break;
    case 98:
    case 99:
    case 100:
      cout << "cases b to d\n";
      break;
    case 'e':
      cout << "case e\n";
  }

cout << endl;

cout << "A repeat/until loop.\n";

// Demonstrate a repeat/until loop.
int k = 0;
do {
  k++;
  cout << "k: " << k << " ";
} while(!(k==10));

cout << "\n\n";

cout << "Use typeof.\n";
```

```
// Demonstrate typeof.
A *aPtr;
B *bPtr, bObj;

// Assign a base pointer to derived object.
aPtr = &bObj;
bPtr = &bObj;

if(typeid(*aPtr) == typeid(*bPtr))
  cout << "aPtr points to same type of object as bPtr\n";

if(typeid(*aPtr) == typeid(B))
 cout << "aPtr points to B object\n";

return 0;
}
```

The C++ version can be compiled by any modern C++ compiler and produces the following output:

```
Using a foreach loop.
1 2 3 4 5 6 7 8 9 10

Using nested foreach loops.
1.1 1.21 0.366667 0.733333 1.1 1.46667
2.2 4.84 0.366667 0.733333 1.1 1.46667
3.3 10.89 0.366667 0.733333 1.1 1.46667
4.4 19.36 0.366667 0.733333 1.1 1.46667

Demonstrate cases statement.
A cases statement that uses integer constants:
case 0
cases 1 to 6
cases 1 to 6
cases 1 to 6
cases 1 to 6
cases 1 to 6
cases 1 to 6
case 7
cases 8 to 10
cases 8 to 10
cases 8 to 10
case 11

A cases statement that uses character constants:
case a
```

```
cases b to d
cases b to d
cases b to d
case e

A repeat/until loop.
k: 1 k: 2 k: 3 k: 4 k: 5 k: 6 k: 7 k: 8 k: 9 k: 10

Use typeof.
aPtr points to same type of object as bPtr
aPtr points to B object
```

Some Things to Try

As explained at the start of this chapter, the purpose of the translator is to enable you to experiment with your own ideas for new language features or intriguing alternatives to existing features. To add your own experimental keyword to the translator, first create a function that handles the translation. Then, inside the main loop, add another **else if** statement that calls that function when the keyword is encountered.

The constructs with which you can experiment are limited only by your imagination. Here are some ideas to get you started:

▶ A **breakon** statement, which breaks from a loop when some condition is true. It might use a syntax like this:

```
breakon(x == 99);
```

▶ A **breakto** statement, which transfers control out of a loop or **switch** to the specified label. It might use a syntax like this:

```
breakto jmp12;
```

▶ An **ignore** statement, which causes the early iteration of a loop when a certain value is encountered. Thus, it streamlines an **if**...**continue** statement. It might use a syntax like this:

```
ignore(n == 12);
```

Of course, not all experimental features will turn out to be good ones. That's what makes them experimental—and enjoyable to play with!

One last point: If you are interested in designing your own language, you will find Chapter 9 especially valuable because it develops an interpreter for a small subset of C++. You can use this interpreter as the starting point for language features more advanced than can be easily handled by the translator found in this chapter.

CHAPTER 5

An Internet File Downloader

159

The Internet has irreversibly altered the course of programming. Prior to the rise of the Internet, most applications executed in isolation on individual machines, or made use of small, local area networks. The Internet changed this. Today, most computers are Internet-enabled, and many programs make use of the vast resources of the World Wide Web. For the modern programmer, incorporating Internet functionality into an application is no longer an option, it is a necessity.

Despite the importance of the Internet, C++ does not provide built-in support for it. This is because C++ came to maturity before the Internet reached critical mass in the late 1990s. However, this is not a hindrance. In fact, it's actually a benefit. Instead of dictating a single approach that all programmers must use, C++ lets you access the Internet capabilities of the operating system. Not only does this offer the potential for greater efficiency and flexibility by letting you choose the best way to interface to the Internet, it also lets you write an Internet-enabled program in a way that is most compatible with the underlying execution environment. Therefore, if you want to create high-performance, Internet-enabled code, C++ is your first choice.

To illustrate the ease with which C++ handles the Internet, this chapter develops a file download subsystem that can be integrated into a number of different Internet-based applications. The file downloader retrieves a file from the Internet, given that file's URL. It is a self-contained subsystem that handles all the details of opening an Internet connection, reading the file, and then closing the connection. The file downloader has one special feature: it is restartable. For example, if in the middle of a long download, the connection to the Internet is lost, the download can be resumed at the point at which it was interrupted when the connection is reestablished. This is especially useful when downloading very long files over a slow modem connection!

After developing the download subsystem, two applications that use it are created. The first is a very simple, console-based application that simply demonstrates the downloader. The second is a GUI application that you can use to download files.

Because Internet support is provided by the operating system, it is necessary to choose one. The one operating system that is available to virtually all readers of this book is Windows, and it is used in this chapter. However, the basic techniques can be translated into other environments.

NOTE

This chapter assumes that the reader has a general understanding of the Internet and a working knowledge of Windows programming. It is far beyond the scope of this book to teach either.

The WinINet Library

To access the Internet, this chapter takes advantage of an easy-to-use library provided by Windows. This library is called Windows Internet, or *WinINet* for short. The WinINet API offers a rich assortment of high-level functions that handle the various protocols, such as HTTP and FTP, in a consistent, stable way. Windows handles the low-level details for you. (This is somewhat similar to the way that **<fstream>** presents a consistent interface for file operations while handling the details for you.) As you will see, if you follow a few rules, it is easy to add Internet access to any Windows application.

Although WinINet is a large library, you need to use only a few of its functions:

InternetAttemptConnect	Checks if an Internet connection is available.
InternetOpen	Opens an Internet connection and returns a handle to it.
InternetOpenUrl	Opens a URL and returns a handle to it.
HttpQueryInfo	Obtains information from the last response header.
InternetReadFile	Reads bytes from an open URL.
InternetCloseHandle	Closes an Internet handle.

Each of these will be described in detail during the discussion of the code for the file downloader.

To use WinINet, you must include **wininet.h** in your program and link **wininet.lib** with your application.

The File Downloader Subsystem

The entire code for the file downloader subsystem is shown here. Put this code in a file called **dl.cpp**.

```cpp
// A file download subsystem.
#include <iostream>
#include <windows.h>
#include <wininet.h>
#include <fstream>
#include <cstdio>

using namespace std;

const int MAX_ERRMSG_SIZE = 80;
const int MAX_FILENAME_SIZE = 512;
const int BUF_SIZE = 1024;

// Exception class for download errors.
class DLExc {
  char err[MAX_ERRMSG_SIZE];
public:
  DLExc(char *exc) {
    if(strlen(exc) < MAX_ERRMSG_SIZE)
      strcpy(err, exc);
  }

  // Return a pointer to the error message.
```

```cpp
  const char * geterr() {
    return err;
  }
};


// A class for downloading files from the Internet.
class Download {
  static bool ishttp(char *url);
  static bool httpverOK(HINTERNET hIurl);
  static bool getfname(char *url, char *fname);
  static unsigned long openfile(char *url, bool reload,
                                ofstream &fout);
public:
  static bool download(char *url, bool restart=false,
     void (*update)(unsigned long, unsigned long)=NULL);
};


// Download a file.
//
// Pass the URL of the file to url.
//
// To reload a file, pass true to reload.
//
// To specify an update function that is called after
// each buffer is read, pass a pointer to that
// function as the third parameter.  If no update
// function is desired, then let the third parameter
// default to null.
bool Download::download(char *url, bool reload,
        void (*update)(unsigned long, unsigned long)) {

  ofstream fout;            // output stream
  unsigned char buf[BUF_SIZE]; // input buffer
  unsigned long numrcved;   // number of bytes read
  unsigned long filelen;    // length of file on disk
  HINTERNET hIurl, hInet;   // Internet handles
  unsigned long contentlen;// length of content
  unsigned long len;        // length of contentlen
  unsigned long total = 0;  // running total of bytes received
  char header[80];          // holds Range header

  try {
    if(!ishttp(url))
      throw DLExc("Must be HTTP url.");
```

```
// Open the file specified by url.
// The open stream will be returned
// in fout.  If reload is true, then
// any preexisting file will be truncated.
// The length of any preexisting file (after
// possible truncation) is returned.
filelen = openfile(url, reload, fout);

// See if Internet connection available.
if(InternetAttemptConnect(0) != ERROR_SUCCESS)
  throw DLExc("Can't connect.");

// Open Internet connection.
hInet = InternetOpen("downloader",
                     INTERNET_OPEN_TYPE_DIRECT,
                     NULL, NULL,  0);

if(hInet == NULL)
  throw DLExc("Can't open connection.");

// Construct header requesting range of data.
sprintf(header, "Range:bytes=%d-", filelen);

// Open the URL and request range.
hIurl = InternetOpenUrl(hInet, url,
          header, -1,
          INTERNET_FLAG_NO_CACHE_WRITE, 0);

if(hIurl == NULL) throw DLExc("Can't open url.");

// Confirm that HTTP/1.1 or greater is supported.
if(!httpverOK(hIurl))
  throw DLExc("HTTP/1.1 not supported.");

// Get content length.
len = sizeof contentlen;
if(!HttpQueryInfo(hIurl,
                  HTTP_QUERY_CONTENT_LENGTH |
                  HTTP_QUERY_FLAG_NUMBER,
                  &contentlen, &len, NULL))
  throw DLExc("File or content length not found.");

// If existing file (if any) is not complete,
// then finish downloading.
if(filelen != contentlen && contentlen)
```

```
        do {
          // Read a buffer of info.
          if(!InternetReadFile(hIurl, &buf,
                                 BUF_SIZE, &numrcved))
            throw DLExc("Error occurred during download.");

            // Write buffer to disk.
            fout.write((const char *) buf, numrcved);
            if(!fout.good())
              throw DLExc("Error writing file.");

            total += numrcved; // update running total

            // Call update function, if specified.
            if(update && numrcved > 0)
              update(contentlen+filelen, total+filelen);

        } while(numrcved > 0);
      else
        if(update)
          update(filelen, filelen);

    } catch(DLExc) {
      fout.close();
      InternetCloseHandle(hIurl);
      InternetCloseHandle(hInet);

      throw; // rethrow the exception for use by caller
    }

    fout.close();
    InternetCloseHandle(hIurl);
    InternetCloseHandle(hInet);

    return true;
  }

// Return true if HTTP version of 1.1 or greater.
bool Download::httpverOK(HINTERNET hIurl) {
  char str[80];
  unsigned long len = 79;

  // Get HTTP version.
  if(!HttpQueryInfo(hIurl, HTTP_QUERY_VERSION, &str, &len, NULL))
    return false;
```

```
    // First, check major version number.
    char *p = strchr(str, '/');
    p++;
    if(*p == '0') return false; // can't use HTTP 0.x

    // Now, find start of minor HTTP version number.
    p = strchr(str, '.');
    p++;

    // Convert to int.
    int minorVerNum = atoi(p);

    if(minorVerNum > 0) return true;
    return false;
}

// Extract the filename from the URL.  Return false if
// the filename cannot be found.
bool Download::getfname(char *url, char *fname) {
    // Find last /.
    char *p = strrchr(url, '/');

    // Copy filename after the last /.
    if(p && (strlen(p) < MAX_FILENAME_SIZE)) {
        p++;
        strcpy(fname, p);
        return true;
    }
    else
        return false;
}

// Open the output file, initialize the output
// stream, and return the file's length.  If
// reload is true, first truncate any preexisting
// file.
unsigned long Download::openfile(char *url,
                                 bool reload,
                                 ofstream &fout) {
    char fname[MAX_FILENAME_SIZE];

    if(!getfname(url, fname))
        throw DLExc("File name error.");

    if(!reload)
```

```
    fout.open(fname, ios::binary | ios::out |
                    ios::app | ios::ate);
  else
    fout.open(fname, ios::binary | ios::out |
                    ios::trunc);

  if(!fout)
    throw DLExc("Can't open output file.");

  // Get current file length.
  return fout.tellp();
}


// Confirm that the URL specifies HTTP.
bool Download::ishttp(char *url) {
  char str[5] = "";

  // Get first four characters from URL.
  strncpy(str, url, 4);

  // Convert to lowercase
  for(char *p=str; *p; p++) *p = tolower(*p);

  return !strcmp("http", str);
}
```

Notice that this file defines two classes. The first is **DLExc**, which is a class that encapsulates exceptions thrown by the downloader. The **DLExc** constructor is passed a pointer to a string that describes the exception, and it stores that string. A pointer to the error message is obtained by calling the member function **geterr( )**.

The second class is **Download**, which is the class that handles the downloading of files. Notice that the **Download** class consists solely of **static** functions. Thus, putting the downloader into a class is more of an organizational technique than it is a means of encapsulation. In fact, it would have been possible to use a namespace rather than a class for this purpose. However, by using a class, it is possible to make several of the functions private, thus preventing their use by other code. Also, using a class facilitates the addition of new features at a later date.

The following sections examine each part of **Download** in detail.

General Theory of Operation

Before examining the various pieces of **Download**, it will be helpful to understand its general theory of operation. To download a file, the URL of that file is passed to the **download( )** function. If no preexisting file by that name exists on disk, then the file is downloaded in its entirety. However, if a partially downloaded file by that name is found, then only the remainder of the file is downloaded. It is the ability to download the remainder of a file that makes it possible to resume a download that has been interrupted.

To perform partial downloads, **Download** relies upon a feature provided by HTTP version 1.1 (or greater) that allows a range of data to be downloaded: the Range header. Therefore, the downloader only works with URLs that support HTTP version 1.1 or above. It is the Range header that allows an interrupted download to be restarted from the point at which it left off. Because HTTP, version 1.1 is required, only HTTP downloads are supported by the downloader.

As it relates to an HTTP request, a *header* is information that accompanies a request. The Range header is a string that has this general form:

Range:bytes=*start-end*

Here, *start* specifies the beginning of the range, and *end* specifies the end. If *end* is left off, then the range runs from *start* to the end of the file.

Download defines one public function, **download( )**, which is the function called to download a file. Thus, it is the entry point for downloading. **Download** defines four support functions:

ishttp	Determines if the URL specifies an HTTP request.
httpverOK	Determines if HTTP version 1.1 or greater is being used.
getfname	Obtains the filename portion of the URL.
openfile	Opens the file and returns its length, which will be greater than zero if a partial download already exits.

These support functions are declared **private** within **Download**.

The download( ) Function

The **download( )** function is the only public function defined by **Download**. It is called by user code and handles the downloading of a file. Thus, to download a file, you call **download( )**. Because of its importance, we will examine it line-by-line. It begins with

```
bool Download::download(char *url, bool reload,
void (*update)(unsigned long, unsigned long)) {
```

The **download( )** function has three parameters. The first, **url**, is a pointer to a string that contains the complete URL for the file (including the filename). The filename is assumed to be the name that follows the last / in the URL. For example, in this URL the filename is MyFile.dat:

http://www.SoeSite.com/SomeDir/MyFile.dat

Keep in mind that you must specify the entire URL using the canonical form, which includes **http://**.

The second parameter, **reload**, determines if a file that has already been downloaded will be downloaded again. If **reload** is true, then the file is downloaded in its entirety, whether or not it already exists on disk (either completely or partially). If **reload** is false, then only the remaining portion of the file (if any) is downloaded. Thus, if you want to retrieve a fresh copy of a file that you have already downloaded, pass true to **reload**.

The third parameter is **update**. It is a pointer to a function that will be periodically called by **download( )** as a means of keeping user code apprised of the download progress. If this parameter is null, then no update function is used. We will examine the requirements for the **update** function parameter a bit later.

Next, the following local variables are declared:

```
ofstream fout;            // output stream
unsigned char buf[BUF_SIZE]; // input buffer
unsigned long numrcved;   // number of bytes read
unsigned long filelen;    // length of file on disk
HINTERNET hIurl, hInet;   // Internet handles
unsigned long contentlen;// length of content
unsigned long len;        // length of contentlen
unsigned long total = 0;  // running total of bytes received
char header[80];          // holds Range header
```

Notice the variables **hIurl** and **hInet**. These hold handles to the URL being downloaded and the Internet connection, respectively. One or the other of these handles is used by the WinINet API functions.

The main function code begins as shown here. Notice that the entire download code is wrapped in a **try/catch** block, which handles communication and/or file errors.

```
try {
  if(!ishttp(url))
    throw DLExc("Must be HTTP url.");
```

The first thing that **download( )** does is call **ishttp( )** to determine if the URL specifies an HTTP request by confirming that it begins with "http". As explained, only HTTP requests are handled by the downloader.

Next, the receiving file is opened and its length is obtained.

```
// Open the file specified by url.
// The open stream will be returned
// in fout.  If reload is true, then
// any preexisting file will be truncated.
// The length of any preexisting file (after
// possible truncation) is returned.
filelen = openfile(url, reload, fout);
```

As the comments explain, if the file does not exist or is being reloaded, then any preexisting file by the specified name will be truncated to zero. In this case, the length of the file returned by **openfile( )** will be zero. Otherwise, if the file already exists, its length will be returned.

Remember, if a download was interrupted, then a partial file may already exist when the download is restarted.

After the file is opened, a connection with the Internet is established by the following code:

```
// See if Internet connection available.
if(InternetAttemptConnect(0) != ERROR_SUCCESS)
  throw DLExc("Can't connect.");


// Open Internet connection.
hInet = InternetOpen("downloader",
                   INTERNET_OPEN_TYPE_DIRECT,
                   NULL, NULL,  0);


if(hInet == NULL)
  throw DLExc("Can't open connection.");
```

First, an attempt is made to connect to the Internet by calling the WinINet API function **InternetAttemptConnect( )**. This function returns **ERROR_SUCCESS** if it is possible to establish a connection. Its only argument is reserved and must be zero. If the computer is not currently connected, then (depending upon your computer's settings) you will see a dialog box asking if you want to connect. If no connection is available, **InternetAttemptConnect( )** returns an error, which causes an exception to be thrown.

Assuming that a connection is available, **InternetOpen( )** is called to open the connection. It is another WinINet function and has this prototype:

> HINTERNET InternetOpen(LPCTSTR *agent*, DWORD *access*,
> LPCTSTR *proxy*, LPCTSTR *proxopt*,
> DWORD *options*)

Here, *agent* specifies the application name, and *access* specifies what type of access is used. For the downloader, the access is **INTERNET_OPEN_TYPE_DIRECT**. Neither *proxy* nor *proxopt* are used when *access* is **INTERNET_OPEN_TYPE_DIRECT** and must be null. The *options* parameter specifies any options, none of which are needed by the downloader. It returns a handle to the open connection. Null is returned if the connection can't be opened.

Once the connection is open, a Range header is generated:

```
// Construct header requesting range of data.
sprintf(header, "Range:bytes=%d-", filelen);
```

This header is then passed to the WinINet function **InternetOpenUrl( )**, shown next, which opens the URL specified in **url**:

```
// Open the URL and request range.
hIurl = InternetOpenUrl(hInet, url,
          header, -1,
          INTERNET_FLAG_NO_CACHE_WRITE, 0);


if(hIurl == NULL) throw DLExc("Can't open url.");
```

The **InternetOpenUrl( )** function has this prototype:

HINTERNET InternetOpenUrl(HINTERNET *hInet*, LPCTSTR *url*,
LPCTSTR *headerstr*, DWORD *headlen*,
DWORD *options*, LPDWORD *extra*);

The Internet handle obtained from **InternetOpen( )** is passed in *hInet*. A pointer to the string containing the URL to open is passed in *url*. A pointer to a string containing one or more additional headers to be incorporated into the request is passed in *headerstr*. The length of *headerstr* is passed in *headlen*, which can be –1 if *headerstr* points to a null-terminated string, as it does for the downloader. Various option flags can be specified in *options*. The one used by the downloader is

INTERNET_FLAG_NO_CACHE_WRITE

which prevents the downloaded file from being cached. Any additional, application-specific information can be passed in *extra*. Because the downloader does not require any, zero is used. The function returns a handle to the open URL, or null on failure.

Each response from the server carries with it a header. One component of this header contains the HTTP version. Because the downloader requires that the server support HTTP, version 1.1 or higher, a check of the HTTP version is necessary before proceeding. This is accomplished by calling **httpverOK( )**, as shown here:

```
// Confirm that HTTP/1.1 or greater is supported.
if(!httpverOK(hIurl))
   throw DLExc("HTTP/1.1 not supported.");
```

Assuming that the HTTP version is acceptable, the next step obtains the amount of content that is being downloaded. This is accomplished by calling the WinINet function **HttpQueryInfo( )**, as shown here:

```
// Get content length.
len = sizeof contentlen;
if(!HttpQueryInfo(hIurl,
                HTTP_QUERY_CONTENT_LENGTH |
                HTTP_QUERY_FLAG_NUMBER,
                &contentlen, &len, NULL))
   throw DLExc("File or content length not found.");
```

When **HttpQueryInfo( )** returns, the content length (in bytes) will be in **contentlen**. The content length automatically takes into account the range requested by the Range header. Therefore, if the entire file is being downloaded, the requested range will be "0-" (which specifies the entire file) and the content length will equal the length of the file. When an interrupted download is being resumed, the range value will specify a starting point somewhere in the middle of the file and the content length will equal the number of bytes remaining.

HttpQueryInfo( ) obtains information from a header. It has the following prototype:

BOOL HttpQueryInfo(HINTERNET *hIurl*, DWORD *what*, LPVOID *buf*,
LPDWORD *buflen*, LPDWORD *index*)

The handle of the request, which in this case is the one returned by **InternetOpenUrl( )**, is passed to *hIurl*. A value specifying the item of information to obtain is passed in *what*. For the downloader, two values are needed. The first is

HTTP_QUERY_CONTENT_LENGTH

which obtains the length of the content being requested (which in this case is the file), and

HTTP_QUERY_FLAG_NUMBER

which requests that this value be represented as an integer value. A pointer to a buffer that will receive the information is passed in *buf*, and a pointer to an integer that specifies the length of that buffer is passed in *buflen*. The *index* parameter allows you to specify the index of a header, but the downloader does not require this feature, so null is passed. The function returns true if it can obtain the requested information. The content length may not be available, in which case **HttpQueryInfo( )** returns false.

Assuming that the content length is available, if the length of any preexisting file on disk is less than the content length, and the content length does not equal zero, the file (or the remaining portion of the file) is downloaded by the following lines of code:

```
// If existing file (if any) is not complete,
// then finish downloading.
if(filelen != contentlen && contentlen)
  do {
    // Read a buffer of info.
    if(!InternetReadFile(hIurl, &buf,
                         BUF_SIZE, &numrcved))
      throw DLExc("Error occurred during download.");

    // Write buffer to disk.
    fout.write((const char *) buf, numrcved);
    if(!fout.good())
      throw DLExc("Error writing file.");

    total += numrcved; // update running total

// Call update function, if specified.
    if(update && numrcved > 0)
      update(contentlen+filelen, total+filelen);

  } while(numrcved > 0);
```

```
else
  if(update)
    update(filelen, filelen);
```

This code uses the WinINet function **InternetReadFile( )** to read the file, one buffer at a time. Each time through the loop, the function pointed to by **update** is called, unless **update** is null. As explained, the function pointed to by **update** is used to report on the progress of the file download.

InternetReadFile( ) is a very useful function because it lets you read a file from the Internet in much the same way that you read a file from disk. Its prototype is shown here:

BOOL InternetReadFile(HINTERNET *hIurl*, LPVOID *buf*, DWORD *numbytes*,
LPDWORD *numrcvd*);

The handle of the file is passed in *hIurl*. For the downloader, this is the handle returned by **InternetOpenUrl( )**. A pointer to a buffer that will receive the data is passed in *buf*, and the number of bytes to read is passed in *numbytes*. This value must not exceed the size of *buf*. The number of bytes actually read is returned in the variable pointed to by *numrcvd*. This value will be zero when there are no more bytes to retrieve. The function returns true if successful and false otherwise.

The **download( )** function ends with the following lines:

```
  } catch(DLExc) {
fout.close();
    InternetCloseHandle(hIurl);
    InternetCloseHandle(hInet);

    throw; // rethrow the exception for use by caller
  }

  fout.close();
  InternetCloseHandle(hIurl);
  InternetCloseHandle(hInet);

  return true;
}
```

Assuming successful completion, the **download( )** function ends by closing the file and Internet handles and returning true. If an error has occurred, the handles are still closed and then the exception is rethrown. This allows user code to respond to the error.

The ishttp( ) Function

As explained, only HTTP file downloads are supported by the downloader. **Download** uses the **ishttp( )** function, shown here, to confirm that the URL of the file specifies the HTTP protocol:

```
// Confirm that the URL specifies HTTP.
bool Download::ishttp(char *url) {
  char str[5] = "";

  // Get first four characters from URL.
  strncpy(str, url, 4);

  // Convert to lowercase
  for(char *p=str; *p; p++) *p = tolower(*p);

  return !strcmp("http", str);
}
```

The operation of **ishttp( )** is straightforward. It simply checks that the first four characters in the URL contain the string "http". It returns true if this is the case and false otherwise.

The httpverOK( ) Function

The **httpverOK( )** function, shown here, confirms that the server handling the request supports HTTP version 1.1:

```
// Return true if HTTP version of 1.1 or greater.
bool Download::httpverOK(HINTERNET hIurl) {
  char str[80];
  unsigned long len = 79;

  // Get HTTP version.
  if(!HttpQueryInfo(hIurl, HTTP_QUERY_VERSION, &str, &len, NULL))
    return false;

  // First, check major version number.
  char *p = strchr(str, '/');
  p++;
  if(*p == '0') return false; // can't use HTTP 0.x

  // Now, find start of minor HTTP version number.
  p = strchr(str, '.');
  p++;

  // Convert to int.
  int minorVerNum = atoi(p);

  if(minorVerNum > 0) return true;
  return false;
}
```

A handle to the URL is passed to **httpverOK( )**. Next, the HTTP version is obtained (in string form) by calling **HttpQueryInfo( )** on this handle, specifying **HTTP_QUERY_VERSION**, which requests the version information. This query stores the version string in **str**. For HTTP version 1.1, the string will have this form:

HTTP/1.1

The function then sets **p** to point to the / character by calling the standard library function **strchr( )**. It then increments **p** and confirms that the digit it points to is nonzero. Next, a pointer to the period separating the major and minor version numbers is found, and then the pointer is advanced to point to the start of the numeric value that follows the period. Finally, this value is converted into an integer through use of the standard library function **atoi( )**. If the minor version number is greater than or equal to 1, then the HTTP version is greater than or equal to 1.1.

The getfname( ) Function

The **getfname( )** function, shown next, extracts the filename from a URL:

```
// Extract the filename from the URL.  Return false if
// the filename cannot be found.
bool Download::getfname(char *url, char *fname) {
  // Find last /.
  char *p = strrchr(url, '/');

  // Copy filename after the last /.
  if(p && (strlen(p) < MAX_FILENAME_SIZE)) {
    p++;
    strcpy(fname, p);
    return true;
  }
  else
    return false;
}
```

The function is passed a pointer to a string that holds a URL and a pointer to a character array that will hold the filename upon the function's return. The filename is assumed to be that portion of the URL that extends from the last / to the end. The function returns true if successful and false if the filename cannot be found.

The openfile( ) Function

The **openfile( )** function opens a file on disk to which the downloaded file will be written. It also returns the length of any preexisting file. It is shown here:

```
// Open the output file, initialize the output
// stream, and return the file's length.  If
// reload is true, first truncate any existing
// file.
unsigned long Download::openfile(char *url,
                                 bool reload,
                                 ofstream &fout) {
  char fname[MAX_FILENAME_SIZE];

  if(!getfname(url, fname))
    throw DLExc("File name error.");

  if(!reload)
    fout.open(fname, ios::binary | ios::out |
                     ios::app | ios::ate);
  else
    fout.open(fname, ios::binary | ios::out |
                     ios::trunc);

  if(!fout)
    throw DLExc("Can't open output file.");

  // Get current file length.
  return fout.tellp();
}
```

The **openfile( )** function has three parameters: **url**, **reload**, and **fout**. A pointer to the string that contains the URL is passed to **url**. A value that determines if any preexisting file of the same name is truncated is passed in **reload**. A pointer to a variable that will contain the opened file stream when **openfile( )** returns is passed in **fout**.

First, **openfile( )** obtains the filename from the string pointed to by **url**. Then it checks the value of **reload**. If **reload** is true, the file is opened for output, with the contents of any preexisting file being truncated to zero. If **reload** is false, it opens the file without truncating any preexisting contents and specifies that all output occur at the end of the file. It then advances the file pointer to the end of the file. Next, the length of the file is obtained by calling **tellp( )**. For a new file, this value will be zero. However, if a preexisting file was found, this value gives the length of the file because the file pointer was advanced to the end of the file when it was opened. The length of the file is returned.

The update( ) Function

As explained earlier, if you want to track the progress of the download, you must pass to **download( )**'s **update** parameter a pointer to a function that will receive the tracking information. (For silent operation, **update** can simply be allowed to default to null.) The tracking function must have this prototype. (Of course, the name of the function can be different.)

> void update(unsigned long *total*, unsigned long *part*);

When **update( )** is called, the total length of the file is passed in *total* and the amount currently downloaded is passed in *part*. You can use this information to monitor the progress of the download and to keep the user informed.

The Download Header File

The following header file must be included in any file that uses the downloader. Call this file **dl.h**.

```
// Header file for downloader.  Call this file dl.h.
#include <iostream>
#include <string>
#include <windows.h>
#include <wininet.h>
#include <fstream>
using namespace std;

const int MAX_ERRMSG_SIZE = 80;

// Exception class for downloading errors.
class DLExc {
  char err[MAX_ERRMSG_SIZE];
public:
  DLExc(char *exc) {
    if(strlen(exc) < MAX_ERRMSG_SIZE)
      strcpy(err, exc);
  }

  const char * geterr() {
    return err;
  }
};

class Download {
  static bool httpverOK(HINTERNET hIurl);
  static bool getfname(char *url, char *fname);
  static unsigned long openfile(char *url, bool reload,
                                ofstream &fout);
public:
```

```
       static bool download(char *url, bool restart=false,
         void (*update)(unsigned long, unsigned long)=NULL);
};
```

Demonstrating the File Downloader

The following program demonstrates the file downloader by creating a simple console-based
application that downloads a file. To follow along, call this file **dltest.cpp**.

```cpp
// A Sample program that uses Download.
#include <iostream>
#include "dl.h"

// This function displays the download progress as a percentage.
void showprogress(unsigned long total, unsigned long part) {
  int val = (int) ((double) part/total*100);
  cout << val << "%" << endl;
}

int main(int argc, char *argv[])
{

  // This URL is for demonstration purposes only.  Substitute
  // the URL of the file that you want to download.
  char url[] =
   "http://www.osborne.com/products/0072226803/0072226803_code.zip";

  bool reload = false;

  if(argc==2 && !strcmp(argv[1], "reload"))
      reload = true;

  cout << "Beginning download.\n";

  try {
    if(Download::download(url, reload, showprogress))
      cout << "Download Complete\n";
  } catch(DLExc exc) {
    cout << exc.geterr() << endl;
    cout << "Download Interrupted\n";
  }

  return 0;
}
```

There are three things of interest in this program. First, notice that it includes a hard-coded URL. This URL specifies the file that contains the free, online code for another of my books, *C++: The Complete Reference, 4th Edition*. This file makes a convenient test of the downloader. Of course, you can specify a URL of your own choosing.

Next, notice the **showprogress( )** function. A pointer to this function is passed to **download( )**'s **update** parameter. This means that it is called each time a buffer of data is downloaded. It displays a value that indicates the percentage of completion.

Finally, notice that **dltest** accepts one command-line argument. If this argument is "reload", then the file is downloaded in its entirety whether or not it already exists on disk. If this argument is not present, the file (or the remaining portion of the file) is downloaded only if the file on disk is not complete.

To compile **dltest.cpp**, you must remember to link in **wininet.lib**. For example, if you are compiling from the command line using Visual C++, then you will use this command line to compile this program:

```
cl -GX dl.cpp dltest.cpp wininet.lib
```

If you are using an IDE, then you must remember to add **wininet.lib** to the link.

A GUI-Based Downloader

The **Download** class can be used whenever you need to download a file from the Internet from within program code. For example, you might use the downloader to obtain a weekly sales report. If you add a user interface front end, it can also be used as a stand-alone Internet utility. To illustrate this second use, this chapter concludes by developing a complete, GUI-based file downloader for Windows called WinDL.

WinDL displays a dialog box that allows the user to enter the URL of the file to download. It has a progress bar that shows the status of the download. It also includes a check box that lets the user request that the file be fully reloaded. Figure 5-1 shows the file download dialog box.

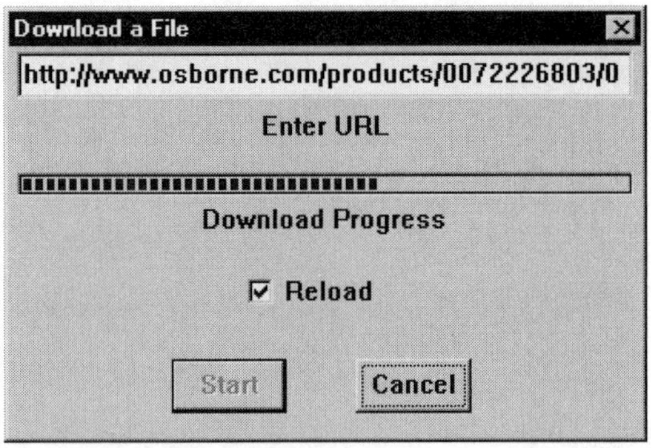

Figure 5-1   *The File Download dialog box*

The WinDL Code

WinDL consists of two main parts. The first is, of course, the code for **Download**, which was described earlier. The second is the code that handles the GUI interface. This code is shown here. To follow along, call this file **windl.cpp**.

```cpp
// WinDL: A GUI-based file download utility.

#include <windows.h>
#include <commctrl.h>
#include <cstring>
#include <cstdio>
#include "windl.h"
#include <process.h>
#include "dl.h"

const int URL_BUF_SIZE = 1024;

LRESULT CALLBACK WindowFunc(HWND, UINT, WPARAM, LPARAM);
BOOL CALLBACK DialogFunc(HWND, UINT, WPARAM, LPARAM);

void showprogress(unsigned long total,
                  unsigned long part);
void resetprogress();
unsigned __stdcall dlstart(void * reload);

char szWinName[] = "Download"; // name of window class

HINSTANCE hInst; // instance handle
HWND hwnd;        // handle of main window
HWND hProgWnd;    // handle of progress bar

HANDLE hThrd = 0;  // thread handle
unsigned long Tid; // thread ID

// Progress counters.
int percentdone = 0;
int oldpercentdone = 0;

// A small struct for passing info to dlstart().
struct ThrdInfo {
  char *url;      // pointer to URL string
  int reload;     // reload flag
  HWND hPBStart;  // handle of Start button
};
```

```cpp
int WINAPI WinMain(HINSTANCE hThisInst, HINSTANCE hPrevInst,
                   LPSTR lpszArgs, int nWinMode)
{
  MSG msg;
  WNDCLASSEX wcl;
  INITCOMMONCONTROLSEX cc;

  // Define a window class.
  wcl.cbSize = sizeof(WNDCLASSEX);

  wcl.hInstance = hThisInst;      // handle to this instance
  wcl.lpszClassName = szWinName; // window class name
  wcl.lpfnWndProc = WindowFunc;  // window function
  wcl.style = 0;                 // default style

  wcl.hIcon = LoadIcon(NULL, IDI_APPLICATION); // large icon
  wcl.hIconSm = NULL; // use small version of large icon
  wcl.hCursor = LoadCursor(NULL, IDC_ARROW);  // cursor style

  wcl.lpszMenuName = NULL; // no menu

  wcl.cbClsExtra = 0; // no extras
  wcl.cbWndExtra = 0;

  wcl.hbrBackground = NULL; // not used

  // Register the window class.
  if(!RegisterClassEx(&wcl)) return 0;

  // Create a main window that won't be visible.
  hwnd = CreateWindow(
    szWinName,  // name of window class
    "File Downloader", // title
    0,          // no style needed
    0, 0, 0, 0, // no dimensions
    NULL,       // no parent window
    NULL,       // no menu
    hThisInst,  // instance handle
    NULL        // no additional arguments
  );

  hInst = hThisInst; // save the current instance handle

  // Initialize the common controls. This is
  // needed because of the progress bar.
```

```
    cc.dwSize = sizeof(INITCOMMONCONTROLSEX);
    cc.dwICC = ICC_PROGRESS_CLASS;
    InitCommonControlsEx(&cc);

    // Show the window minimized.
    ShowWindow(hwnd, SW_SHOWMINIMIZED);

    // Create the download dialog box.
    DialogBox(hInst, "DLDB", hwnd, (DLGPROC) DialogFunc);

    // Create the message loop.
    while(GetMessage(&msg, NULL, 0, 0))
    {
      TranslateMessage(&msg); // translate keyboard messages
      DispatchMessage(&msg); // return control to Windows
    }

    return msg.wParam;
}


// Window function.
LRESULT CALLBACK WindowFunc(HWND hwnd, UINT message,
                            WPARAM wParam, LPARAM lParam)
{
  switch(message) {
    case WM_DESTROY:
      PostQuitMessage(0); // terminate the program
      break;
    default:
      return DefWindowProc(hwnd, message, wParam, lParam);
  }
  return 0;
}


// Downloader Dialog function.
BOOL CALLBACK DialogFunc(HWND hdwnd, UINT message,
                         WPARAM wParam, LPARAM lParam)
{
  // Here, url is initialized with a sample url for
  // demonstration purposes only.
  static char url[URL_BUF_SIZE] =
    "http://www.osborne.com/products/0072226803/0072226803_code.zip";

  static ThrdInfo ti;
```

```
switch(message) {
  case WM_INITDIALOG:
    // Initialize edit box with URL.
    SetDlgItemText(hdwnd, IDD_EB1, url);

    // Create progress bar.
    hProgWnd = CreateWindow(PROGRESS_CLASS,
                 "",
                 WS_CHILD | WS_VISIBLE | WS_BORDER,
                 4, 64, 320, 12,
                 hdwnd, NULL, hInst, NULL);

    // Set step increment to 1.
    SendMessage(hProgWnd, PBM_SETSTEP, 1, 0);

    return 1;
  case WM_COMMAND:
    switch(LOWORD(wParam)) {
      case IDCANCEL:
        EndDialog(hdwnd, 0);
        PostQuitMessage(0);

        return 1;

      case IDD_START: // start download
        // Set position to zero.
        SendMessage(hProgWnd, PBM_SETPOS, 0, 0);

        // Get URL from edit box.
        GetDlgItemText(hdwnd, IDD_EB1, url, URL_BUF_SIZE);
        ti.url = url;

        // Get reload status.
        ti.reload = SendDlgItemMessage(hdwnd, IDD_CB1,
                  BM_GETCHECK, 0, 0);

        // Get handle to Start button.
        ti.hPBStart = GetDlgItem(hdwnd, IDD_START);

        // Reset progress counters.
        resetprogress();

        // Start download thread.
        if(!hThrd)
          hThrd = (HANDLE) _beginthreadex(NULL, 0, dlstart,
```

```
                    (void *) &ti, 0, (unsigned *) &Tid);

          return 1;
      }
  }

  return 0;
}

// Show progress in the progress bar.  This is called
// by the download() function.
void showprogress(unsigned long total,
                  unsigned long part) {

  percentdone = (part*100)/total;

  if(percentdone > oldpercentdone) {
    for(int i= oldpercentdone; i < percentdone; i++) {
      // Advance the progress bar.
      SendMessage(hProgWnd, PBM_STEPIT, 0, 0);
    }
    oldpercentdone = percentdone;
  }
}

// Reset the progress counters.
void resetprogress() {
  percentdone = 0;
  oldpercentdone = 0;
}

// Thread entry function that begins downloading.
unsigned __stdcall dlstart(void * param) {
  ThrdInfo *tip = (ThrdInfo *) param;

  // Disable Start button.
  EnableWindow(tip->hPBStart, 0);

  try {
    if(tip->reload == BST_CHECKED)
      Download::download(tip->url, true, showprogress);
    else
      Download::download(tip->url, false, showprogress);
  } catch(DLExc exc) {
      MessageBox(hwnd, exc.geterr(),
```

```
                       "Download Error", MB_OK);
  }

  // Enable Start button.
  EnableWindow(tip->hPBStart, 1);

  CloseHandle(hThrd); // close the thread handle
  hThrd = 0; // set thread handle to inactive

  return 0;
}
```

WinDL uses this resource file:

```
// Resources for file downloader.
#include <windows.h>
#include "windl.h"

DLDB DIALOGEX 18, 18, 164, 100
CAPTION "Download a File"
STYLE DS_MODALFRAME | WS_POPUP | WS_CAPTION |
      WS_SYSMENU | WS_VISIBLE
{
  PUSHBUTTON "Start", IDD_START, 42, 80, 30, 14
  PUSHBUTTON "Cancel", IDCANCEL, 90, 80, 30, 14

  CTEXT "Download Progress", IDD_TEXT2, 2, 40, 160, 12

CTEXT "Enter URL", IDD_TEXT1, 2, 16, 160, 12
  EDITTEXT IDD_EB1, 2, 1, 160, 12, ES_LEFT | WS_CHILD |
          WS_VISIBLE | WS_BORDER | ES_AUTOHSCROLL

  AUTOCHECKBOX "Reload", IDD_CB1, 62, 56, 36, 14
}
```

Both the resource file and program code require the header file **windl.h**, shown here:

```
#define IDD_START       100

#define IDD_CB1         200

#define IDD_EB1         300

#define IDD_TEXT1       401
#define IDD_TEXT2       402
```

To compile WinDL, you must create a project that contains these files:

dl.cpp   windl.cpp   windl.rc

The header files **dl.h** and **windl.h** must also be available. You must also remember to link in **wininet.lib** and **comctl32.lib**. (The **comctl32.lib** library is required by the progress control.) Finally, because **download( )** runs in its own thread, you must link in the multithreaded libraries.

How WinDL Works

WinDL provides a visual front end to the **Download** class that handles user input and displays the progress of the download. WinDL begins by creating a minimized main window and then displays the download dialog box. Thus, WinDL is a dialog box–based application that never displays a main window. As mentioned, it is beyond the scope of this book to describe the parts of WinDL that support the basic Windows framework common to all Windows programs. However, those portions of the code relating specifically to the downloader are described next.

The function that handles user interaction with the dialog box is **DialogFunc( )**. It declares two **static** variables. The first is an array called **url** that provides the backing array for the edit box. The second is **ti**, which is a small structure that contains information that will be passed to the thread entry function.

When the dialog box is created, it initializes the edit box and the progress bar. As the comments suggest, the edit box is initialized with a URL simply for the sake of demonstration. (Normally, this edit box will not contain an initial string.) The progress bar increment is set to 1. By default, progress bars have a range of 0 to 100, so by setting the increment to 1, each increment of the bar equals 1 percent.

To download a file, enter the URL of the desired file into the edit box and then click the Start button. This initiates the following sequence of events. First, the progress bar is reset to zero. Next, a string containing the URL is obtained from the edit box, the reload status is obtained from the check box, and a handle to the Start pushbutton is obtained. These are stored in **ti**, which will be passed to the thread entry function. Next, the progress counters are reset to zero. These are the global variables **percentdone** and **oldpercentdone**. They are used to update the position of the progress bar during the download. Finally, a new thread that will handle the download is started.

It is necessary to run **download( )** in a thread of its own because the Windows messaging system assumes that control will pass back to Windows relatively quickly. (That is, **DialogFunc( )** can't undertake some extended operation that prevents new messages from being processed.) The entry function for the thread is **dlstart( )**. As explained in Chapter 3, in Windows all thread entry functions take precisely one **void *** parameter. This parameter can be passed anything needed by the function. In this case, it is passed a pointer to the **ti** structure, which contains three fields: **url**, **reload**, and **hPBStart**. The URL to download is pointed to by the **url** field. The status of the Reload check box is in the **reload** field. It determines if the file will be reloaded in its entirety. The Start button handle is in the **hPBStart** field. It is used by

dlstart( ) to disable the Start button when a download begins and to enable it when the download ends.

The **dlstart( )** function calls **download( )** to handle the downloading of the file. When it does so, it passes the address of **showprogress** to the **update** parameter. When **download( )** ends, the Start button is enabled and the thread handle is closed.

The **showprogress( )** function is called by **download( )** to display the progress of the download. It simply increments the progress bar each time another percent of the file is downloaded.

Some Things to Try

Several enhancements can be added to **Download**. One of the first things you might want to try is adding the ability to download files given an FTP address. Because **InternetOpenUrl( )** supports FTP, this is a relatively simple matter. Although HTTP version 1.0 is becoming increasingly rare, you might also want to try adding support for it. This is easy to do because it just means that the file will always be downloaded in its entirety. Another useful enhancement to **Download** is to enable it to retrieve a list of files. One way to do this is to have it read the URLs from a disk file. Finally, you might want to add an automatic retry feature that attempts to finish a download that was interrupted.

The general file download mechanism has applications beyond being the basis of a file downloader. The **Download** class can be used whenever a file must be retrieved. For example, you could use **Download** to create a remote data acquisition program that downloads a data file, such as an inventory report, from a remote site on a regular basis.

Financial Calculations in C++

Despite all of the large, sophisticated applications, such as compilers, Internet browsers, word processors, databases, and accounting packages that dominate much of the computing landscape, there has remained a class of programs that are both popular and small. These perform various financial calculations, such as computing the regular payments on a loan, the future value of an investment, or the remaining balance on a loan. None of these calculations are very complicated or require much code, yet they yield information that is quite useful.

Because C++ excels in the creation of high-powered system software, it is often overlooked for financial applications, but this is a mistake. C++ has excellent capabilities in this area, supporting a complete range of math functions and efficient floating-point arithmetic. Furthermore, because of its ability to produce extremely fast executable code, C++ is a perfect fit for programs performing sophisticated financial analysis and modeling.

To illustrate the ease with which C++ handles financial calculations, this chapter develops a number of small programs that perform the financial computations shown here:

1. Regular payments on a loan

2. Future value of an investment

3. Initial investment needed to attain a desired future value

4. Investment necessary for a desired annuity

5. The maximum annuity from an investment

6. Remaining balance on a loan

These programs can be used as-is, or tweaked to fit your specific need. Frankly, even though these are the simplest programs in this book, they are also the ones that you may find yourself using the most!

Finding the Payments for a Loan

Perhaps the most popular financial calculation is the one that computes the regular payments on a loan, such as a car or house loan. The payments on a loan are found by using the following formula:

$$\text{Payment} = \frac{(\text{intRate} * (\text{principal} / \text{payPerYear}))}{(1 - ((\text{intRate} / \text{payPerYear}) + 1)^{-\text{payPerYear} * \text{numYears}})}$$

where *intRate* specifies the interest rate, *principal* contains the starting balance, *payPerYear* specifies the number of payments per year, and *numYears* specifies the length of the loan in years.

In the following program, the function called **regpay( )** uses the preceding formula to compute the payments on a loan. It is passed the principal, the interest rate, the term of the loan in years, and the number of payments per year. It returns the payment.

```
#include <iostream>
#include <cmath>
```

```cpp
#include <iomanip>
#include <locale>

using namespace std;

// Compute the regular payments on a loan.
double regpay(double principal, double intRate,
              int numYears, int payPerYear) {
  double numer;
  double denom;
  double b, e;

  intRate /= 100.0; // convert percentage to fraction

  numer = intRate * principal / payPerYear;

  e = -(payPerYear * numYears);
  b = (intRate / payPerYear) + 1.0;

  denom = 1.0 - pow(b, e);

  return numer / denom;
}

int main() {
  double p, r;
  int y, ppy;

  // Set locale to English.  Adjust as necessary
  // for your language and/or region.
  cout.imbue(locale("english"));

  cout << "Enter principal: ";
  cin >> p;

  cout << "Enter interest rate (as a percentage): ";
  cin >> r;

  cout << "Enter number years: ";
  cin >> y;

  cout << "Enter number of payments per year: ";
  cin >> ppy;

  cout << "\nPayment: " << fixed << setprecision(2)
```

```
          << regpay(p, r, y, ppy) << endl;

  return 0;
}
```

To compute a loan payment, simply enter the information requested by the prompts. Here is a sample run:

```
Enter principal: 1000
Enter interest rate (as a percentage): 9
Enter number years: 5
Enter number of payments per year: 12


Payment: 20.76
```

There are a couple of points of interest to notice in **main( )**. First, the locale associated with **cout** is set to English. This is accomplished by calling the **imbue( )** member function and passing the **locale** object for English. This ensures that monetary values are displayed using the conventions defined by English, which is the comma as the thousands separator and the period as a decimal point. Second, before the loan payment is displayed, the number format is changed to fixed with a precision of 2. This causes the output to have two decimal places, with appropriate rounding. The decimal places are also padded with zeros as necessary. All of the financial programs use this same approach. To change the format to reflect a different language or region, simply change the language/region of the **locale** object passed to **imbue( )**.

Finding the Future Value of an Investment

Another popular financial calculation finds the future value of an investment given the initial investment, the rate of return, the number of compounding periods per year, and the number of years the investment is held. For example, you might want to know what your retirement account will be worth in 12 years if it currently contains $98,000 and has an average annual rate of return of 6 percent. The program shown here will supply the answer.

To compute the future value, use the following formula:

$$\text{Future Value} = \text{principal} * ((\text{rateOfRet} / \text{compPerYear}) + 1)^{\text{compPerYear} * \text{numYears}}$$

where *rateOfRet* specifies the rate of return, *principal* contains the initial value of the investment, *compPerYear* specifies the number of compounding periods per year, and *numYears* specifies the length of the investment in years. If you use an annualized rate of return for *rateOfRet*, then the number of compounding periods is 1.

In the following program, the **futval( )** function uses the preceding formula to compute the future value of an investment. It is passed the principal, the rate of return, the term of the investment in years, and the number of compoundings per year. It returns the future value.

```
#include <iostream>
#include <cmath>
```

```cpp
#include <iomanip>
#include <locale>

using namespace std;

// Compute the future value of an investment.
double futval(double principal, double rateOfRet,
              int numYears, int compPerYear) {
  double b, e;

  rateOfRet /= 100.0; // convert percentage to fraction

  b = (1 + rateOfRet/compPerYear);
  e = compPerYear * numYears;

  return principal * pow(b, e);
}

int main() {
  double p, r;
  int y, cpy;

  // Set locale to English.  Adjust as necessary
  // for your language and/or region.
  cout.imbue(locale("english"));

  cout << "Enter principal: ";
  cin >> p;

  cout << "Enter rate of return (as a percentage): ";
  cin >> r;

  cout << "Enter number years: ";
  cin >> y;

  cout << "Enter number of compoundings per year: ";
  cin >> cpy;

  cout << "\nFuture value: " << fixed << setprecision(2)
       << futval(p, r, y, cpy) << endl;

  return 0;
}
```

Here is a sample run:

```
Enter principal: 10000
Enter rate of return (as a percentage): 6
Enter number years: 5
Enter number of compoundings per year: 12

Future value: 13,488.50
```

Finding the Initial Investment Required to Achieve a Future Value

Sometimes you will want to know how large of an initial investment is required to achieve some future value. For example, if you are saving for your child's college education and you know that you will need $75,000 in five years, how much money do you need to invest at 7 percent to reach that goal? The program developed here can answer that question.

The formula to compute an initial investment is shown here:

$$\text{Initial Investment} = \text{targetValue} / (((\text{rateOfRet} / \text{compPerYear}) + 1)^{\text{compPerYear} * \text{numYears}})$$

where *rateOfRet* specifies the rate of return, *targetValue* contains the desired future value, *compPerYear* specifies the number of compounding periods per year, and *numYears* specifies the length of the investment in years. If you use an annualized rate of return for *rateOfRet*, then the number of compounding periods is 1.

In the following program, the **initval( )** function uses the preceding formula to compute the initial investment required to reach a desired future value. It is passed the target value, the rate of return, the term of the investment in years, and the number of compoundings per year. It returns the initial investment required to reach the target value.

```
#include <iostream>
#include <cmath>
#include <iomanip>
#include <locale>

using namespace std;

// Compute the initial investment necessary for
// a specified future value.
double initval(double targetValue, double rateOfRet,
               int numYears, int compPerYear) {
  double b, e;
```

```cpp
  rateOfRet /= 100.0; // convert percentage to fraction

  b = (1 + rateOfRet/compPerYear);
  e = compPerYear * numYears;

  return targetValue / pow(b, e);
}

int main() {
  double p, r;
  int y, cpy;

  // Set locale to English.  Adjust as necessary
  // for your language and/or region.
  cout.imbue(locale("english"));

  cout << "Enter desired future value: ";
  cin >> p;

  cout << "Enter rate of return: ";
  cin >> r;

  cout << "Enter number years: ";
  cin >> y;

  cout << "Enter number of compoundings per year: ";
  cin >> cpy;

  cout << "\nInitial investment required: "
       << fixed << setprecision(2)
       << initval(p, r, y, cpy) << endl;

  return 0;
}
```

Here is a sample run:

```
Enter desired future value: 75000
Enter rate of return (as a percentage): 7
Enter number years: 5
Enter number of compoundings per year: 4

Initial investment required: 53,011.84
```

Finding the Initial Investment Needed for a Desired Annuity

Another common financial calculation computes the amount of money that one must invest so that a desired annuity, in terms of a regular withdrawal, can be paid. For example, you might decide that you need $5,000 per month at retirement, and that you will need that amount for 20 years. The question is how much will you need to invest to secure that annuity? The answer can be found using the following formula:

$$\text{Initial Investment} = ((\text{regWD} * \text{wdPerYear}) / \text{rateOfRet}) * (1 - (1 / (\text{rateOfRet} / \text{wdPerYear} + 1)^{\text{wdPerYear} * \text{numYears}}))$$

where *rateOfRet* specifies the rate of return, *regWD* contains the desired regular withdrawal, *wdPerYear* specifies the number of withdrawals per year, and *numYears* specifies the length of the annuity in years.

In the next program, the **annuity( )** function computes the initial investment required to produce the desired annuity. It is passed the desired withdrawal, the rate of return, the term of the annuity in years, and the number of compoundings per year. It returns the minimum investment needed to produce the annuity.

```cpp
#include <iostream>
#include <cmath>
#include <iomanip>
#include <locale>

using namespace std;

// Compute the initial investment necessary for
// a desired annuity. In other words, it finds
// the initial amount needed to allow the regular
// withdrawals of a desired amount over a period
// of time.
double annuity(double regWD, double rateOfRet,
               int numYears, int numPerYear) {

  double b, e;
  double t1, t2;

  rateOfRet /= 100.0; // convert percentage to fraction

  t1 = (regWD * numPerYear) / rateOfRet;

  b = (1 + rateOfRet/numPerYear);
```

```
    e = numPerYear * numYears;

    t2 = 1 - (1 / pow(b, e));

    return t1 * t2;
}

int main() {
    double wd, r;
    int y, wpy;

    // Set locale to English.  Adjust as necessary
    // for your language and/or region.
    cout.imbue(locale("english"));

    cout << "Enter desired withdrawal: ";
    cin >> wd;

    cout << "Enter rate of return (as a percentage): ";
    cin >> r;

    cout << "Enter number years: ";
    cin >> y;

    cout << "Enter number of withdrawals per year: ";
    cin >> wpy;

    cout << "\nInitial investment required: "
         << fixed << setprecision(2)
         << annuity(wd, r, y, wpy) << endl;

    return 0;
}
```

Here is a sample run.

```
Enter desired withdrawal: 5000
Enter rate of return (as a percentage): 6
Enter number years: 20
Enter number of withdrawals per year: 12

Initial investment required: 697,903.86
```

Finding the Maximum Annuity for a Given Investment

Another annuity calculation computes the maximum annuity (in terms of a regular withdrawal) available from a given investment over a specified period of time. For example, if you have $500,000 in a retirement account, how much can you take out each month for 20 years, assuming a 6 percent rate of return? The formula that computes the maximum withdrawal is shown here:

$$\text{Maximum Withdrawal} = \text{principal} * (((\text{rateOfRet} / \text{wdPerYear}) / (-1 + ((\text{rateOfRet} / \text{wdPerYear}) + 1)^{\text{wdPerYear} * \text{numYears}})) + (\text{rateOfRet} / \text{wdPerYear}))$$

where *rateOfRet* specifies the rate of return, *principal* contains the value of the initial investment, *wdPerYear* specifies the number of withdrawals per year, and *numYears* specifies the length of the annuity in years.

The **maxwd( )** function, shown in the following program, computes the maximum periodic withdrawals that can be made over a specified length of time for an assumed rate of return. It is passed the principal, the rate of return, the term of the annuity in years, and the number of compoundings per year. It returns the maximum annuity.

```cpp
#include <iostream>
#include <cmath>
#include <iomanip>
#include <locale>

using namespace std;

// Compute the maximum annuity that can
// be withdrawn from an investment over
// a period of time.
double maxwd(double principal, double rateOfRet,
             int numYears, int numPerYear) {

  double b, e;
  double t1, t2;

  rateOfRet /= 100.0; // convert percentage to fraction

  t1 = rateOfRet / numPerYear;

  b = (1 + t1);
  e = numPerYear * numYears;

  t2 = pow(b, e) - 1;
```

```
    return principal * (t1/t2 + t1);
}

int main() {
  double p, r;
  int y, wpy;

  // Set locale to English.  Adjust as necessary
  // for your language and/or region.
  cout.imbue(locale("english"));

  cout << "Enter principal: ";
  cin >> p;

  cout << "Enter rate of return (as a percentage): ";
  cin >> r;

  cout << "Enter number years: ";
  cin >> y;

  cout << "Enter number of withdrawals per year: ";
  cin >> wpy;

  cout << "\nMaximum withdrawal: " << fixed << setprecision(2)
       << maxwd(p, r, y, wpy) << endl;

  return 0;
}
```

Here is a sample run:

```
Enter principal: 500000
Enter rate of return (as a percentage): 6
Enter number years: 20
Enter number of withdrawals per year: 12

Maximum withdrawal: 3,582.16
```

Finding the Remaining Balance on a Loan

Often you will want to know the remaining balance on a loan. This is easily calculated if you know the original principal, the interest rate, the loan length, and the number of payments made. To find the remaining balance, you must sum the payments, subtracting from each payment the amount allocated to interest, and then subtract that result from the principal.

The **balance( )** function shown here, finds the remaining balance of a loan. It is passed the principal, the interest rate, the payment, the number of payments per year, and the number of payments that have been made. It returns the remaining balance.

```cpp
#include <iostream>
#include <cmath>
#include <iomanip>
#include <locale>

using namespace std;

// Find the remaining balance on a loan.
double balance(double principal, double intRate,
               double payment, int payPerYear,
               int numPayments) {

  double bal = principal;
  double rate = intRate / payPerYear;

  rate /= 100.0; // convert percentage to fraction

  for(int i = 0; i < numPayments; i++)
    bal -= payment - (bal * rate);

  return bal;
}

int main() {
  double p, r, pmt;
  int ppy, npmt;

  // Set locale to English.  Adjust as necessary
  // for your language and/or region.
  cout.imbue(locale("english"));

  cout << "Enter original principal: ";
  cin >> p;

  cout << "Enter interest rate (as a percentage): ";
  cin >> r;

  cout << "Enter payment: ";
  cin >> pmt;

  cout << "Enter number of payments per year: ";
```

```
  cin >> ppy;

  cout << "Enter number of payments made: ";
  cin >> npmt;

  cout << "Remaining balance: " << fixed << setprecision(2)
       << balance(p, r, pmt, ppy, npmt) << endl;

  return 0;
}
```

A sample run is shown here:

```
Enter original principal: 10000
Enter interest rate (as a percentage): 9
Enter payment: 207.58
Enter number of payments per year: 12
Enter number of payments made: 30

Remaining balance: 5,558.19
```

Some Things to Try

There are many other financial calculations that you might find useful. For example, the rate of return of an investment or the amount of a regular deposit over time to reach a future value would be useful additions. You could also print a loan amortization chart.

You might want to try creating a larger application that offers all of the calculations presented in this chapter, allowing the user to select the desired calculation from a menu.

AI-Based Problem Solving

T his chapter examines a topic from an interesting discipline of programming: artificial intelligence (AI). One of the goals of this book is to show the range and versatility of C++. Perhaps nothing demonstrates this better than its application to the demanding realm of artificial intelligence.

The field of artificial intelligence is comprised of several fascinating areas, but fundamental to many AI-based applications is problem solving. Essentially, there are two types of problems. The first type can be solved through the use of some sort of deterministic procedure that is guaranteed success, such as the computation of the sine of an angle or the square root of a value. These types of problems are easily translated into algorithms that a computer can execute. In the real world, however, few problems lend themselves to such straightforward solutions. Instead, many problems can be solved only by *searching for a solution*. It is this type of problem solving with which AI is concerned. It is also the type of searching that is explored in this chapter.

To understand why searching is so important to AI, consider the following. One of the early goals of AI research was the creation of a *general problem solver*. A general problem solver is a program that can produce solutions to all sorts of different problems about which it has no specific, designed-in knowledge. It is an understatement to say that such a program would be highly desirable. Unfortunately, a general problem solver is as difficult to realize as it is tantalizing. One trouble is the sheer size and complexity of many real-world situations. Because a general problem solver must search for a solution through what might be a very large, maze-like universe of possibilities, finding ways to search such an environment was a priority. Although we won't attempt something as ambitious as a general problem solver in this chapter, we will explore several AI-based search techniques that are applicable to a wide variety of problems.

C++ is a language well suited to the AI developer. The reason is because C++ offers significant support for the program elements that AI-based applications typically use: recursion, lists, and stacks. As you know, C++ handles recursion with both ease and efficiency. Add to that the power of the various STL containers, and you have a programming environment that streamlines AI development.

Representation and Terminology

Imagine that you have lost your car keys. You know that they are somewhere in your house, which looks like this:

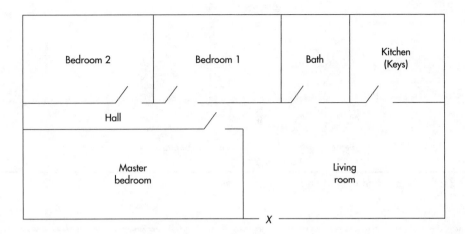

You are standing at the front door (where the *X* is). As you begin your search, you check the living room. Then you go down the hall to the first bedroom, through the hall to the second bedroom, back to the hall, and to the master bedroom. Not having found your keys, you backtrack further by going back through the living room. Finally, you find your keys in the kitchen. This situation is easily represented by a graph, as shown in Figure 7-1. Representing search problems in a graphical form is helpful because it provides a convenient way to depict the way a solution was found.

With the preceding discussion in mind, consider the following terms, which will be used throughout this chapter:

Node	A discrete point
Terminal node	A node that ends a path
Search space	The set of all nodes
Goal	The node that is the object of the search
Heuristics	Information about whether any specific node is a better next choice than another
Solution path	A directed graph of the nodes visited en route to the goal

In the example of the lost keys, each room in the house is a node; the entire house is the search space; the goal, as it turns out, is the kitchen; and the solution path is shown in Figure 7-1. The bedrooms, kitchen, and the bath are terminal nodes because they lead nowhere. Heuristics are not represented on a graph. Rather, they are techniques that you might employ to help you better choose a path.

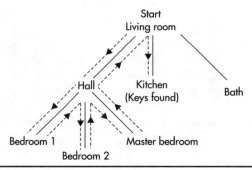

Figure 7-1   *The solution path to find the missing keys*

Combinatorial Explosions

Given the preceding example, you may think that searching for a solution is easy—you start at the beginning and work your way to the conclusion. In the extremely simple case of the lost keys, this is not a bad approach because the search space is so small. But for many problems (especially those for which you would want to use a computer), the number of nodes in the search space is very large, and as the search space grows, so does the number of possible paths to the goal. The trouble is that often adding another node to the search space adds more than one path. That is, the number of potential pathways to the goal can increase in a nonlinear fashion as the size of the search space grows. In a nonlinear situation, the number of possible paths can quickly become very large.

For instance, consider the number of ways three objects—A, B, and C—can be arranged on a table. The six possible permutations are

A	B	C
A	C	B
B	C	A
B	A	C
C	B	A
C	A	B

You can quickly prove to yourself that these six are the only ways that A, B, and C can be arranged. However, you can derive the same number by using a theorem from the branch of mathematics called *combinatorics*—the study of the way that things can be combined. According to the theorem, the number of ways that N objects can be arranged is equal to *N*! (*N* factorial). The factorial of a number is the product of all whole numbers equal to or less than itself down to 1. Therefore, 3! is $3 \times 2 \times 1$, or 6. If you had four objects to arrange, there would be 4!, or 24, permutations. With five objects, the number is 120, and with six it is 720. With 1000 objects the number of possible permutations is huge! The graph in Figure 7-2 gives you a visual feel for what is sometimes referred to as a *combinatoric explosion*. Once there are

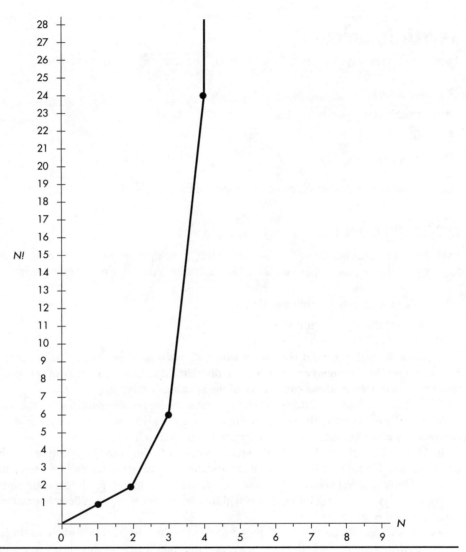

Figure 7-2   *A combinatoric explosion with factorials*

more than a handful of possibilities, it very quickly becomes difficult to examine (indeed, even to enumerate) all the arrangements.

This same sort of combinatorial explosion can occur in paths through search spaces. Because of this, only the simplest of problems lend themselves to *exhaustive searches*. An exhaustive search is one that examines all nodes. Thus, it is a "brute-force" technique. Brute force always works, but it is not often practical for large problems because it consumes too much time, too many computing resources, or both. For this reason, AI-based search techniques were developed.

Search Techniques

There are several ways to search for a solution. The four most fundamental are

- ► Depth first
- ► Breadth first
- ► Hill climbing
- ► Least cost

In the course of this chapter, each of these searches is examined.

Evaluating a Search

Evaluating the performance of an AI-based search technique can be complicated. Fortunately, for the purposes of this chapter, we are concerned with only these two measurements:

- ► How quickly is a solution found?
- ► How good is the solution?

There are several types of problems for which all that matters is that a solution, any solution, be found with the minimum effort. For these problems, the first measurement is especially important. In other situations, the quality of the solution is more important.

The speed of a search is affected both by the size of the search space and by the number of nodes actually traversed in the process of finding the solution. Because backtracking from dead ends is wasted effort, you want a search that seldom retraces its steps.

In AI-based searching, there is a difference between finding the best solution and finding a good solution. Finding the best solution can require an exhaustive search because sometimes this is the only way to know that the best solution has been found. Finding a good solution, in contrast, means finding a solution that is within a set of constraints—it does not matter if a better solution might exist.

As you will see, the search techniques described in this chapter all work better in certain situations than in others. It is difficult to say whether one search method is *always* superior to another, but some search techniques have a greater probability of being better for the average case. In addition, the way a problem is defined can sometimes help you choose an appropriate search method.

The Problem

Now, let us consider the problem that we will use various searches to solve. Imagine that you are a travel agent, and a rather quarrelsome customer wants you to book a flight from New York to Los Angeles with XYZ Airlines. You try to tell the customer that XYZ does not have a direct flight from New York to Los Angeles, but the customer insists that XYZ is the only airline that he will fly. Thus, you must find connecting flights between New York and Los Angeles. You consult XYZ's scheduled flights, shown here:

Flight	Distance
New York to Chicago	900 miles
Chicago to Denver	1000 miles
New York to Toronto	500 miles
New York to Denver	1800 miles
Toronto to Calgary	1700 miles
Toronto to Los Angeles	2500 miles
Toronto to Chicago	500 miles
Denver to Urbana	1000 miles
Denver to Houston	1000 miles
Houston to Los Angeles	1500 miles
Denver to Los Angeles	1000 miles

You quickly see that there are connections that enable your customer to fly from New York to Los Angeles. The problem is to write C++ programs that do the same thing that you just did in your head!

A Graphic Representation

The flight information in XYZ's schedule can be translated into the directed graph shown in Figure 7-3. A *directed graph* is simply a graph in which the lines connecting each node include an arrow to indicate the direction of motion. In a directed graph, you cannot travel against the direction of the arrow.

To make things easier to understand, this graph is redrawn in a tree-like fashion in Figure 7-4. Refer to this version for the rest of this chapter. The goal, Los Angeles, is circled. Also notice that various cities appear more than once to simplify the construction of the graph. Thus, the tree-like representation *does not* depict a binary tree. It is simply a visual convenience.

Now we are ready to develop the various search techniques that will find routes from New York to Los Angeles.

The FlightInfo Structure and the Search Class

Writing a program to find a route from New York to Los Angeles requires a database that contains the flight information. Each entry in the database must contain the departure and

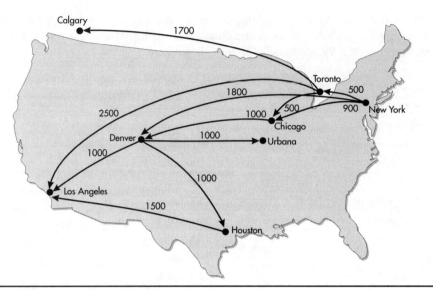

Figure 7-3 *A directed graph of XYZ's flight schedule*

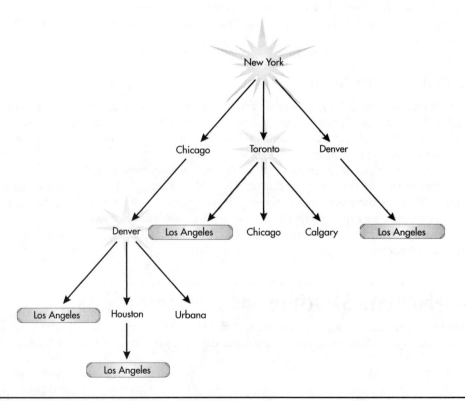

Figure 7-4 *A tree version of XYZ's flight schedule*

destination cities, the distance between them, and a flag that aids in backtracking. This information is held in a structure called **FlightInfo**, shown here:

```
// Flight information.
struct FlightInfo {
  string from;   // departure city
  string to;     // destination city
  int distance; // distance between from and to
  bool skip;     // used in backtracking

  FlightInfo() {
    from = "";
    to = "";
    distance = 0;
    skip = false;
  }

  FlightInfo(string f, string t, int d) {
    from = f;
    to = t;
    distance = d;
    skip = false;
  }
};
```

This structure will be used by all of the search techniques described in the remainder of the chapter.

The AI-based searches are encapsulated within a class called **Search**. The precise implementation of this class will change from one search technique to the next. However, all will share the same general framework, shown here:

```
// An AI-based search class.
class Search {
  // This vector holds the flight information.
  vector<FlightInfo> flights;

  // This stack is used for backtracking.
  stack<FlightInfo> btStack;

  // If there is a flight between from and to,
  // store the distance of the flight in dist.
  // Return true if the flight exists and,
  // false otherwise.
  bool match(string from, string to, int &dist);

  // Given from, find any connection.
```

```
    // Return true if a connection is found,
    // and false otherwise.
    bool find(string from, FlightInfo &f);

public:

    // Put flights into the database.
    void addflight(string from, string to, int dist) {
      flights.push_back(FlightInfo(from, to, dist));
    }

    // Show the route and total distance.
    void route();

    // Determine if there is a route between from and to.
    void findroute(string from, string to);

    // Return true if a route has been found.
    bool routefound() {
      return !btStack.empty();
    }
};
```

Search declares two private instance variables. The first is a **vector** of **FlightInfo** objects, called **flights**, that holds the flight data. (Recall that a **vector** is an STL container that implements a dynamic array.) The second is a stack, called **btStack**, that is used for backtracking. As you will see, the backtrack stack is very important to all of the search techniques.

Search contains two in-line functions: **addflight( )** and **routefound( )**. When a **Search** object is first created, its **flights** vector is empty. Connections are added by repeatedly calling **addflight( )**, specifying the departure city, the destination city, and the distance between the two. The **addflight( )** function simply pushes each connection onto the end of the **flights** vector, which automatically expands in size to accommodate each new entry.

The **routefound( )** function determines if a route exists between the departure and destination cities based on the contents of the backtrack stack. If the backtrack stack is empty, no route exists between the two cities. Otherwise, the backtrack stack contains the route. (The process of constructing the route varies from one search technique to the next.)

The implementation of the remaining members of **Search** are described in the sections that follow. The following table briefly explains their purpose:

match( )	Determines if there is a direct connection between two cities
find( )	Attempts to find a connection from a specified city to anywhere else
findroute( )	Attempts to construct a route from the city of departure to the city of destination
route( )	Displays the route

The Depth-First Search

The *depth-first search* explores each possible path to its conclusion before another path is tried. To understand exactly how this works, consider the tree that follows. F is the goal.

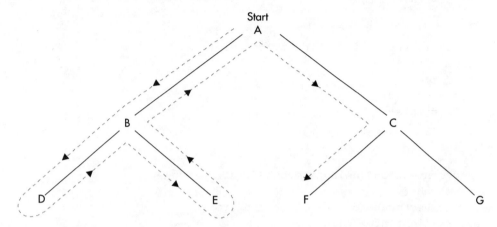

A depth-first search traverses the graph in the following order: ABDBEBACF. If you are familiar with trees, you recognize this type of search as an *inorder* tree traversal. That is, the path goes left until a terminal node is reached or the goal is found. If a terminal node is reached, the path backs up one level, goes right, and then left until either the goal or a terminal node is encountered. This procedure is repeated until the goal is found or the last node in the search space has been examined.

As you can see, a depth-first search is certain to find the goal because in the worst case it degenerates into an exhaustive search. In this example, an exhaustive search would result if G were the goal.

The entire depth-first search program follows:

```
// Search for a route.
#include <iostream>
#include <stack>
#include <string>
#include <vector>

using namespace std;

// Flight information.
struct FlightInfo {
  string from;   // departure city
  string to;     // destination city
  int distance;  // distance between from and to
  bool skip;     // used in backtracking
```

```cpp
  FlightInfo() {
    from = "";
    to = "";
    distance = 0;
    skip = false;
  }

  FlightInfo(string f, string t, int d) {
    from = f;
    to = t;
    distance = d;
    skip = false;
  }
};

// Find connections using a depth-first search.
class Search {
  // This vector holds the flight information.
  vector<FlightInfo> flights;

  // This stack is used for backtracking.
  stack<FlightInfo> btStack;

  // If there is a flight between from and to,
  // store the distance of the flight in dist.
  // Return true if the flight exists and
  // false otherwise.
  bool match(string from, string to, int &dist);

  // Given from, find any connection.
  // Return true if a connection is found,
  // and false otherwise.
  bool find(string from, FlightInfo &f);

public:

  // Put flights into the database.
  void addflight(string from, string to, int dist) {
    flights.push_back(FlightInfo(from, to, dist));
  }

  // Show the route and total distance.
  void route();

  // Determine if there is a route between from and to.
```

```cpp
  void findroute(string from, string to);

  // Return true if a route has been found.
  bool routefound() {
    return !btStack.empty();
  }
};

// Show the route and total distance.
void Search::route()
{
  stack<FlightInfo> rev;
  int dist = 0;
  FlightInfo f;

  // Reverse the stack to display route.
  while(!btStack.empty()) {
    f = btStack.top();
    rev.push(f);
    btStack.pop();
  }

  // Display the route.
  while(!rev.empty()) {
    f = rev.top();
    rev.pop();
    cout << f.from << " to ";
    dist += f.distance;
  }

  cout << f.to << endl;
  cout << "Distance is " << dist << endl;
}

// If there is a flight between from and to,
// store the distance of the flight in dist.
// Return true if the flight exists and,
// false otherwise.
bool Search::match(string from, string to, int &dist)
{
  for(unsigned i=0; i < flights.size(); i++) {
    if(flights[i].from == from &&
       flights[i].to == to && !flights[i].skip)
    {
      flights[i].skip = true; // prevent reuse
```

```
      dist = flights[i].distance;
      return true;
    }
  }

  return false; // not found
}

// Given from, find any connection.
// Return true if a connection is found,
// and false otherwise.
bool Search::find(string from, FlightInfo &f)
{
  for(unsigned i=0; i < flights.size(); i++) {
    if(flights[i].from == from && !flights[i].skip) {
      f = flights[i];
      flights[i].skip = true; // prevent reuse

      return true;
    }
  }

  return false;
}

// Depth-first version.
// Determine if there is a route between from and to.
void Search::findroute(string from, string to)
{
  int dist;
  FlightInfo f;

  // See if at destination.
  if(match(from, to, dist)) {
    btStack.push(FlightInfo(from, to, dist));
    return;
  }

  // Try another connection.
  if(find(from, f)) {
    btStack.push(FlightInfo(from, to, f.distance));
    findroute(f.to, to);
  }
  else if(!btStack.empty()) {
    // Backtrack and try another connection.
```

```
      f = btStack.top();
      btStack.pop();
      findroute(f.from, f.to);
   }
}

int main() {
   char to[40], from[40];
   Search ob;

   // Add flight connections to database.
   ob.addflight("New York", "Chicago", 900);
   ob.addflight("Chicago", "Denver", 1000);
   ob.addflight("New York", "Toronto", 500);
   ob.addflight("New York", "Denver", 1800);
   ob.addflight("Toronto", "Calgary", 1700);
   ob.addflight("Toronto", "Los Angeles", 2500);
   ob.addflight("Toronto", "Chicago", 500);
   ob.addflight("Denver", "Urbana", 1000);
   ob.addflight("Denver", "Houston", 1000);
   ob.addflight("Houston", "Los Angeles", 1500);
   ob.addflight("Denver", "Los Angeles", 1000);

   // Get departure and destination cities.
   cout << "From? ";

   cin.getline(from, 40);
   cout << "To? ";

   cin.getline(to, 40);

   // See if there is a route between from and to.
   ob.findroute(from, to);

   // If there is a route, show it.
   if(ob.routefound())
      ob.route();

   return 0;
}
```

Notice that **main( )** prompts you for both the city of origin and the city of destination. This means that you can use the program to find routes between any two cities. However, the rest of this chapter assumes that New York is the origin and Los Angeles is the destination.

When the program is run with New York as the origin and Los Angeles as the destination, the following solution is displayed:

```
From? New York
To? Los Angeles
New York to Chicago to Denver to Los Angeles
Distance is 2900
```

If you refer to Figure 7-5, you see that this is indeed the first solution that would be found by a depth-first search. It is also a fairly good solution.

As **main( )** illustrates, to use **Search**, first create a **Search** object. Then load the flight database with the connections. Next, call **findroute( )** to attempt to find a route between the point of departure and the destination. To determine if such a route has been found, call **routefound( )**. It returns true if a route exists. To display the route, call **route( )**. Let's now examine each piece of the depth-first search in detail.

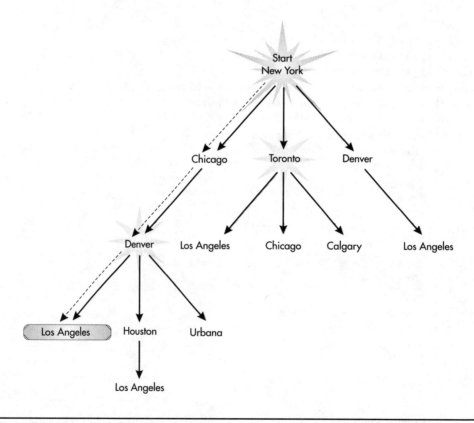

Figure 7-5   *The depth-first path to a solution*

The match( ) Function

The **match( )** function, shown here, determines if there is a flight between two cities, specified by **from** and **to**:

```
// If there is a flight between from and to,
// store the distance of the flight in dist.
// Return true if the flight exists and
// false otherwise.
bool Search::match(string from, string to, int &dist)
{
  for(unsigned i=0; i < flights.size(); i++) {
    if(flights[i].from == from &&
       flights[i].to == to && !flights[i].skip)
    {
      flights[i].skip = true; // prevent reuse
      dist = flights[i].distance;
      return true;
    }
  }

  return false; // not found
}
```

The **match( )** function operates by searching the **flights** vector, looking for any entry in which the departure and destination cities match those passed through **from** and **to**. It returns false if no such flight exists. It returns true if there is a flight, in which case it also obtains the distance between the two cities and stores this value in the variable referenced by its **dist** parameter.

Notice that **match( )** ignores connections that have the **skip** field set to true. Also, if a connection is found, its **skip** field is set. This manages backtracking from dead ends, preventing the same connections from being tried over and over again.

The find( ) Function

The **find( )** function, shown here, searches the database for any connection from a given departure city:

```
// Given from, find any connection.
// Return true if a connection is found,
// and false otherwise.
bool Search::find(string from, FlightInfo &f)
{
  for(unsigned i=0; i < flights.size(); i++) {
    if(flights[i].from == from && !flights[i].skip) {
      f = flights[i];
      flights[i].skip = true; // prevent reuse
```

```
        return true;
      }
    }

    return false;
}
```

The departure city is passed to **from**. If a connecting flight is found, **find( )** returns true, and the **FlightInfo** object associated with that connection is stored in the variable referenced by the second parameter, **f**. Otherwise, **find( )** returns false. The difference between **match( )** and **find( )** is that **match( )** determines if there is a flight between two specific cities; **find( )** determines if there is a flight from a given city to *any other* city.

Like **match( )**, **find( )** also use the **skip** field to manage backtracking from dead ends.

The findroute( ) Function

The code that actually finds the connecting flights is contained in the **findroute( )** function, the key routine in finding a route between two cities. It is called with the names of the departure and destination cities.

```
// Determine if there is a route between from and to
// by using depth-first searching.
void Search::findroute(string from, string to)
{
  int dist;
  FlightInfo f;

  // See if at destination.
  if(match(from, to, dist)) {
    btStack.push(FlightInfo(from, to, dist));
    return;
  }

  // Try another connection.
  if(find(from, f)) {
    btStack.push(FlightInfo(from, to, f.distance));
    findroute(f.to, to);
  }
  else if(!btStack.empty()) {
    // Backtrack and try another connection.
    f = btStack.top();
    btStack.pop();
    findroute(f.from, f.to);
  }
}
```

Let's examine **findroute( )** closely. First, the flight database is checked by **match( )** to see if there is a flight between **from** and **to**. If there is, the goal has been reached, the connection is pushed onto the stack, and the function returns. Otherwise, **findroute( )** calls **find( )** to find a connection between **from** and *any place else*. The **find( )** function returns true if such a connection is found, in which case it stores the **FlightInfo** object describing the connection in **f**. If no connecting flight is available, **find( )** returns false. If there is a connecting flight, the current flight is pushed onto the backtrack stack, and **findroute( )** is called recursively, with the city in **f.to** becoming the new departure city. Otherwise, backtracking takes place. The previous node is removed from the stack and **findroute( )** is called recursively. This process continues until the goal is found, or the database is exhausted.

For example, if **findroute( )** is called with New York and Chicago, the first **if** would succeed and **findroute( )** would terminate because there is a direct flight from New York to Chicago. The situation is more complex when **findroute( )** is called with New York and Calgary. In this case, the first **if** would fail because there is no direct flight connecting these two cities. Next, the second **if** is tried by attempting to find a connection between New York and any other city. In this case, **find( )** first finds the New York to Chicago connection, this connection is pushed onto the backtrack stack, and **findroute( )** is called recursively with Chicago as the starting point. Unfortunately, there is no path from Chicago to Calgary and several false paths are followed. Eventually, after several recursive calls to **findroute( )** and substantial backtracking, the connection from New York to Toronto is found, and Toronto connects to Calgary. This causes **findroute( )** to return, unraveling all recursive calls in the process. Finally, the original call to **findroute( )** returns. You might want to try adding **cout** statements in **findroute( )** to see precisely how it works with various other departure and destination cities.

It is important to understand that **findroute( )** does not actually *return* the solution—it *generates* it. Upon exit from **findroute( )**, the backtrack stack contains the route between the point of departure and the destination. That is, the solution is contained in **btStack**. Furthermore, the success or failure of **findroute( )** is determined by the state of the stack. An empty stack indicates failure; otherwise, the stack holds a solution.

In general, backtracking is a crucial ingredient in AI-based search techniques. In **Search**, backtracking is accomplished through the use of recursion and a backtrack stack. (This is why C++'s support for recursion and the STL make it good choice for AI development.) Almost all backtracking situations are stack-like in operation—that is, they are first-in, last-out. As a path is explored, nodes are pushed onto the stack as they are encountered. At each dead end, the last node is popped off the stack and a new path, from that point, is tried. This process continues until either the goal is reached or all paths have been exhausted.

Displaying the Route

The **route( )** function displays the path and the total distance. It is shown here:

```
// Show the route and total distance.
void Search::route()
{
  stack<FlightInfo> rev;
```

```
   int dist = 0;
   FlightInfo f;

   // Reverse the stack to display route.
   while(!btStack.empty()) {
     f = btStack.top();
     rev.push(f);
     btStack.pop();
   }

   // Display the route.
   while(!rev.empty()) {
     f = rev.top();
     rev.pop();
     cout << f.from << " to ";
     dist += f.distance;
   }

   cout << f.to << endl;
   cout << "Distance is " << dist << endl;
}
```

Notice the use of a second stack called **rev**. The solution stored in **btStack** is in reverse order, with the top of the stack holding the last connection, the bottom of the stack holding the first connection. Thus, it must be reversed in order to display the connection in the proper sequence. To put the solution into its proper order, the connections are popped from **btStack** and pushed onto **rev**.

An Analysis of the Depth-First Search

The depth-first approach found a good solution. Also, relative to this specific problem, depth-first searching found this solution on its first try with no backtracking—this is very good. However, had the data been organized differently, finding a solution might have involved considerable backtracking. Thus, the outcome of this example cannot be generalized. Moreover, the performance of depth-first searches can be quite poor when a particularly long branch with no solution at the end is explored. In this case, a depth-first search wastes time not only exploring this chain, but also backtracking to the goal.

The Breadth-First Search

The opposite of the depth-first search is the *breadth-first search*. In this method, each node on the same level is checked before the search proceeds to the next deeper level. This traversal method is shown here with C as the goal:

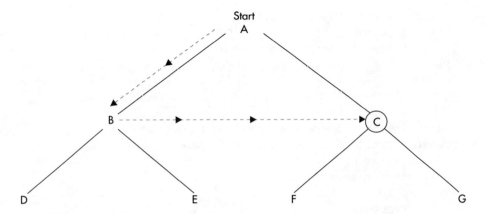

Although thinking in terms of a binary tree-structured search space makes it easy to describe the actions of a breadth-first search, many search spaces, including the flight example, are not binary trees. Therefore, precisely what constitutes "breadth" is a bit subjective, being defined by the problem at hand. As it relates to the flight example, the breadth-first approach is implemented by checking if any flight leaving the departure city connects to a flight that reaches the destination. In other words, before advancing to another level, the destinations of all connections of connecting flights are checked.

To make **Search** perform a breadth-first search, you need to make an alteration to **findroute( )**, as shown here:

```
// Breadth-first version.
// Determine if there is a route between from and to.
void Search::findroute(string from, string to)
{
  int dist;
  FlightInfo f;

  // This stack is needed by the breadth-first search.
  stack<FlightInfo> resetStck;

  // See if at destination.
  if(match(from, to, dist)) {
    btStack.push(FlightInfo(from, to, dist));
    return;
  }

  // Following is the first part of the breadth-first
  // modification.  It checks all connecting flights
  // from a specified node.
  while(find(from, f)) {
    resetStck.push(f);
    if(match(f.to, to, dist)) {
```

```
      resetStck.push(FlightInfo(f));
      btStack.push(FlightInfo(from, f.to, f.distance));
      btStack.push(FlightInfo(f.to, to, dist));
      return;
    }
  }

  // The following code resets the skip fields set by
  // preceding while loop. This is also part of the
  // breadth-first modification.
  while(!resetStck.empty()) {
    resetSkip(resetStck.top());
    resetStck.pop();
  }

  // Try another connection.
  if(find(from, f)) {
    btStack.push(FlightInfo(from, to, f.distance));
    findroute(f.to, to);
  }
  else if(!btStack.empty()) {
    // Backtrack and try another connection.
    f = btStack.top();
    btStack.pop();
    findroute(f.from, f.to);
  }
}
```

Two changes have been made. First, the **for** loop checks all flights leaving from the departure city (**from**) to see if they connect with flights that arrive at the destination city. Second, if the destination is not found, the **skip** fields of those connecting flights are cleared by calling **resetSkip( )**, which is a new function that must be added to **Search**. The connections that need to be reset are stored on their own stack, called **resetStck**, which is local to **findroute( )**. Resetting the **skip** flags is necessary to enable alternative paths that might involve those connections.

The **resetSkip( )** function is shown here:

```
// Reset the skip fields in flights vector.
void Search::resetSkip(FlightInfo f) {
  for(unsigned i=0; i < flights.size(); i++)
    if(flights[i].from == f.from &&
       flights[i].to == f.to)
         flights[i].skip = false;
}
```

You need to add this function (and its prototype) to **Search**.

To try the breadth-first search, substitute the new version of **findroute( )** into the preceding search program and then add the **resetSkip( )** function. When run, it produces the following solution:

```
From? New York
To? Los Angeles
New York to Toronto to Los Angeles
Distance is 3000
```

Figure 7-6 shows the breadth-first path to the solution.

An Analysis of the Breadth-First Search

In this example, the breadth-first search performed fairly well, finding a reasonable solution. As before, this result cannot be generalized because the first path to be found depends upon the physical organization of the information. The example does illustrate, however, how depth-first and breadth-first searches often find different paths through the same search space.

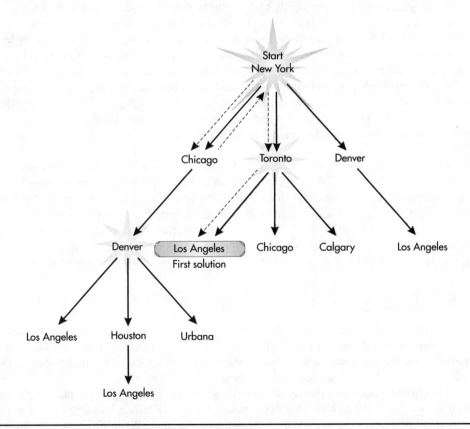

Figure 7-6   *The breadth-first path to a solution*

Breadth-first searching works well when the goal is not buried too deeply in the search space. It works poorly when the goal is several layers deep. In this case, a breadth-first search expends substantial effort during the backtrack stage.

Adding Heuristics

Neither the depth-first nor the breadth-first search attempts to make any educated guesses about whether one node in the search space is closer to the goal than another. Instead, they simply move from one node to the next using a prescribed pattern until the goal is finally found. This may be the best you can do for some situations, but often a search space contains information that you can use to increase the probability that a search will reach its goal faster. To take advantage of such information, you must add heuristic capabilities to the search.

Heuristics are simply rules that increase the likelihood that a search is proceeding in the correct direction. For example, imagine that you are lost in the woods and need a drink of water. The woods are so thick that you cannot see far ahead, and the trees are too big to climb to get a look around. However, you know that rivers, streams, and ponds are most likely in valleys; that animals frequently make paths to their watering places; that when you are near water it is possible to "smell" it; and that you can hear running water. So, you begin by moving downhill because water is unlikely to be uphill. Next you come across a deer trail that also runs downhill. Knowing that this may lead to water, you follow it. You begin to hear a slight rushing off to your left. Knowing that this may be water, you cautiously move in that direction. As you move, you begin to detect the increased humidity in the air; you can smell the water. Finally, you find a stream and have your drink. In this situation, the heuristic information used to find the water did not guarantee success, but it did increase the probability of an early success. In general, heuristics improve the odds in favor of quickly finding the goal.

Most often, heuristic search methods are based on maximizing or minimizing some constraint. In the problem of scheduling a flight from New York to Los Angeles, there are two possible constraints that a passenger may want to minimize. The first is the number of connections that have to be made. The second is the length of the route. Remember, the shortest route does not necessarily imply the fewest connections, or vice versa. In this section, two heuristic searches are developed. The first minimizes the number of connections. The second minimizes the length of the route. Both heuristic searches are built upon the depth-first search framework.

The Hill-Climbing Search

A search algorithm that attempts to find a route that minimizes the number of connections uses the heuristic that the longer the length of the flight, the greater the likelihood that it takes the traveler closer to the destination; therefore, the number of connections is minimized. In the language of AI, this is an example of *hill climbing*.

The hill-climbing algorithm chooses as its next step the node that appears to place it closest to the goal (that is, farthest away from the current position). It derives its name from the analogy of a hiker being lost in the dark, halfway up a mountain. Assuming that the hiker's camp is at the top of the mountain, even in the dark the hiker knows that each step that goes up is a step in the right direction.

Working only with the information contained in the flight-scheduling database, here is how to incorporate the hill-climbing heuristic into the routing program: Choose the connecting flight that is as far away as possible from the current position in the hope that it will be closer to the destination. To do this, begin with the depth-first version of **Search** and modify the **find( )** routine, as shown here:

```
// Hill-climbing version.
// Given from, find the farthest away connection.
// Return true if a connection is found,
// and false otherwise.
bool Search::find(string from, FlightInfo &f)
{
  int pos = -1;
  int dist = 0;

  for(unsigned i=0; i < flights.size(); i++) {
    if(flights[i].from == from && !flights[i].skip) {
      // Use the longest flight.
      if(flights[i].distance > dist) {
        pos = i;
        dist = flights[i].distance;
      }
    }
  }

  if(pos != -1) {
    f = flights[pos];
    flights[pos].skip = true; // prevent reuse

    return true;
  }

  return false;
}
```

The **find( )** routine now searches the entire database, looking for the connection that is farthest away from the departure city.

For the sake of clarity, the entire hill-climbing program follows:

```
// Search for a connection by hill climbing.
#include <iostream>
#include <stack>
#include <string>
#include <vector>
```

```cpp
using namespace std;

// Flight information.
struct FlightInfo {
  string from;  // departure city
  string to;    // destination city
  int distance; // distance between from and to
  bool skip;    // used in backtracking

  FlightInfo() {
    from = "";
    to = "";
    distance = 0;
    skip = false;
  }

  FlightInfo(string f, string t, int d) {
    from = f;
    to = t;
    distance = d;
    skip = false;
  }
};

// This version of search finds connections
// through the heuristic of hill climbing.
class Search {
  // This vector holds the flight information.
  vector<FlightInfo> flights;

  // This stack is used for backtracking.
  stack<FlightInfo> btStack;

  // If there is a flight between from and to,
  // store the distance of the flight in dist.
  // Return true if the flight exists and
  // false otherwise.
  bool match(string from, string to, int &dist);

  // Hill-climbing version.
  // Given from, find the farthest away connection.
  // Return true if a connection is found,
  // and false otherwise.
  bool find(string from, FlightInfo &f);
```

```
public:

  // Put flights into the database.
  void addflight(string from, string to, int dist) {
    flights.push_back(FlightInfo(from, to, dist));
  }

  // Show the route and total distance.
  void route();

  // Determine if there is a route between from and to.
  void findroute(string from, string to);

  // Return true if a route has been found.
  bool routefound() {
    return btStack.size() != 0;
  }
};

// Show the route and total distance.
void Search::route()
{
  stack<FlightInfo> rev;
  int dist = 0;
  FlightInfo f;

  // Reverse the stack to display route.
  while(!btStack.empty()) {
    f = btStack.top();
    rev.push(f);
    btStack.pop();
  }

  // Display the route.
  while(!rev.empty()) {
    f = rev.top();
    rev.pop();
    cout << f.from << " to ";
    dist += f.distance;
  }

  cout << f.to << endl;
  cout << "Distance is " << dist << endl;
}
```

```cpp
// If there is a flight between from and to,
// store the distance of the flight in dist.
// Return true if the flight exists and
// false otherwise.
bool Search::match(string from, string to, int &dist)
{
  for(unsigned i=0; i < flights.size(); i++) {
    if(flights[i].from == from &&
       flights[i].to == to && !flights[i].skip)
    {
      flights[i].skip = true; // prevent reuse
      dist = flights[i].distance;
      return true;
    }
  }

  return false; // not found
}

// Hill-climbing version.
// Given from, find the farthest away connection.
// Return true if a connection is found,
// and false otherwise.
bool Search::find(string from, FlightInfo &f)
{
  int pos = -1;
  int dist = 0;

  for(unsigned i=0; i < flights.size(); i++) {
    if(flights[i].from == from && !flights[i].skip) {
      // Use the longest flight.
      if(flights[i].distance > dist) {
        pos = i;
        dist = flights[i].distance;
      }
    }
  }

  if(pos != -1) {
    f = flights[pos];
    flights[pos].skip = true; // prevent reuse

    return true;
  }
```

```
    return false;
}

// Determine if there is a route between from and to.
void Search::findroute(string from, string to)
{
  int dist;
  FlightInfo f;

  // See if at destination.
  if(match(from, to, dist)) {
    btStack.push(FlightInfo(from, to, dist));
    return;
  }

  // Try another connection.
  if(find(from, f)) {
    btStack.push(FlightInfo(from, to, f.distance));
    findroute(f.to, to);
  }
  else if(!btStack.empty()) {
    // Backtrack and try another connection.
    f = btStack.top();
    btStack.pop();
    findroute(f.from, f.to);
  }
}

int main() {
  char to[40], from[40];
  Search ob;

  // Add flight connections to database.
  ob.addflight("New York", "Chicago", 900);
  ob.addflight("Chicago", "Denver", 1000);
  ob.addflight("New York", "Toronto", 500);
  ob.addflight("New York", "Denver", 1800);
  ob.addflight("Toronto", "Calgary", 1700);
  ob.addflight("Toronto", "Los Angeles", 2500);
  ob.addflight("Toronto", "Chicago", 500);
  ob.addflight("Denver", "Urbana", 1000);
  ob.addflight("Denver", "Houston", 1000);
  ob.addflight("Houston", "Los Angeles", 1500);
  ob.addflight("Denver", "Los Angeles", 1000);
```

```
    // Get departure and destination cities.
    cout << "From? ";

    cin.getline(from, 40);
    cout << "To? ";

    cin.getline(to, 40);

    // See if there is a route between from and to.
    ob.findroute(from, to);

    // If there is a route, show it.
    if(ob.routefound())
        ob.route();

    return 0;
}
```

When the program is run, the solution is

```
From? New York
To? Los Angeles
New York to Denver to Los Angeles
Distance is 2800
```

This is quite good! The route contains the minimal number of stops on the way (only one), and it is the shortest route. Thus, it found the best possible route.

However, if the Denver to Los Angeles connection did not exist, the solution would not be quite so good. It would be New York to Denver to Houston to Los Angeles—a distance of 4300 miles! In this case, the solution climbs a "false peak," because the connection to Houston does not take us closer to the goal of Los Angeles. Figure 7-7 shows the first solution as well as the path to the false peak.

An Analysis of Hill Climbing

Hill climbing provides fairly good solutions in many circumstances because it tends to reduce the number of nodes that need to be visited before a solution is found. However, it can suffer from three maladies. First, there is the problem of false peaks, as just described. In this case, extensive backtracking may result. The second problem relates to plateaus, a situation in which all next steps look equally good (or bad). In this case, hill climbing is no better than depth-first searching. The final problem is that of a ridge. In this case, hill climbing really performs poorly because the algorithm causes the ridge to be crossed several times as backtracking occurs. In spite of these potential troubles, hill climbing often increases the probability of finding a good solution.

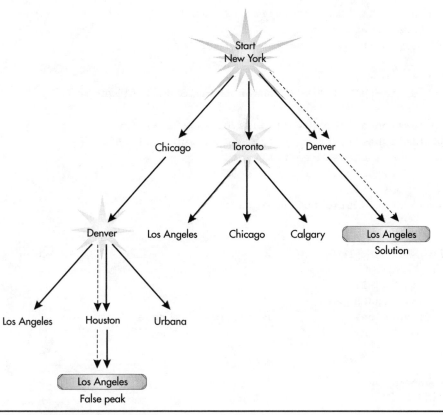

Figure 7-7   *The hill-climbing path to a solution and to a false peak*

The Least-Cost Search

The opposite of a hill-climbing search is a *least-cost search*. This strategy is similar to standing in the middle of a street on a big hill while wearing roller skates. You have the definite feeling that it's a lot easier to go down rather than up! In other words, a least-cost search takes the path of least resistance.

Applying a least-cost search to the flight-scheduling problem implies that the shortest connecting flight is taken in all cases so that the route found has a good chance of covering the shortest distance. Unlike hill climbing, which attempts to minimize the number of connections, a least-cost search attempts to minimize the number of miles.

To use a least-cost search, you must alter **find( )** in the previous program, as shown here:

```
const int MAXDIST = 100000;


// Least-cost version.
// Given from, find the closest connection.
```

```
// Return true if a connection is found,
// and false otherwise.
bool Search::find(string from, FlightInfo &f)
{
  int pos = -1;
  int dist = MAXDIST; // longer than longest flight

  for(unsigned i=0; i < flights.size(); i++) {
    if(flights[i].from == from && !flights[i].skip) {
      // Use the shortest flight.
      if(flights[i].distance < dist) {
        pos = i;
        dist = flights[i].distance;
      }
    }
  }

  if(pos != -1) {
    f = flights[pos];
    flights[pos].skip = true; // prevent reuse

    return true;
  }

  return false;
}
```

Using this version of **find( )**, the solution is

```
From? New York
To? Los Angeles
New York to Toronto to Los Angeles
Distance is 3000
```

As you can see, the search found a good route—not the best, but acceptable. Figure 7-8 shows the least-cost path to the goal.

An Analysis of the Least-Cost Search

Least-cost searches and hill climbing have the same advantages and disadvantages, but in reverse. In the least-cost search there can be false valleys, lowlands, and gorges. In this specific case, it worked about as well as hill climbing.

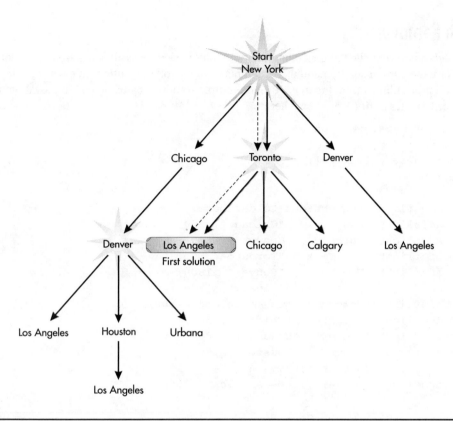

Figure 7-8   *The least-cost path to a solution*

Finding Multiple Solutions

Sometimes it is valuable to find several solutions to the same problem. This is not the same as finding all solutions (an exhaustive search). Instead, multiple solutions offer a representative sample of the solutions present in the search space.

There are several ways to generate multiple solutions, but only two are examined here. The first is path removal, and the second is node removal. As their names imply, generating multiple solutions without redundancy requires that already found solutions be removed from the system. Remember that neither of these techniques attempts to find all solutions. Finding all solutions is a different problem that is usually not attempted because it implies an exhaustive search.

Path Removal

The *path-removal* method of generating multiple solutions removes all nodes from the database that form the current solution and then attempts to find another solution. In essence, path removal prunes limbs from the tree. To find multiple solutions by using path removal, you just need to alter **main( )**, as shown here:

```
// Path removal version.
int main() {
  char to[40], from[40];
  Search ob;

  // Add flight connections to database.
  ob.addflight("New York", "Chicago", 900);
  ob.addflight("Chicago", "Denver", 1000);
  ob.addflight("New York", "Toronto", 500);
  ob.addflight("New York", "Denver", 1800);
  ob.addflight("Toronto", "Calgary", 1700);
  ob.addflight("Toronto", "Los Angeles", 2500);
  ob.addflight("Toronto", "Chicago", 500);
  ob.addflight("Denver", "Urbana", 1000);
  ob.addflight("Denver", "Houston", 1000);
  ob.addflight("Houston", "Los Angeles", 1500);
  ob.addflight("Denver", "Los Angeles", 1000);

  // Get departure and destination cities.
  cout << "From? ";

  cin.getline(from, 40);
  cout << "To? ";

  cin.getline(to, 40);

  // Find multiple solutions.
  for(;;) {
    // See if there is a connection.
    ob.findroute(from, to);

    // If no new route was found, then end.
    if(!ob.routefound()) break;

    ob.route();
  }

  return 0;
}
```

Here, a **for** loop is added that iterates until the backtrack stack is empty. Recall that when the backtrack stack is empty, no solution (in this case, no additional solution) has been found. No other modifications are needed because any connection that is part of a solution will have its **skip** field marked. Consequently, such a connection can no longer be found by **find( )** and cannot be part of the next solution; it cannot be refound.

If you use the original depth-first version of **Search** (shown first in this chapter) with the preceding **main( )**, the following solutions will be found:

```
From? New York
To? Los Angeles
New York to Chicago to Denver to Los Angeles
Distance is 2900
New York to Toronto to Los Angeles
Distance is 3000
New York to Denver to Houston to Los Angeles
Distance is 4300
```

The search found the three solutions. Notice, however, that none are the best solution.

Node Removal

The second way to force the generation of additional solutions, *node removal*, simply removes the last node in the current solution path and tries again. To do this, **main( )** is changed so that it removes the last connection from the flight database, clears all of the **skip** fields, and obtains a new, empty stack which is used to hold the next solution. The updated **main( )** function is shown here:

```
// Node removal version
int main() {
  char to[40], from[40];
  Search ob;
  FlightInfo f;

  // Add flight connections to database.
  ob.addflight("New York", "Chicago", 900);
  ob.addflight("Chicago", "Denver", 1000);
  ob.addflight("New York", "Toronto", 500);
  ob.addflight("New York", "Denver", 1800);
  ob.addflight("Toronto", "Calgary", 1700);
  ob.addflight("Toronto", "Los Angeles", 2500);
  ob.addflight("Toronto", "Chicago", 500);
  ob.addflight("Denver", "Urbana", 1000);
  ob.addflight("Denver", "Houston", 1000);
  ob.addflight("Houston", "Los Angeles", 1500);
  ob.addflight("Denver", "Los Angeles", 1000);
```

```
  // Get departure and destination cities.
  cout << "From? ";

  cin.getline(from, 40);
  cout << "To? ";

  cin.getline(to, 40);

  // Find multiple solutions.
  for(;;) {
    // See if there is a connection.
    ob.findroute(from, to);

    // If no new route was found, then end.
    if(!ob.routefound()) break;

    // Save the flight on top-of-stack.
    f = ob.getTOS();

    ob.route(); // display the current route.

    ob.resetAllSkip(); // reset the skip fields

    // Remove last flight in previous solution
    // from the flight database.
    ob.remove(f);
  }

  return 0;
}
```

To remove the last connection of the previous solution from the flight database, **main( )** first obtains that connection by calling **getTOS( )**, which is declared in-line within the **Search** class, as shown here:

```
// Return flight on top of stack.
FlightInfo getTOS() {
  return btStack.top();
}
```

It returns the flight information found on the top of the backtrack stack, which is the last connection in the route.

To actually remove this connection, **main( )** calls **remove( )**, shown here:

```
// Remove a connection.
void Search::remove(FlightInfo f) {
```

```
  for(unsigned i=0; i< flights.size(); i++)
    if(flights[i].from == f.from &&
       flights[i].to == f.to)
         flights[i].from = "";
}
```

Removing a connection is accomplished by assigning a zero-length string to the name of the departure city.

To clear the **skip** fields, **main( )** calls **resetAllSkip( )**, shown next:

```
// Reset all skip fields.
void Search::resetAllSkip() {
  for(unsigned i=0; i< flights.size(); i++)
    flights[i].skip = false;
}
```

It simply sets the **skip** fields to false. (Remember to add the prototypes for **resetAllSkip( )** and **remove( )** to the **Search** class declaration.)

Because so many changes are required, the entire node-removal program is shown here for the sake of clarity. Notice that it too uses the original depth-first version of **Search**.

```
// Search for multiple routes by use of node removal.
#include <iostream>
#include <stack>
#include <string>
#include <vector>

using namespace std;

// Flight information.
struct FlightInfo {
  string from;   // departure city
  string to;     // destination city
  int distance;  // distance between from and to
  bool skip;     // used in backtracking

  FlightInfo() {
    from = "";
    to = "";
    distance = 0;
    skip = false;
  }

  FlightInfo(string f, string t, int d) {
    from = f;
    to = t;
```

```
      distance = d;
      skip = false;
    }
};

// Find multiple solutions via node removal.
class Search {
  // This vector holds the flight information.
  vector<FlightInfo> flights;

  // This stack is used for backtracking.
  stack<FlightInfo> btStack;

  // If there is a flight between from and to,
  // store the distance of the flight in dist.
  // Return true if the flight exists and
  // false otherwise.
  bool match(string from, string to, int &dist);

  // Given from, find any connection.
  // Return true if a connection is found,
  // and false otherwise.
  bool find(string from, FlightInfo &f);

public:

  // Put flights into the database.
  void addflight(string from, string to, int dist) {
    flights.push_back(FlightInfo(from, to, dist));
  }

  // Show the route and total distance.
  void route();

  // Determine if there is a route between from and to.
  void findroute(string from, string to);

  // Return true if a route has been found.
  bool routefound() {
    return btStack.size() != 0;
  }

  // Return flight on top of stack.
  FlightInfo getTOS() {
    return btStack.top();
```

```
    }

    // Reset all skip fields.
    void resetAllSkip();

    // Remove a connection.
    void remove(FlightInfo f);
};

// Show the route and total distance.
void Search::route()
{
    stack<FlightInfo> rev;
    int dist = 0;
    FlightInfo f;

    // Reverse the stack to display route.
    while(!btStack.empty()) {
        f = btStack.top();
        rev.push(f);
        btStack.pop();
    }

    // Display the route.
    while(!rev.empty()) {
        f = rev.top();
        rev.pop();
        cout << f.from << " to ";
        dist += f.distance;
    }

    cout << f.to << endl;
    cout << "Distance is " << dist << endl;
}

// If there is a flight between from and to,
// store the distance of the flight in dist.
// Return true if the flight exists and
// false otherwise.
bool Search::match(string from, string to, int &dist)
{
    for(unsigned i=0; i < flights.size(); i++) {
        if(flights[i].from == from &&
            flights[i].to == to && !flights[i].skip)
        {
```

```
        flights[i].skip = true; // prevent reuse
        dist = flights[i].distance;
        return true;
      }
    }

    return false; // not found
}

// Given from, find any connection.
// Return true if a connection is found,
// and false otherwise.
bool Search::find(string from, FlightInfo &f)
{
  for(unsigned i=0; i < flights.size(); i++) {
    if(flights[i].from == from && !flights[i].skip) {
      f = flights[i];
      flights[i].skip = true; // prevent reuse

      return true;
    }
  }

  return false;
}

// Determine if there is a route between from and to.
void Search::findroute(string from, string to)
{
  int dist;
  FlightInfo f;

  // See if at destination.
  if(match(from, to, dist)) {
    btStack.push(FlightInfo(from, to, dist));
    return;
  }

  // Try another connection.
  if(find(from, f)) {
    btStack.push(FlightInfo(from, to, f.distance));
    findroute(f.to, to);
  }
  else if(!btStack.empty()) {
    // Backtrack and try another connection.
```

```
      f = btStack.top();
      btStack.pop();
      findroute(f.from, f.to);
    }
  }

// Reset all skip fields.
void Search::resetAllSkip() {
  for(unsigned i=0; i< flights.size(); i++)
    flights[i].skip = false;
}

// Remove a connection.
void Search::remove(FlightInfo f) {
  for(unsigned i=0; i< flights.size(); i++)
    if(flights[i].from == f.from &&
       flights[i].to == f.to)
         flights[i].from = "";
}


// Node removal version.
int main() {
  char to[40], from[40];
  Search ob;
  FlightInfo f;

  // Add flight connections to database.
  ob.addflight("New York", "Chicago", 900);
  ob.addflight("Chicago", "Denver", 1000);
  ob.addflight("New York", "Toronto", 500);
  ob.addflight("New York", "Denver", 1800);
  ob.addflight("Toronto", "Calgary", 1700);
  ob.addflight("Toronto", "Los Angeles", 2500);
  ob.addflight("Toronto", "Chicago", 500);
  ob.addflight("Denver", "Urbana", 1000);
  ob.addflight("Denver", "Houston", 1000);
  ob.addflight("Houston", "Los Angeles", 1500);
  ob.addflight("Denver", "Los Angeles", 1000);

  // Get departure and destination cities.
  cout << "From? ";

  cin.getline(from, 40);
  cout << "To? ";
```

```
   cin.getline(to, 40);

   // Find multiple solutions.
   for(;;) {
     // See if there is a connection.
     ob.findroute(from, to);

     // If no new route was found, then end.
     if(!ob.routefound()) break;

     // Save the flight on top-of-stack.
     f = ob.getTOS();

     ob.route(); // display the current route.

     ob.resetAllSkip(); // reset the skip fields

     // Remove last flight in previous solution
     // from the flight database.
     ob.remove(f);
   }

   return 0;
}
```

This program finds the following routes:

```
From? New York
To? Los Angeles
New York to Chicago to Denver to Los Angeles
Distance is 2900
New York to Chicago to Denver to Houston to Los Angeles
Distance is 4400
New York to Toronto to Los Angeles
Distance is 3000
```

In this case, the second solution is the worst possible route, but two fairly good solutions are also found. Notice that the set of solutions found by the node-removal method differs from that found by the path-removal approach. Different approaches to generating multiple solutions can often yield different results.

Finding the "Optimal" Solution

All of the previous search techniques were concerned, first and foremost, with finding a solution—any solution. As you saw with the heuristic searches, efforts can be made to improve the likelihood of finding a good solution. But no attempt was made to ensure that the optimal solution was found. However, at times you may want *only* the optimal solution. Keep in mind that "optimal," as it is used here, simply means the best route that can be found by using one of the multiple-solution generation techniques—it may not actually be the best solution. (Finding the best solution would, of course, require the prohibitively time-consuming exhaustive search.)

Before leaving the well-used flight scheduling example, consider a program that finds the optimal route given the constraint that distance is to be minimized. To do this, the program employs the path-removal method of generating multiple solutions and uses a least-cost search to minimize distance. The key to finding the shortest path is to keep a solution that is shorter than the previously generated solution. When there are no more solutions to generate, the optimal solution remains.

The entire "optimal solution" program is shown here. Notice that the program creates an additional stack, called **optimal**, which holds the optimal solution, and an instance variable, called **minDist**, which keeps track of the distance. There are also changes to **route( )** and some minor modifications to **main( )**.

```cpp
// Find an "optimal" solution using least-cost with path removal.
#include <iostream>
#include <stack>
#include <string>
#include <vector>

using namespace std;

// Flight information.
struct FlightInfo {
  string from;   // departure city
  string to;     // destination city
  int distance; // distance between from and to
  bool skip;     // used in backtracking

  FlightInfo() {
    from = "";
    to = "";
    distance = 0;
    skip = false;
  }

  FlightInfo(string f, string t, int d) {
    from = f;
```

```
      to = t;
      distance = d;
      skip = false;
   }
};

const int MAXDIST = 100000;

// Find connections using least cost.
class Optimal {
  // This vector holds the flight information.
  vector<FlightInfo> flights;

  // This stack is used for backtracking.
  stack<FlightInfo> btStack;

  // This stack holds the optimal solution.
  stack<FlightInfo> optimal;

  int minDist;

  // If there is a flight between from and to,
  // store the distance of the flight in dist.
  // Return true if the flight exists and
  // false otherwise.
  bool match(string from, string to, int &dist);

  // Least-cost version.
  // Given from, find the closest connection.
  // Return true if a connection is found,
  // and false otherwise.
  bool find(string from, FlightInfo &f);

public:

  // Constructor
  Optimal() {
    minDist = MAXDIST;
  }

  // Put flights into the database.
  void addflight(string from, string to, int dist) {
    flights.push_back(FlightInfo(from, to, dist));
  }
```

```cpp
  // Show the route and total distance.
  void route();

  // Display the optimal route.
  void Optimal::showOpt();

  // Determine if there is a route between from and to.
  void findroute(string from, string to);

  // Return true if a route has been found.
  bool routefound() {
    return btStack.size() != 0;
  }
};

// Show the route and total distance.
void Optimal::route()
{
  stack<FlightInfo> optTemp;
  int dist = 0;
  FlightInfo f;

  // Reverse the stack to display route.
  while(!btStack.empty()) {
    f = btStack.top();
    optTemp.push(f);
    btStack.pop();
    dist += f.distance;
  }

  // If shorter, keep this route.
  if(minDist > dist) {
    optimal = optTemp;
    minDist = dist;
  }
}

// Display the optimal route.
void Optimal::showOpt()
{
  FlightInfo f;
  int dist = 0;

  cout <<"Optimal solution is:\n";
```

```
  // Display the optimal route.
  while(!optimal.empty()) {
    f = optimal.top();
    optimal.pop();
    cout << f.from << " to ";
    dist += f.distance;
  }

  cout << f.to << endl;
  cout << "Distance is " << dist << endl;
}


// If there is a flight between from and to,
// store the distance of the flight in dist.
// Return true if the flight exists and
// false otherwise.
bool Optimal::match(string from, string to, int &dist)
{
  for(unsigned i=0; i < flights.size(); i++) {
    if(flights[i].from == from &&
       flights[i].to == to && !flights[i].skip)
    {
      flights[i].skip = true; // prevent reuse
      dist = flights[i].distance;
      return true;
    }
  }

  return false; // not found
}


// Least-cost version.
// Given from, find the closest connection.
// Return true if a connection is found,
// and false otherwise.
bool Optimal::find(string from, FlightInfo &f)
{
  int pos = -1;
  int dist = MAXDIST; // longer than longest flight

  for(unsigned i=0; i < flights.size(); i++) {
    if(flights[i].from == from && !flights[i].skip)
    {
      // Use the shortest flight.
      if(flights[i].distance < dist) {
```

```
        pos = i;
        dist = flights[i].distance;
      }
    }
  }

  if(pos != -1) {
    f = flights[pos];
    flights[pos].skip = true; // prevent reuse

    return true;
  }

  return false;
}

// Determine if there is a route between from and to.
void Optimal::findroute(string from, string to)
{
  int dist;
  FlightInfo f;

  // See if at destination.
  if(match(from, to, dist)) {
    btStack.push(FlightInfo(from, to, dist));
    return;
  }

  // Try another connection.
  if(find(from, f)) {
    btStack.push(FlightInfo(from, to, f.distance));
    findroute(f.to, to);
  }
  else if(!btStack.empty()) {
    // Backtrack and try another connection.
    f = btStack.top();
    btStack.pop();
    findroute(f.from, f.to);
  }
}

// Find "optimal" solution by using least-cost with path removal.
int main() {
  char to[40], from[40];
  Optimal ob;
```

```
   // Add flight connections to database.
   ob.addflight("New York", "Chicago", 900);
   ob.addflight("Chicago", "Denver", 1000);
   ob.addflight("New York", "Toronto", 500);
   ob.addflight("New York", "Denver", 1800);
   ob.addflight("Toronto", "Calgary", 1700);
   ob.addflight("Toronto", "Los Angeles", 2500);
   ob.addflight("Toronto", "Chicago", 500);
   ob.addflight("Denver", "Urbana", 1000);
   ob.addflight("Denver", "Houston", 1000);
   ob.addflight("Houston", "Los Angeles", 1500);
   ob.addflight("Denver", "Los Angeles", 1000);

   // Get departure and destination cities.
   cout << "From? ";

   cin.getline(from, 40);
   cout << "To? ";

   cin.getline(to, 40);

   // Find multiple solutions.
   for(;;) {
     // See if there is a connection.
     ob.findroute(from, to);

     // If no route found, then end.
     if(!ob.routefound()) break;

     ob.route();
   }

   // Display optimal solution.
   ob.showOpt();

   return 0;

}
```

The output from the program is shown here:

```
From? New York
To? Los Angeles
Optimal solution is:
```

```
New York to Chicago to Denver to Los Angeles
Distance is 2900
```

In this case, the "optimal" solution is not quite the very best one, but it is still a very good one. As explained, when using AI-based searches, the best solution to be found by one search technique will not always be the very best one that might exist. You might want to try substituting another search technique in the preceding program, observing what type of "optimal" solution it finds.

The one inefficiency in the preceding method is that all paths are followed to their conclusion. An improved method would stop following a path as soon as the length equaled or exceeded the current minimum. You might want to modify this program to accommodate such an enhancement.

Back to the Lost Keys

To conclude this chapter on problem solving, it seems only fitting to provide a C++ program that finds the lost car keys described in the first example. The following code employs the same techniques used in the problem of finding a route between two cities, so the program is presented without further explanation:

```cpp
// Search for the lost keys.
#include <iostream>
#include <stack>
#include <string>
#include <vector>

using namespace std;

// Room information.
struct RoomInfo {
  string from;
  string to;
  bool skip;

  RoomInfo() {
    from = "";
    to = "";
    skip = false;
  }

  RoomInfo(string f, string t) {
    from = f;
    to = t;
    skip = false;
  }
```

```cpp
};

// Find the keys using a depth-first search.
class Search {
  // This vector holds the room information.
  vector<RoomInfo> rooms;

  // This stack is used for backtracking.
  stack<RoomInfo> btStack;

  // Return true if a path exists between
  // from and to.  Return false otherwise.
  bool match(string from, string to);

  // Given from, find any path.
  // Return true if a path is found,
  // and false otherwise.
  bool find(string from, RoomInfo &f);

public:

  // Put rooms into the database.
  void addroom(string from, string to)
  {
    rooms.push_back(RoomInfo(from, to));
  }

  // Show the route taken.
  void route();

  // Determine if there is a path between from and to.
  void findkeys(string from, string to);

  // Return true if the keys have been found.
  bool keysfound() {
    return !btStack.empty();
  }
};

// Show the route.
void Search::route()
{
  stack<RoomInfo> rev;
  RoomInfo f;
```

```
    // Reverse the stack to display route.
    while(!btStack.empty()) {
      f = btStack.top();
      rev.push(f);
      btStack.pop();
    }

    // Display the route.
    while(!rev.empty()) {
      f = rev.top();
      rev.pop();
      cout << f.from << " to ";
    }

    cout << f.to << endl;
}

// Return true if a path exists between
// from and to.  Return false otherwise.
bool Search::match(string from, string to)
{
    for(unsigned i=0; i < rooms.size(); i++) {
      if(rooms[i].from == from &&
          rooms[i].to == to && !rooms[i].skip)
      {
        rooms[i].skip = true; // prevent reuse
        return true;
      }
    }

    return false; // not found
}

// Given from, find any path.
// Return true if a path is found,
// and false otherwise.
bool Search::find(string from, RoomInfo &f)
{
    for(unsigned i=0; i < rooms.size(); i++) {
      if(rooms[i].from == from && !rooms[i].skip) {
        f = rooms[i];
        rooms[i].skip = true; // prevent reuse

        return true;
      }
```

```
  }

  return false;
}

// Find the keys.
void Search::findkeys(string from, string to)
{
  RoomInfo f;

  // See if keys are found.
  if(match(from, to)) {
    btStack.push(RoomInfo(from, to));
    return;
  }

  // Try another room.
  if(find(from, f)) {
    btStack.push(RoomInfo(from, to));
    findkeys(f.to, to);
  }
  else if(!btStack.empty()) {
    // Backtrack and try another path.
    f = btStack.top();
    btStack.pop();
    findkeys(f.from, f.to);
  }
}

int main() {
  Search ob;

  // Add rooms to database.
  ob.addroom("front_door", "lr");
  ob.addroom("lr", "bath");
  ob.addroom("lr", "hall");
  ob.addroom("hall", "bd1");
  ob.addroom("hall", "bd2");
  ob.addroom("hall", "mb");
  ob.addroom("lr", "kitchen");
  ob.addroom("kitchen", "keys");

  // Find the keys.
  ob.findkeys("front_door", "keys");
```

```
// If keys are found, show the path.
if(ob.keysfound())
    ob.route();

return 0;
}
```

Some Things to Try

Because AI-based searching is an engaging, yet challenging area of computer science, it is enjoyable to experiment with. Here are some things you might want to try. First, experiment with the heuristic searches by substituting the breadth-first technique and observe the results. Second, substitute breadth-first searching when finding multiple solutions or when finding an "optimal" solution. Finally, try handling other real-world search situations.

Building a Custom STL Container

A central theme of this book is the raw power that C++ puts into the hands of the programmer. Perhaps nothing illustrates this better than the Standard Template Library (STL), which is reshaping the way that programs are written. The STL is a sophisticated set of template classes and functions that implement many popular and commonly used data structures and algorithms. Because the STL offers off-the-shelf solutions to a variety of programming problems that involve the storage and retrieval of data, STL-based code is becoming commonplace. For example, the garbage collection subsystem in Chapter 2 and the thread control panel in Chapter 3 both make use of the STL, which greatly simplifies their code. In the past, if a data structure such as a list, stack, or queue was needed, it would have to be coded manually. Today, the programmer can simply use one provided by the STL.

At the core of the STL is the *container*. A container is an object that holds other objects. The STL offers several built-in containers that support such data structures as stacks, queues, lists, and vectors. Because containers are templatized, they can hold any type of object, including objects of classes that you create.

Although the built-in containers are quite useful, you are not limited to them. One of the most impressive aspects of the STL is that it allows you to create your own containers. Thus, the STL is extensible. Once you have created a container, it is automatically fully compatible with the rest of the STL.

In this chapter, you will see how to create your own custom STL container. Although custom containers are not difficult to create, many programmers are initially intimidated by the prospect. One reason for this is that the STL's template-based syntax can be a bit overwhelming at first glance. In actuality the STL is a conceptually clean and easy-to-understand subsystem. If you follow a few rules, you will have no trouble creating your own containers.

The custom container developed here implements a range-selectable dynamic array called **RangeArray**. When using **RangeArray**, you can specify the beginning and ending indices. For example, **RangeArray** lets you create an array that runs from −10 to 10.

A Brief Review of the STL

The STL is a very large topic that would require hundreds of pages to describe in detail, and a complete description of the STL is far beyond the scope of this chapter. Therefore, this chapter assumes that you have a basic working knowledge of the STL. The foregoing not withstanding, a brief review of the main STL terms and constituents is given here so that all readers will be on an even footing.

The STL is based on three main features: containers, iterators, and algorithms. As mentioned, containers are objects that hold other objects. *Iterators* are pointer-like objects that enable you to cycle through a container in much the same way that you cycle through an array using a pointer. *Algorithms* operate on containers, modifying, copying, or otherwise manipulating their elements.

In addition to containers, algorithms, and iterators, the STL relies upon several other standard components for support, such as *allocators*, *adaptors*, *predicates*, and *function objects*. The following sections take a closer look at the main STL constituents.

NOTE

For a complete discussion of the STL, I recommend my book STL Programming From the Ground Up, *McGraw-Hill/Osborne.*

Containers

The STL defines two types of containers: *sequence* and *associative*. Sequence containers hold a linear list of objects. The STL provides several built-in sequence containers, including **vector**, which defines a dynamic array, **deque,** which creates a double-ended queue, and **list**, which implements a linked list. The associative containers store key/value pairs. Thus, the associative containers allow efficient retrieval of values based on keys. For example, a **map** provides access to values with unique keys. Therefore, a **map** stores a key/value pair and allows a value to be retrieved given its key.

Each container class defines a set of functions that may be applied to the container. For example, a **list** container includes functions that insert, delete, and merge elements. A **stack** includes functions that push and pop values.

Algorithms

Algorithms act on containers. They provide the means by which you can manipulate the contents of containers. Their capabilities include initialization, sorting, searching, and transforming the contents of containers. Many algorithms operate on a range of elements within a container rather than the entire container. Examples of algorithms include **copy( )**, **remove( )**, **replace( )**, and **find( )**.

Iterators

Iterators are objects that are similar to pointers. You can increment and decrement them. You can apply the * operator to them. Iterators are declared using the **iterator** type defined by the various containers.

The STL also supports *reverse iterators*. Reverse iterators move through a sequence in the reverse direction. Thus, if a reverse iterator points to the end of a sequence, incrementing that iterator will cause it to point to one element before the end.

Other STL Entities

In addition to containers, iterators, and algorithms, there are several other STL elements that play important roles: allocators, function objects, adaptors, predicates, binders, and negators.

Each container has defined for it an *allocator*. Allocators manage memory allocation for a container. The default allocator is an object of class **allocator**, but you can define your own allocator if one is needed by a specialized application. For most uses, the default allocator is sufficient.

Function objects are classes that define **operator( )**. There are several predefined function objects, such as **less( )**, **greater( )**, **plus( )**, **minus( )**, **multiplies( )**, and **divides( )**. Perhaps the most widely used function object is **less( )**, which determines when one object is less than another. Function objects can be used in place of function pointers when using STL algorithms.

In the most general sense, an *adaptor* transforms one thing into another. There are container adaptors, iterator adaptors, and function adaptors. An example of a container adaptor is **queue**, which adapts the **deque** container for use as a standard queue. Adaptors simplify a number of difficult situations.

Several of the algorithms and containers use a special type of function called a *predicate*. There are two variations of predicates: unary and binary. A unary predicate takes one argument; a binary predicate takes two arguments. These functions return true/false results, but the precise conditions that make them return true or false are defined by you. Some algorithms use a special type of binary predicate that compares two elements. These *comparison functions* return true if their first argument is less than their second.

Two other entities that populate the STL are binders and negators. A *binder* binds an argument to a function object. There are two binders defined by the STL: **bind2nd( )** and **bind1st( )**. A *negator* returns the complement of a predicate. There are two negators: **not1( )** and **not2( )**. Both binders and negators increase the versatility of the STL.

Custom Container Requirements

Before designing a custom container, it is necessary to know precisely what it must provide. According to Standard C++, all containers must supply a prescribed set of types, operators, and member functions. In addition to these common elements, both sequence and associative containers add several specific requirements. If you follow all the rules, then your custom container can make use of all of the other entities defined by the STL, including such things as allocators, function objects, predicates, and binders. Thus, a properly constructed custom container will be fully integrated into the STL landscape. The following sections describe the requirements for a container.

General Requirements

Every container (sequence or associative) must manage memory through an allocator rather than by using **new** and **delete**. Thus, the container must use the allocator's member functions to allocate and release memory. The allocator is specified as a parameter when a container is created. However, a default allocator class, called **allocator**, is provided by C++, and the allocator parameter can be allowed to default to an object of type **allocator**, which is what all of the standard containers do. All allocators must provide the same member functions as **allocator** (but, of course, may vary in implementation). This way, a container can use any allocator that the programmer supplies. The allocator functions used by the container in this chapter are shown in Table 8-1.

Function	Description
pointer allocate(size_type *num*, typename allocator<void>::const_pointer *h* = 0);	Returns a pointer to allocated memory that is large enough to hold *num* objects of type T. The value of *h* is a hint to the function that can be used to help satisfy the request or ignored.
void construct(pointer *ptr*, const_reference *val*);	Constructs an object of type T at *ptr*.
void deallocate(pointer *ptr*, size_type *num*);	Deallocates *num* objects of type T starting at *ptr*. The value of *ptr* must have been obtained from **allocate( )**.
void destroy(pointer *ptr*);	Destroys the object at *ptr*. Its destructor is automatically called.
size_type max_size( ) const throw( );	Returns the maximum number of objects of type T that can be allocated.

Table 8-1   *The allocator Functions Used in This Chapter*

Every container must provide these types:

iterator	const_iterator	reference	const_reference
value_type	size_type	difference_type	

A reversible container (one that supports bidirectional iterators) must also supply these types:

reverse_iterator   const_reverse_iterator

All containers must provide a default constructor, which creates a zero-length container, and a copy constructor. Various parameterized constructors are also needed, the precise form of which differs between sequence and associative containers. A destructor is also required.

The following member functions must be supported:

begin( )	clear( )	empty( )	end( )
erase( )	insert( )	max_size( )	rbegin( )
rend( )	size( )	swap( )	

Of course, **rbegin( )** and **rend( )** are needed only by reversible containers. Some functions have overloaded forms.

NOTE

*All of the built-in STL containers supply a function called **get_allocator( )**, but this is not a requirement for custom containers.*

The fact that a container must define the iterator functions, such as **begin( )**, implies that the container must support all required iterator operations.

The following operators must be supported by all containers:

=	==	!=	>
<	<=	>=	

Additional Sequence Container Requirements

In addition to a default constructor and a copy constructor, a sequence container must supply a constructor that creates and initializes a specified number of elements. It must also provide a constructor that creates and initializes an object given a range of elements. That is, the following forms of constructors must be supported:

Cnt( )

Cnt(*c*)

Cnt(*num*, *val*)

Cnt(*start*, *end*)

Here, *c* is an object of type *Cnt*, *num* is an integer specifying a count, *val* is a value compatible with the type of objects stored in *Cnt*, and *start* and *end* are iterators to a range of elements that will be used to initialize the container. A custom container can specify additional constructors.

NOTE

*With the exception of the copy constructor, the constructors for the built-in STL sequence containers accept an argument that specifies an allocator (which defaults to **allocator**), but this is not a requirement.*

Standard C++ defines the following optional member functions for sequence containers:

at( )	back( )	front( )	pop_back( )
pop_front( )	push_back( )	push_front( )	

The subscript operator **[ ]** is also optional. Of course, you can also add other member functions of your own design.

Associative Container Requirements

All associative containers must define these additional types:

key_compare	key_type	value_compare

Along with a default constructor and a copy constructor, an associative container must supply constructors that allow you to specify a comparison function. You must also define a constructor that creates and initializes an object given a range of elements. One version of this constructor must use the default comparison function. Another must allow the user to specify the comparison function. That is, the following forms of constructors must be supported:

Cnt( )

Cnt(*c*)

Cnt(*comp*)

Cnt(*start*, *end*)

Cnt(*start*, *end*, *comp*)

Here, *c* is an object of type *Cnt*, *start* and *end* are iterators to a range of elements that will be used to initialize the container, and *comp* is a comparison function. A custom container can specify additional constructors.

NOTE

*With the exception of the copy constructor, the constructors for the built-in STL associative containers accept an argument that specifies an allocator (which defaults to **allocator**), but this is not a requirement.*

Associative containers must provide these additional member functions:

count( )	equal_range( )	find( )	key_comp( )
lower_bound( )	upper_bound( )	value_comp( )	

Creating a Range-Selectable, Dynamic Array Container

The remainder of this chapter develops a custom sequence container called **RangeArray** that provides a range-selectable dynamic array. While the example shown here illustrates the creation of a sequence container, most of the concepts can be applied to the implementation of associative containers as well.

How RangeArray Works

As you know, in C++ all arrays begin at zero, and negative indexes are not allowed. However, some applications would benefit from an array that allows the programmer to specify different endpoints. Consider the Cartesian coordinate plane: each axis is a line that has both positive and negative values. A convenient way to represent such a line in a program would be to use an array that allows negative as well as positive indices. For example, given a line that runs from –5 to 5, you would like to use an array that could be indexed as shown here:

-5	-4	-3	-2	-1	0	1	2	3	4	5

The **RangeArray** container developed here enables you to create such an array. More generally, **RangeArray** lets you specify any arbitrary lower and upper bounds for the array indices.

RangeArray is a dynamic container that allows the array to grow in both the positive and negative directions. In this regard, it is similar to the built-in container **vector**. **RangeArray** supports all of the required sequence container operations, plus the optional **[ ]** operator and the optional functions **at( )**, **push_front( )**, **pop_front( )**, and so on.

Using **RangeArray**, you can write code like this:

```
// This creates an array that runs from -3 to 4
// and is initialized to zero.
RangeArray<int> ob(-3, 4, 0);

// Load the values -3 to 4 into ob.
for(int i = -3; i < 5; i++) ob[i] = i;
// ...
cout << ob[-2];
// ...
ob[2] = ob[-1] % 2;
```

As you might surmise, the first line constructs a **RangeArray** object that runs from –3 to 4, with each element in the array initialized to zero. The other lines of code illustrate that the array can be accessed via indices ranging from –3 to 4.

In general, **RangeArray** allows you to construct objects by specifying the lower and upper bounds of the array and the value that is used to initialize each element in the array. That is, **RangeArray** supports the following form of constructor:

RangeArray(*lowerbound*, *upperbound*, *initvalue*)

Once the array has been constructed, it can be indexed by any value that is within its range. This means that arbitrary indices, including negative indices, are allowed.

Because **RangeArray** is dynamic, it allows elements to be inserted or removed. When either of these operations occur, the array grows or shrinks as needed. The key point, however, is that the array can grow or shrink in either direction. If an element is added to the negative side, the negative side grows. If an element is removed from the positive side, the positive shrinks.

Before starting, it is necessary to point out that the implementation of the **RangeArray** container is, by intent, not optimized for high performance. Rather, it is optimized for clarity.

Its purpose is to clearly show the steps required to create a custom container. As such, it is designed for ease of understanding and straightforwardness of implementation. You might find it enjoyable to enhance its performance on your own.

The Entire RangeArray Class

To begin, the entire code for **RangeArray** is shown here. As you will find when you create your own container classes, even a simple container turns into a fairly large class. The reason for this is, of course, that several requirements must be met. While no single requirement is difficult, combined they present a fair bit of code. Don't be intimidated; each part is examined piece by piece in the sections that follow.

```
// A custom container that implements a
// range-selectable array.
//
// Call this file ra.h
//
#include <iostream>
#include <iterator>
#include <algorithm>
#include <cstdlib>
#include <stdexcept>

using namespace std;

// An exception class for RangeArray.
class RAExc {
  string err;
public:

  RAExc(string e) {
    err = e;
  }

  string geterr() { return err; }
};

// A range-selectable array container.
template<class T, class Allocator = allocator<T> >
class RangeArray {
  T *arrayptr; // pointer to array that underlies the container

  unsigned len;    // holds length of the container
  int upperbound; // lower bound
  int lowerbound; // upper bound
```

```
    Allocator a; // allocator
public:
  // Required typedefs for container.
  typedef T value_type;
  typedef Allocator allocator_type;
  typedef typename Allocator::reference reference;
  typedef typename Allocator::const_reference const_reference;
  typedef typename Allocator::size_type size_type;
  typedef typename Allocator::difference_type difference_type;
  typedef typename Allocator::pointer pointer;
  typedef typename Allocator::const_pointer const_pointer;

  // Forward iterators.
  typedef T * iterator;
  typedef const T * const_iterator;

  // Note: This container does not support reverse
  // iterators, but you can add them if you like.


  // *****  Constructors and Destructor *****

  // Default constructor.
  RangeArray()
  {
    upperbound = lowerbound = 0;
    len = 0;
    arrayptr = a.allocate(0);
  }

  // Construct an array of the specified range
  // with each element having the specified initial value.
  RangeArray(int low, int high, const T &t);

  // Construct zero-based array of num elements
  // with the value t. This constructor is required
  // for STL compatibility.
  RangeArray(int num, const T &t=T());

  // Construct from range of iterators.
  RangeArray(iterator start, iterator stop);

  // Copy constructor.
  RangeArray(const RangeArray &o);
```

```cpp
// Destructor.
~RangeArray();


// *****  Operator Functions *****

// Return reference to specified element.
T &operator[](int i)
{
  return arrayptr[i - lowerbound];
}


// Return const references to specified element.
const T &operator[](int i) const
{
  return arrayptr[i - lowerbound];
}


// Assign one container to another.
RangeArray &operator=(const RangeArray &o);


// *****  Insert Functions *****

// Insert val at p.
iterator insert(iterator p, const T &val);

// Insert num copies of val at p.
void insert(iterator p, int num, const T &val)
{
  for(; num>0; num--) p = insert(p, val) + 1;
}

// Insert range specified by start and stop at p.
void insert(iterator p, iterator start, iterator stop)
{
  while(start != stop) {
    p = insert(p, *start) + 1;
    start++;
  }
}


// *****  Erase Functions *****
```

```cpp
// Erase element at p.
iterator erase(iterator p);

// Erase specified range.
iterator erase(iterator start, iterator stop)
{
  iterator p = end();

  for(int i=stop-start; i > 0; i--)
    p = erase(start);

  return p;
}


// *****  Push and Pop Functions *****

// Add element to end.
void push_back(const T &val)
{
  insert(end(), val);
}

// Remove element from end.
void pop_back()
{
  erase(end()-1);
}

// Add element to front.
void push_front(const T &val)
{
  insert(begin(), val);
}

// Remove element from front.
void pop_front()
{
  erase(begin());
}


// *****  front() and back() functions *****

// Return reference to first element.
T &front()
```

```
{
  return arrayptr[0];
}

// Return const reference to first element.
const T &front() const
{
  return arrayptr[0];
}

// Return reference to last element.
T &back()
{
  return arrayptr[len-1];
}

// Return const reference to last element.
const T &back() const
{
  return arrayptr[len-1];
}


// *****  Iterator Functions *****

// Return iterator to first element.
iterator begin()
{
  return &arrayptr[0];
}

// Return iterator to last element.
iterator end()
{
  return &arrayptr[upperbound - lowerbound];
}

// Return const iterator to first element.
const_iterator begin() const
{
  return &arrayptr[0];
}

// Return const iterator to last element.
const_iterator end() const
```

```
{
  return &arrayptr[upperbound - lowerbound];
}


// *****  Misc. Functions *****

// The at() function performs a range check.
// Return a reference to the specified element.
T &at(int i)
{
  if(i < lowerbound || i >= upperbound)
    throw out_of_range("Index Out of Range");

  return arrayptr[i - lowerbound];
}

// Return a const reference to the specified element.
const T &at(int i) const
{
  if(i < lowerbound || i >= upperbound)
    throw out_of_range("Index Out of Range");

  return arrayptr[i - lowerbound];
}

// Return the size of the container.
size_type size() const
{
  return end() - begin();
}

// Return the maximum size of a RangeArray.
size_type max_size()
{
  return a.max_size();
}

// Return true if container is empty.
bool empty()
{
  return size() == 0;
}

// Exchange the values of two containers.
```

```cpp
  void swap(RangeArray &b)
  {
    RangeArray<T> tmp;

    tmp = *this;
    *this = b;
    b = tmp;
  }

  // Remove and destroy all elements.
  void clear()
  {
    erase(begin(), end());
  }

  // ***** Non-STL functions *****

  // Return endpoints.
  int getlowerbound()
  {
    return lowerbound;
  }

  int getupperbound()
  {
    return upperbound;
  }

};


// ***** Implementations of non-inline functions *****

// Construct an array of the specified range
// with each element having the specified initial value.
template <class T, class A>
RangeArray<T, A>::RangeArray(int low, int high,
                                 const T &t)
{
  if(high <= low) throw RAExc("Invalid Range");

  high++;

  // Save endpoints.
  upperbound = high;
```

```
    lowerbound = low;

    // Allocate memory for the container.
    arrayptr = a.allocate(high - low);

    // Save the length of the container.
    len = high - low;

    // Construct the elements.
    for(size_type i=0; i < size(); i++)
      a.construct(&arrayptr[i], t);
}


// Construct zero-based array of num elements
// with the value t. This constructor is required
// for STL compatibility.
template <class T, class A>
RangeArray<T, A>::RangeArray(int num, const T &t) {

  // Save endpoints.
  upperbound = num;
  lowerbound = 0;

  // Allocate memory for the container.
  arrayptr = a.allocate(num);

  // Save the length of the container.
  len = num;

  // Construct the elements.
  for(size_type i=0; i < size(); i++)
    a.construct(&arrayptr[i], t);

}


// Construct zero-based array from range of iterators.
// This constructor is required for STL compatibility.
template <class T, class A>
RangeArray<T, A>::RangeArray(iterator start,
                            iterator stop)
{
  // Allocate sufficient memory.
  arrayptr = a.allocate(stop - start);

  upperbound = stop - start;
```

```
  lowerbound = 0;

  len = stop - start;

  // Construct the elements using those
  // specified by the range of iterators.
  for(size_type i=0; i < size(); i++)
    a.construct(&arrayptr[i], *start++);
}

// Copy constructor.
template <class T, class A>
RangeArray<T, A>::RangeArray(const RangeArray<T, A> &o)
{
  // Allocate memory for the copy.
  arrayptr = a.allocate(o.size());

  upperbound = o.upperbound;
  lowerbound = o.lowerbound;
  len = o.len;

  // Make the copy.
  for(size_type i=0; i < size(); i++)
    a.construct(&arrayptr[i], o.arrayptr[i]);
}

// Destructor.
template <class T, class A>
RangeArray<T, A>::~RangeArray()
{
  // Call destructors for elements in the container.
  for(size_type i=0; i < size(); i++)
    a.destroy(&arrayptr[i]);

  // Release memory.
  a.deallocate(arrayptr, size());
}

// Assign one container to another.
template <class T, class A> RangeArray<T, A> &
RangeArray<T, A>::operator=(const RangeArray<T, A> &o)
{
  // Call destructors for elements in target container.
  for(size_type i=0; i < size(); i++)
    a.destroy(&arrayptr[i]);
```

```
  // Release original memory.
  a.deallocate(arrayptr, size());

  // Allocate memory for new size.
  arrayptr = a.allocate(o.size());

  upperbound = o.upperbound;
  lowerbound = o.lowerbound;
  len = o.len;

  // Make copy.
  for(size_type i=0; i < size(); i++)
    arrayptr[i] = o.arrayptr[i];

  return *this;
}

// Insert val at p.
template <class T, class A>
typename RangeArray<T, A>::iterator
RangeArray<T, A>::insert(iterator p, const T &val)
{
  iterator q;
  size_type i, j;

  // Get sufficient memory.
  T *tmp = a.allocate(size() + 1);

  // Copy existing elements to new array,
  // inserting new element if possible.
  for(i=j=0; i < size(); i++, j++) {
    if(&arrayptr[i] == p) {
      tmp[j] = val;
      q = &tmp[j];
      j++;
    }
    tmp[j] = arrayptr[i];
  }

  // Otherwise, the new element goes on end.
  if(p == end()) {
    tmp[j] = val;
    q = &tmp[j];
  }
```

```cpp
  // Adjust len and bounds.
  len++;
  if(p < &arrayptr[abs(lowerbound)])
    lowerbound--;
  else
    upperbound++;

  // Call destructors for elements in old container.
  for(size_type i=0; i < size()-1; i++)
    a.destroy(&arrayptr[i]);

  // Release memory for old container.
  a.deallocate(arrayptr, size()-1);

  arrayptr = tmp;

  return q;
}

// Erase element at p.
template <class T, class A>
typename RangeArray<T, A>::iterator
RangeArray<T, A>::erase(iterator p)
{
  iterator q = p;

  // Destruct element being erased.
  if(p != end()) a.destroy(p);

  // Adjust len and bounds.
  len--;
  if(p < &arrayptr[abs(lowerbound)])
    lowerbound++;
  else
    upperbound--;

  // Compact remaining elements.
  for( ; p < end(); p++)
    *p = *(p+1);

  return q;
}


// ********  Relational Operators **************
```

```cpp
template<class T, class Allocator>
  bool operator==(const RangeArray<T, Allocator> &a,
                  const RangeArray<T, Allocator> &b)
{
  if(a.size() != b.size()) return false;

  return equal(a.begin(), a.end(), b.begin());
}

template<class T, class Allocator>
  bool operator!=(const RangeArray<T, Allocator> &a,
                  const RangeArray<T, Allocator> &b)
{
  if(a.size() != b.size()) return true;

  return !equal(a.begin(), a.end(), b.begin());
}

template<class T, class Allocator>
  bool operator<(const RangeArray<T, Allocator> &a,
                 const RangeArray<T, Allocator> &b)
{
  return lexicographical_compare(a.begin(), a.end(),
                                 b.begin(), b.end());
}

template<class T, class Allocator>
  bool operator>(const RangeArray<T, Allocator> &a,
                 const RangeArray<T, Allocator> &b)
{
  return b < a;
}

template<class T, class Allocator>
  bool operator<=(const RangeArray<T, Allocator> &a,
                  const RangeArray<T, Allocator> &b)
{
  return !(a > b);
}

template<class T, class Allocator>
  bool operator>=(const RangeArray<T, Allocator> &a,
                  const RangeArray<T, Allocator> &b)
{
  return !(a < b);
}
```

As the comment at the beginning of the code indicates, you should put all of this code into a file called **ra.h**. It will be used by the sample programs shown later.

The preceding code contains two classes. The first is the **RAExc** exception class. This is the type of exception that is thrown if there is an attempt to create a **RangeArray** with invalid bounds, such as if the lower bound is greater than the upper bound. The second is the **RangeArray** container class, which we will examine closely in the sections that follow.

The RangeArray Class in Detail

Like all of the built-in STL sequence containers, **RangeArray** begins with the following template specification:

> template<class T, class Allocator = allocator<T> >

T is the type of data stored in the container and **Allocator** is the allocator, which defaults to the standard allocator.

The Private Members

The **RangeArray** array class begins with the following private declarations:

```
T *arrayptr; // pointer to array that underlies the container

unsigned len;    // holds length of the container
int upperbound; // lower bound
int lowerbound; // upper bound

Allocator a; // allocator
```

The pointer **arrayptr** stores a pointer to the memory that will contain an array of elements of type **T**. This memory will store the elements held by an object of type **RangeArray**. This array is indexed as usual, from zero. Indexes to a **RangeArray** object will be translated into zero-based indexes into the array pointed to by **arrayptr**.

The current length of a **RangeArray** is stored in **len**. The upper and lower bounds of the array are stored in **upperbound** and **lowerbound**, respectively. For the purposes of **RangeArray**, zero is counted as a positive value. The allocator for the container is stored in **a**.

The Required Type Definitions

After the private members, **RangeArray** defines the various **typedefs** required by all sequence containers, as shown here:

```
// Required typedefs for container.
typedef T value_type;
typedef Allocator allocator_type;
typedef typename Allocator::reference reference;
typedef typename Allocator::const_reference const_reference;
typedef typename Allocator::size_type size_type;
typedef typename Allocator::difference_type difference_type;
```

```
typedef typename Allocator::pointer pointer;
typedef typename Allocator::const_pointer const_pointer;

// Forward iterators.
typedef T * iterator;
typedef const T * const_iterator;
```

These **typedef**s are similar to the ones used by the built-in STL containers. Notice that the forward iterators are simply pointers to objects of type **T**. This is sufficient for the purposes of **RangeArray**, but it might not be for more complicated containers. Also, reverse iterators are not provided, but you might want to try adding them as an interesting exercise.

The RangeArray Constructors and Destructor

To create a compliant container, you must support the four constructors defined for sequence containers described earlier. **RangeArray** also defines a fifth constructor, which enables you to construct an array of a specified range. The constructors are shown here:

```
// Default constructor.
RangeArray()
{
  upperbound = lowerbound = 0;
  len = 0;
  arrayptr = a.allocate(0);
}

// Construct an array of the specified range
// with each element having the specified initial value.
template <class T, class A>
RangeArray<T, A>::RangeArray(int low, int high,
                            const T &t)
{
  if(high <= low) throw RAExc("Invalid Range");

  high++;

  // Save endpoints.
  upperbound = high;
  lowerbound = low;

  // Allocate memory for the container.
  arrayptr = a.allocate(high - low);

  // Save the length of the container.
  len = high - low;

  // Construct the elements.
```

```
    for(size_type i=0; i < size(); i++)
      a.construct(&arrayptr[i], t);
}


// Construct zero-based array of num elements
// with the value t. This constructor is required
// for STL compatibility.
template <class T, class A>
RangeArray<T, A>::RangeArray(int num, const T &t) {

  // Save endpoints.
  upperbound = num;
  lowerbound = 0;

  // Allocate memory for the container.
  arrayptr = a.allocate(num);

  // Save the length of the container.
  len = num;

  // Construct the elements.
  for(size_type i=0; i < size(); i++)
    a.construct(&arrayptr[i], t);

}


// Construct zero-based array from range of iterators.
// This constructor is required for STL compatibility.
template <class T, class A>
RangeArray<T, A>::RangeArray(iterator start,
                            iterator stop)
{
  // Allocate sufficient memory.
  arrayptr = a.allocate(stop - start);

  upperbound = stop - start;
  lowerbound = 0;

  len = stop - start;

  // Construct the elements using those
  // specified by the range of iterators.
  for(size_type i=0; i < size(); i++)
    a.construct(&arrayptr[i], *start++);
}
```

```
// Copy constructor.
template <class T, class A>
RangeArray<T, A>::RangeArray(const RangeArray<T, A> &o)
{
  // Allocate memory for the copy.
  arrayptr = a.allocate(o.size());

  upperbound = o.upperbound;
  lowerbound = o.lowerbound;
  len = o.len;

  // Make the copy.
  for(size_type i=0; i < size(); i++)
    a.construct(&arrayptr[i], o.arrayptr[i]);
}
```

The first constructor, which is the default constructor, creates an empty object. One of the constraints specified by the STL is that the result of calling **size( )** on a default object must be zero. Therefore, the default constructor sets the lower and upper bounds to zero. It also sets **len** to zero and constructs a zero-length array using the **allocate( )** function provided by the allocator. The last two steps ensure that a fully formed object exists in all cases.

The second constructor is unique to **RangeArray**. It creates an object with a specified range, with each element given the specified initial value. The lower bound is specified in the first parameter; the upper bound is specified in the second. Notice that a **RAExc** is thrown if the upper bound is less than or equal to the lower bound. The third parameter is passed the initialization value. Thus, this statement:

```
RangeArray<char> ch(-2, 10, 'X');
```

creates an array of characters that begins at –2 and runs through 10, with each element having the initial value of X. The array is allocated using **allocate( )**, which is a member function of the **allocator** class. To be a compliant container, you must use the allocator functions, rather than **new**, to obtain memory required by the container. Once allocated, each element in the array is constructed using the value passed as the third parameter. (Although it would be more convenient if the initialization value was allowed to default so that it would not always have to be specified, doing so would cause ambiguity with the third constructor, which is required by the STL.) The construction is accomplished using the allocator function **construct( )**, another allocator function.

The third constructor creates a zero-based array that has a specified number of elements, each initialized with a specified value. The initialization value can be allowed to default. This constructor is not particularly useful for **RangeArray** but is required by the STL container specification.

The fourth constructor creates a zero-based array from a range of values. The range is specified by passing an iterator to the beginning and end of the range. This constructor is also not particularly useful for **RangeArray** but is required by the STL container specification.

Last is the copy constructor. It allocates memory for the new object and then copies the bounds, the length, and elements from the source object. Thus, the copy has its own memory but is otherwise identical to the source.

The **RangeArray** destructor is shown here:

```
// Destructor.
template <class T, class A>
RangeArray<T, A>::~RangeArray()
{
  // Call destructors for elements in the container.
  for(size_type i=0; i < size(); i++)
    a.destroy(&arrayptr[i]);

  // Release memory.
  a.deallocate(arrayptr, size());
}
```

It first destroys each element in the array by calling the allocator's **destroy( )** function. It then frees the memory used by the array by calling the allocator's **deallocate( )** function.

Remember: the constructors for **RangeArray** do not use **new** to allocate memory. Nor does the destructor use **delete** to release memory. Instead, they use the appropriate member functions provided by the allocator. This approach lets the user specify an alternative means of managing memory for the container.

The RangeArray Operator Functions

There are three member operator functions defined by **RangeArray**. The first two are the **operator[ ]( )** functions shown here:

```
// Return reference to specified element.
T &operator[](int i)
{
  return arrayptr[i - lowerbound];
}

// Return const references to specified element.
const T &operator[](int i) const
{
  return arrayptr[i - lowerbound];
}
```

For a fully formed container, both **const** and non-**const** versions of the **[ ]** operator are required. These functions provide the mechanism by which the **RangeArray** can be indexed. Pay special attention to the way that **arrayptr** is indexed. Remember that **arrayptr** points to a standard C++ array. Thus, the index passed in **i** must be converted into a zero-based index into **arrayptr**. Recall that **lowerbound** holds the value that corresponds to the lowest index within the **RangeArray**. Thus, to obtain a zero-based index, **lowerbound** is subtracted from **i**.

One other point: notice that no bounds checking is performed by **operator[ ]( )**. Bounds checking by this operator is not required by the STL, and none is included here. This is reasonable because, aside from having a user-specifiable range, a **RangeArray** will behave just a like a normal array in this regard. (Remember, normal C++ arrays do not provide boundary checks.) Of course, if you want, you can add bounds checks to **operator[ ] ( )**.

The **operator=( )** function shown next is a bit more complex:

```
// Assign one container to another.
template <class T, class A> RangeArray<T, A> &
RangeArray<T, A>::operator=(const RangeArray<T, A> &o)
{
  // Call destructors for elements in target container.
  for(size_type i=0; i < size(); i++)
    a.destroy(&arrayptr[i]);

  // Release original memory.
  a.deallocate(arrayptr, size());

  // Allocate memory for new size.
  arrayptr = a.allocate(o.size());

  upperbound = o.upperbound;
  lowerbound = o.lowerbound;
  len = o.len;

  // Make copy.
  for(size_type i=0; i < size(); i++)
    arrayptr[i] = o.arrayptr[i];

  return *this;
}
```

It first destroys and frees any preexisting objects in the target object. It then allocates sufficient memory to hold the contents of the source object. Next, it sets the member variables appropriately and then copies the elements. Finally, a reference to the target object is returned.

The Insert Functions

The STL requires that a sequence container support three forms of **insert( )**: one that inserts a value, one that inserts multiple copies of a value, and one that inserts a range. The first version of **insert( )** is shown here:

```
// Insert val at p.
template <class T, class A>
typename RangeArray<T, A>::iterator
RangeArray<T, A>::insert(iterator p, const T &val)
{
  iterator q;
  size_type i, j;
```

```
  // Get sufficient memory.
  T *tmp = a.allocate(size() + 1);

  // Copy existing elements to new array,
  // inserting new element if possible.
  for(i=j=0; i < size(); i++, j++) {
    if(&arrayptr[i] == p) {
      tmp[j] = val;
      q = &tmp[j];
      j++;
    }
    tmp[j] = arrayptr[i];
  }


  // Otherwise, the new element goes on end.
  if(p == end()) {
    tmp[j] = val;
    q = &tmp[j];
  }


  // Adjust len and bounds.
  len++;
  if(p < &arrayptr[abs(lowerbound)])
    lowerbound--;
  else
    upperbound++;

  // Call destructors for elements in old container.
  for(size_type i=0; i < size()-1; i++)
    a.destroy(&arrayptr[i]);

  // Release memory for old container.
  a.deallocate(arrayptr, size()-1);

  arrayptr = tmp;

  return q;
}
```

The first version inserts an element at the location specified by the iterator passed as its first parameter. It returns an iterator to the inserted element. It operates by allocating a new segment of memory that is large enough to hold all of the existing elements plus the new one. It then copies the existing elements to the newly allocated memory, inserting the new element at the proper location. It then updates **len** and **upperbound** or **lowerbound** appropriately. Next, it destroys and deallocates the objects from the original **RangeArray** and assigns to **arrayptr** the address of the new memory. Finally, it returns a pointer to the inserted object.

Now, look closely at the code that updates the **lowerbound** or **upperbound** variable. Remember that the array can grow in either the positive or negative direction, based upon whether the new element is inserted on the positive side or the negative size of the array. Thus it is necessary to determine where the insertion takes place and change the proper value. This is determined by comparing the iterator passed in **p** to the address of the element at **arrayptr[lowerbound]**. If the iterator is less than that element, the negative side is expanding; otherwise, the positive end is growing.

The second two versions of **insert( )**, shown next, are defined in terms of the first:

```
// Insert num copies of val at p.
void insert(iterator p, int num, const T &val)
{
  for(; num>0; num--) p = insert(p, val) + 1;
}


// Insert range specified by start and stop at p.
void insert(iterator p, iterator start, iterator stop)
{
  while(start != stop) {
    p = insert(p, *start) + 1;
    start++;
  }
}
```

The Erase Functions

Sequence containers must support two **erase( )** functions. The first removes the element pointed to by an iterator. It returns an iterator to the element immediately after the one removed, or **end( )** if the last element is removed. This version is shown here:

```
// Erase element at p.
template <class T, class A>
typename RangeArray<T, A>::iterator
RangeArray<T, A>::erase(iterator p)
{
  iterator q = p;

  // Destruct element being erased.
  if(p != end()) a.destroy(p);

  // Adjust len and bounds.
  len--;
  if(p < &arrayptr[abs(lowerbound)])
    lowerbound++;
  else
    upperbound--;
```

```
  // Compact remaining elements.
  for( ; p < end(); p++)
    *p = *(p+1);

  return q;
}
```

This version operates by destroying the deleted element, adjusting the lower and upper bounds appropriately, and then compacting the remaining elements.

The second version, shown next, is framed in terms of the first. It removes a range of elements. It returns an iterator to the last element in the range (that is, the one pointed to by **stop**). Thus, it removes the elements between **start** and **stop**–1, inclusive.

```
// Erase specified range.
iterator erase(iterator start, iterator stop)
{
  iterator p = end();

  for(int i=stop-start; i > 0; i--)
    p = erase(start);

  return p;
}
```

The Push and Pop Functions

RangeArray implements **push_back( )**, **pop_back( )**, **push_front( )**, and **pop_front( )**, shown next. As you can see, they are implemented in terms of **insert( )** and **erase( )**, and their operation is straightforward.

```
// Add element to end.
void push_back(const T &val)
{
  insert(end(), val);
}

// Remove element from end.
void pop_back()
{
  erase(end()-1);
}

// Add element to front.
void push_front(const T &val)
{
  insert(begin(), val);
}
```

```
// Remove element from front.
void pop_front()
{
  erase(begin());
}
```

The front( ) and back( ) Functions

The **front( )** and **back( )** functions, shown here, simply return an iterator to the start or end of the array, respectively. Their implementation is straightforward. Notice, however, that both **const** and non-**const** versions are required.

```
// Return reference to first element.
T &front()
{
  return arrayptr[0];
}


// Return const reference to first element.
const T &front() const
{
  return arrayptr[0];
}


// Return reference to last element.
T &back()
{
  return arrayptr[len-1];
}


// Return const reference to last element.
const T &back() const
{
  return arrayptr[len-1];
}
```

The Iterator Functions

Because iterators for the **RangeArray** container are simply pointers into the memory pointed to by **arrayptr**, the iterator functions **begin( )** and **end( )** are trivial. Notice that both **const** and non-**const** versions are required.

```
// Return iterator to first element.
iterator begin()
{
  return &arrayptr[0];
}
```

```
// Return iterator to last element.
iterator end()
{
  return &arrayptr[upperbound - lowerbound];
}


// Return const iterator to first element.
const_iterator begin() const
{
  return &arrayptr[0];
}


// Return const iterator to last element.
const_iterator end() const
{
  return &arrayptr[upperbound - lowerbound];
}
```

Miscellaneous Functions

All sequence containers must implement **size( )**, **max_size( )**, **empty( )**, **swap( )**, and **clear( )**. These functions are shown here:

```
// Return the size of the container.
size_type size() const
{
  return end() - begin();
}


// Return the maximum size of a RangeArray.
size_type max_size()
{
  return a.max_size();
}


// Return true if container is empty.
bool empty()
{
  return size() == 0;
}


// Exchange the values of two containers.
void swap(RangeArray &b)
{
  RangeArray<T> tmp;
```

```
    tmp = *this;
    *this = b;
    b = tmp;
}


// Remove and destroy all elements.
void clear()
{
    erase(begin(), end());
}
```

In general, the operation of these functions is intuitive. However, **max_size( )** deserves a few words. It returns the number of elements of type **T** that can be held by the largest container that can be created. This value is obtained by calling the **max_size( )** function defined by the allocator.

RangeArray also implements the optional **at( )** function, shown next:

```
// The at() function performs a range check.
// Return a reference to the specified element.
T &at(int i)
{
    if(i < lowerbound || i >= upperbound)
        throw out_of_range("Index Out of Range");

    return arrayptr[i - lowerbound];
}


// Return a const reference to the specified element.
const T &at(int i) const
{
    if(i < lowerbound || i >= upperbound)
        throw out_of_range("Index Out of Range");

    return arrayptr[i - lowerbound];
}
```

The **at( )** function returns a reference to the element located at the specified index. It differs from **operator[ ]( )** only in that it performs a range check on the index. If the index is out of bounds, **at( )** throws an **out_of_range** exception. This exception is defined by C++ in the header **<stdexcept>**.

RangeArray also provides the non-STL functions **getlowerbound( )** and **getupperbound( )**. These obtain the lower and upper bounds, respectively, of the **RangeArray**. They are shown here:

```
// Return endpoints.
int getlowerbound()
{
    return lowerbound;
```

```
}

int getupperbound()
{
  return upperbound;
}
```

The Relational Operators

The relational operators defined for **RangeArray** are shown here:

```
template<class T, class Allocator>
  bool operator==(const RangeArray<T, Allocator> &a,
                  const RangeArray<T, Allocator> &b)
{
  if(a.size() != b.size()) return false;

  return equal(a.begin(), a.end(), b.begin());
}

template<class T, class Allocator>
  bool operator!=(const RangeArray<T, Allocator> &a,
                  const RangeArray<T, Allocator> &b)
{
  if(a.size() != b.size()) return true;

  return !equal(a.begin(), a.end(), b.begin());
}

template<class T, class Allocator>
  bool operator<(const RangeArray<T, Allocator> &a,
                 const RangeArray<T, Allocator> &b)
{
  return lexicographical_compare(a.begin(), a.end(),
                                 b.begin(), b.end());
}

template<class T, class Allocator>
  bool operator>(const RangeArray<T, Allocator> &a,
                 const RangeArray<T, Allocator> &b)
{
  return b < a;
}

template<class T, class Allocator>
  bool operator<=(const RangeArray<T, Allocator> &a,
                  const RangeArray<T, Allocator> &b)
```

```
{
  return !(a > b);
}

template<class T, class Allocator>
  bool operator>=(const RangeArray<T, Allocator> &a,
                  const RangeArray<T, Allocator> &b)
{
  return !(a < b);
}
```

Both **operator=( )** and **operator!=( )** use the **equal( )** algorithm to determine equality. As defined by **equal( )**, two objects are the same if each contains the same elements in the same order.

The < operator uses **lexicographical_compare( )** to determine when one object is less than another. The use of this function is recommended by Standard C++. It operates by comparing corresponding elements in the two sequences, searching for the first mismatch. If a mismatch is found, it returns true if the element from the first range is less than the element from the second range. It returns false otherwise.

Some RangeArray Sample Programs

To demonstrate **RangeArray**, three sample programs are shown. The first one, shown next, exercises the various member functions. It also employs three algorithms, a function object, and a binder. The use of these elements demonstrates that **RangeArray** is a fully functional container that is compatible with the rest of the STL.

```
// Demonstrate basic RangeArray operations.
#include <iostream>
#include <algorithm>
#include <functional>
#include "ra.h"
using namespace std;

// Display integers -- for use by for_each.
void display(int v)
{
  cout << v << " ";
}

int main()
{
  RangeArray<int> ob(-5, 5, 0);
  RangeArray<int>::iterator p;
  int i, sum;
```

```
cout << "Size of ob is: " << ob.size() << endl;

cout << "Initial contents of ob:\n";
for(i=-5; i <= 5; i++) cout << ob[i] << " ";
cout << endl;

// Give ob some values.
for(i=-5; i <= 5; i++) ob[i] = i;

cout << "New values for ob: \n";
p = ob.begin();
do {
  cout << *p++ << " ";
} while (p != ob.end());
cout << endl;

// Display sum of negative indexes.
sum = 0;
for(i = ob.getlowerbound(); i < 0; i++)
  sum += ob[i];
cout << "Sum of values with negative subscripts is: ";
cout << sum << "\n\n";

// Use copy() algorithm to copy one object to another.
cout << "Copy ob to ob2 using copy() algorithm.\n";

RangeArray<int> ob2(-5, 5, 0);
copy(ob.begin(), ob.end(), ob2.begin());

// Use for_each() algorithm to display ob2.
cout << "Contents of ob2: \n";
for_each(ob2.begin(), ob2.end(), display);
cout << "\n\n";

// Use replace_copy_if() algorithm to remove values less than zero.
cout << "Replace values less than zero with zero.\n";
cout << "Put the result into ob3.\n";
RangeArray<int> ob3(ob.begin(), ob.end());

// The next line uses the function object less() and
// the binder bind2nd().
replace_copy_if(ob.begin(), ob.end(), ob3.begin(),
                bind2nd(less<int>(), 0), 0);
cout << "Contents of ob3: \n";
for_each(ob3.begin(), ob3.end(), display);
```

```
      cout << "\n\n";

      cout << "Swap ob and ob3.\n";
      ob.swap(ob3); // swap ob and ob3
      cout << "Here is ob3:\n";
      for_each(ob3.begin(), ob3.end(), display);
      cout << endl;
      cout << "Swap again to restore.\n";
      ob.swap(ob3); // restore
      cout << "Here is ob3 after second swap:\n";
      for_each(ob3.begin(), ob3.end(), display);
      cout << "\n\n";

      // Use insert() member functions.
      cout << "Element at ob[0] is " << ob[0] << endl;
      cout << "Insert values into ob.\n";
      ob.insert(ob.end(), -9999);
      ob.insert(&ob[1], 99);
      ob.insert(&ob[-3], -99);
      for_each(ob.begin(), ob.end(), display);
      cout << endl;
      cout << "Element at ob[0] is " << ob[0] << "\n\n";

      cout << "Insert -7 three times to front of ob.\n";
      ob.insert(ob.begin(), 3, -7);
      for_each(ob.begin(), ob.end(), display);
      cout << endl;
      cout << "Element at ob[0] is " << ob[0] << "\n\n";

      // Use push_back() and pop_back().
      cout << "Push back the value 40 onto ob.\n";
      ob.push_back(40);
      for_each(ob.begin(), ob.end(), display);
      cout << endl;
      cout << "Pop back two values from ob.\n";
      ob.pop_back(); ob.pop_back();
      for_each(ob.begin(), ob.end(), display);
      cout << "\n\n";

      // Use push_front() and pop_front().
      cout << "Push front the value 19 onto ob.\n";
      ob.push_front(19);
      for_each(ob.begin(), ob.end(), display);
      cout << endl;
      cout << "Pop front two values from ob.\n";
```

```
ob.pop_front(); ob.pop_front();
for_each(ob.begin(), ob.end(), display);
cout << "\n\n";

// Use front() and back()
cout << "ob.front(): " << ob.front() << endl;
cout << "ob.back(): " << ob.back() << "\n\n";

// Use erase().
cout << "Erase element at 0.\n";
p = ob.erase(&ob[0]);
for_each(ob.begin(), ob.end(), display);
cout << endl;
cout << "Element at ob[0] is " << ob[0] << endl;
cout << endl;

cout << "Erase many elements in ob.\n";
p = ob.erase(&ob[-2], &ob[3]);
for_each(ob.begin(), ob.end(), display);
cout << endl;
cout << "Element at ob[0] is " << ob[0] << endl;
cout << endl;

cout << "Insert ob4 into ob.\n";
RangeArray<int> ob4(0, 2, 0);
for(i=0; i < 3; i++) ob4[i] = i+100;
ob.insert(&ob[0], ob4.begin(), ob4.end());
for_each(ob.begin(), ob.end(), display);
cout << endl;
cout << "Element at ob[0] is " << ob[0] << endl;
cout << endl;

cout << "Here is ob shown with its indices:\n";
for(i=ob.getlowerbound(); i<ob.getupperbound(); i++)
  cout << "[" << i << "]: " << ob[i] << endl;
cout << endl;

// Use the at() function.
cout << "Use the at() function.\n";
for(i=ob.getlowerbound(); i < ob.getupperbound(); i++)
  ob.at(i) = i * 11;

for(i=ob.getlowerbound(); i < ob.getupperbound(); i++)
  cout << ob.at(i) << " ";
cout << "\n\n";
```

```
    // Use the clear() function.
    cout << "Clear ob.\n";
    ob.clear();
    for_each(ob.begin(), ob.end(), display); // no effect!
    cout << "Size of ob after clear: " << ob.size()
         << "\nBounds: " << ob.getlowerbound()
         << " to " << ob.getupperbound() << "\n\n";

    // Create a copy of an object.
    cout << "Make a copy of ob2.\n";
    RangeArray<int> ob5(ob2);
    for_each(ob5.begin(), ob5.end(), display);
    cout << "\n\n";

    // Construct a new object from a range.
    cout << "Construct object from a range.\n";
    RangeArray<int> ob6(&ob2[-2], ob2.end());
    cout << "Size of ob6: " << ob6.size() << endl;
    for_each(ob6.begin(), ob6.end(), display);
    cout << endl;

    return 0;
}
```

The output from this program is shown here:

```
Size of ob is: 11
Initial contents of ob:
0 0 0 0 0 0 0 0 0 0 0
New values for ob:
-5 -4 -3 -2 -1 0 1 2 3 4 5
Sum of values with negative subscripts is: -15

Copy ob to ob2 using copy() algorithm.
Contents of ob2:
-5 -4 -3 -2 -1 0 1 2 3 4 5

Replace values less than zero with zero.
Put the result into ob3.
Contents of ob3:
0 0 0 0 0 0 1 2 3 4 5

Swap ob and ob3.
Here is ob3:
-5 -4 -3 -2 -1 0 1 2 3 4 5
Swap again to restore.
```

Here is ob3 after second swap:
0 0 0 0 0 0 1 2 3 4 5

Element at ob[0] is 0
Insert values into ob.
-5 -4 -99 -3 -2 -1 0 99 1 2 3 4 5 -9999
Element at ob[0] is 0

Insert -7 three times to front of ob.
-7 -7 -7 -5 -4 -99 -3 -2 -1 0 99 1 2 3 4 5 -9999
Element at ob[0] is 0

Push back the value 40 onto ob.
-7 -7 -7 -5 -4 -99 -3 -2 -1 0 99 1 2 3 4 5 -9999 40
Pop back two values from ob.
-7 -7 -7 -5 -4 -99 -3 -2 -1 0 99 1 2 3 4 5

Push front the value 19 onto ob.
19 -7 -7 -7 -5 -4 -99 -3 -2 -1 0 99 1 2 3 4 5
Pop front two values from ob.
-7 -7 -5 -4 -99 -3 -2 -1 0 99 1 2 3 4 5

ob.front(): -7
ob.back(): 5

Erase element at 0.
-7 -7 -5 -4 -99 -3 -2 -1 99 1 2 3 4 5
Element at ob[0] is 99

Erase many elements in ob.
-7 -7 -5 -4 -99 -3 3 4 5
Element at ob[0] is 3

Insert ob4 into ob.
-7 -7 -5 -4 -99 -3 100 101 102 3 4 5
Element at ob[0] is 100

Here is ob shown with its indices:
[-6]: -7
[-5]: -7
[-4]: -5
[-3]: -4
[-2]: -99
[-1]: -3
[0]: 100

```
[1]: 101
[2]: 102
[3]: 3
[4]: 4
[5]: 5

Use the at() function.
-66 -55 -44 -33 -22 -11 0 11 22 33 44 55

Clear ob.
Size of ob after clear: 0
Bounds: 0 to 0

Make a copy of ob2.
-5 -4 -3 -2 -1 0 1 2 3 4 5

Construct object from a range.
Size of ob6: 8
-2 -1 0 1 2 3 4 5
```

The next sample program demonstrates the relational operators:

```cpp
// Demonstrate the relational operators.
#include <iostream>
#include "ra.h"

using namespace std;

// Display integers -- for use by for_each.
void display(int v)
{
  cout << v << " ";
}

int main()
{
  RangeArray<int> ob1(-3, 2, 0), ob2(-3, 2, 0), ob3(-4, 4, 0);
  int i;

  // Give ob1 and ob2 some values.
  for(i = -3; i < 3; i++) {
    ob1[i] = i;
    ob2[i] = i;
```

```
}

cout << "Contents of ob1 and ob2:\n";
for(i=-3; i < 3; i++)
  cout << ob1[i] << " ";
cout << endl;

for(i=-3; i < 3; i++)
  cout << ob2[i] << " ";
cout << "\n\n";

if(ob1 == ob2) cout << "ob1 == ob2\n";
if(ob1 != ob2) cout << "error\n";
cout << endl;

cout << "Assign ob1[-1] the value 99\n";
ob1[-1] = 99;
cout << "Contents of ob1 are now:\n";
for(i=-3; i < 3; i++)
  cout << ob1[i] << " ";
cout << endl;

if(ob1 == ob2) cout << "error\n";
if(ob1 != ob2) cout << "ob1 != ob2\n";
cout << endl;

if(ob1 < ob2) cout << "ob1 < ob2\n";
if(ob1 <= ob2) cout << "ob1 <= ob2\n";
if(ob1 > ob2) cout << "ob1 > ob2\n";
if(ob1 >= ob2) cout << "ob1 >= ob2\n";

if(ob2 < ob1) cout << "ob2 < ob1\n";
if(ob2 <= ob1) cout << "ob2 <= ob1\n";
if(ob2 > ob1) cout << "ob2 > ob1\n";
if(ob2 >= ob1) cout << "ob2 >= ob1\n";
cout << endl;

// Compare objects of differing sizes.
if(ob3 != ob1) cout << "ob3 != ob1\n";
if(ob3 == ob1) cout << "ob3 == ob1\n";

return 0;
}
```

Its output is shown next:

```
Contents of ob1 and ob2:
-3 -2 -1 0 1 2
-3 -2 -1 0 1 2

ob1 == ob2

Assign ob1[-1] the value 99
Contents of ob1 are now:
-3 -2 99 0 1 2
ob1 != ob2

ob1 > ob2
ob1 >= ob2
ob2 < ob1
ob2 <= ob1

ob3 != ob1
```

The following program stores class objects in a **RangeArray**. It also illustrates when the constructor and destructor functions are called when various operations take place.

```cpp
// Store class objects in a RangeArray.
#include <iostream>
#include "ra.h"

using namespace std;

class test {
public:
  int a;

  test() { cout << "Constructing\n"; a=0; }

  test(const test &o) {
    cout << "Copy Constructor\n";
    a = o.a;
  }

  ~test() { cout << "Destructing\n"; }
};

int main()
```

```
{
  RangeArray<test> t(-3, 1, test());
  int i;

  cout << "Original contents of t:\n";
  for(i=-3; i < 2; i++) cout << t[i].a << " ";
  cout << endl;

  // Give t some new values.
  for(i=-3; i < 2; i++) t[i].a = i;

  cout << "New contents of t:\n";
  for(i=-3; i < 2; i++) cout << t[i].a << " ";
  cout << endl;

  // Copy to new container.
  RangeArray<test> t2(-7, 3, test());
  copy(t.begin(), t.end(), &t2[-2]);

  cout << "Contents of t2:\n";
  for(i=-7; i < 4; i++) cout << t2[i].a << " ";
  cout << endl;

  RangeArray<test> t3(t.begin()+1, t.end()-1);
  cout << "Contents of t3:\n";
  for(i=t3.getlowerbound(); i < t3.getupperbound(); i++)
    cout << t3[i].a << " ";
  cout << endl;

  t.clear();

  cout << "Size after clear(): " << t.size() << endl;

  // Assign container objects.
  t = t3;
  cout << "Contents of t:\n";
  for(i=t.getlowerbound(); i<t.getupperbound(); i++)
    cout << t[i].a << " ";
  cout << endl;

  return 0;
}
```

The output from this program is shown here:

```
Constructing
Copy Constructor
Copy Constructor
Copy Constructor
Copy Constructor
Copy Constructor
Destructing
Original contents of t:
0 0 0 0 0
New contents of t:
-3 -2 -1 0 1
Constructing
Copy Constructor
Copy Constructor
Copy Constructor
Copy Constructor
Copy Constructor
Copy Constructor
Copy Constructor
Copy Constructor
Copy Constructor
Copy Constructor
Destructing
Contents of t2:
0 0 0 0 0 -3 -2 -1 0 1 0
Copy Constructor
Copy Constructor
Copy Constructor
Contents of t3:
-2 -1 0
Destructing
Destructing
Destructing
Destructing
Destructing
Size after clear(): 0
Contents of t:
-2 -1 0
Destructing
Destructing
Destructing
Destructing
```

```
Destructing
Destructing
Destructing
Destructing
Destructing
Destructing
Destructing
Destructing
Destructing
Destructing
Destructing
Destructing
Destructing
```

Some Things to Try

You might want to try enhancing and experimenting with the **RangeArray** class. For example, you can add reverse iterators and the **rbegin( )** and **rend( )** functions. Here are some other ideas. Try optimizing the container. As stated, the code in **RangeArray** was designed for transparency of operation, not for speed, so it can be easily improved. For example, try allocating a little more memory than needed when constructing objects so that not all insert operations force a re-allocation. Try creating member functions that convert a **RangeArray** into a standard, zero-based array. Try adding a constructor that takes a standard array and an index as a parameter. Have the constructor convert the array into a **RangeArray**. Use the index as the location of zero. Finally, try using a **vector**, rather than a standard array, to hold the elements of the **RangeArray**. See if it simplifies the implementation. (You will be pleasantly surprised.)

A Mini C++ Interpreter

THE ART

OF

C++

The preceding chapters have shown the richness and power of the C++ language, focusing on the wide range of tasks to which it can be successfully applied. This, the final chapter of the book, examines C++ from a different point of view: the artistry of its design. At the base of C++'s power lies a profoundly elegant, logically consistent architecture. It is this solid framework that binds the individual features of C++ into a cohesive whole. It is also what gives C++ that rare, almost intangible, formal beauty that all programmers intuitively recognize.

To explore the elegant design of C++, this chapter develops a program that understands a portion of the language. There are two types of programs that are capable of doing this: compilers and interpreters. Although creating a compiler for C++ is far beyond the scope of this book, creating an interpreter is a more manageable task. Therefore, this chapter develops an interpreter for a subset of C++. This interpreter is called *Mini C++*. Because Mini C++ interprets the C++ language, its implementation illustrates in concrete terms the reasons and rationale behind the C++ syntax.

In addition to demonstrating the logically consistent nature of C++, Mini C++ provides a second benefit: it gives you an execution engine that you can enhance or adapt as desired. For example, you can expand Mini C++ to interpret a larger subset of C++, or you can adapt it to interpret a different computer language altogether. You can even use it as a test bench for trying out a computer language of your own design. Its uses are limited only by your imagination.

Interpreters versus Compilers

Before we begin, it is necessary to explain what an interpreter is and how it differs from a compiler. Although both compilers and interpreters take as input the source code for a program, what they do with that source code differs significantly.

A compiler converts the source code of a program into an executable form. Often, as is the case with C++, this executable form consists of actual CPU instructions that are directly executed by the computer. In other cases, the output of a compiler is a portable intermediate form, which is then executed by a runtime system. For example, Java compiles to an intermediate form called *bytecode*, which is then executed by the Java Virtual Machine.

An interpreter works in a completely different way. It reads the source code to a program, executing each statement as it is encountered. Thus, an interpreter does not translate the source code into executable code. Instead, the interpreter directly executes the program. The main drawback to interpretation is loss of execution speed. A program that is interpreted executes more slowly than it does in its compiled form.

Sometimes the term *interpreter* is used in situations other than that just described. For example, the original Java Virtual Machine was called a *bytecode interpreter*. This *is not* the same type of interpreter developed in this chapter. The interpreter developed here is a *source code* interpreter, which means that it executes a program simply by reading its source code.

Although compiled programs execute faster than interpreted ones, interpreters are still commonly used in programming for the following reasons. First, they can provide a truly interactive environment in which program execution can be paused and resumed through user interaction. Such an interactive environment is well suited to robotics, for example. Second, because of the nature of language interpreters, they are especially well suited for interactive debugging. Third, interpreters are excellent for "script languages," such as query languages for databases. Fourth, they allow the same program to run on a variety of different platforms. Only the interpreter's runtime package must be implemented for each new environment.

There is another reason that interpreters are interesting: they are easy to modify, alter, or enhance. This means if you want to create, experiment with, or control your own language, it is easier to do so with an interpreter than with a compiler. Interpreters make great language prototyping environments because you can make a change to the language and quickly see the results.

Of course, for the purposes of this chapter, the greatest benefit of an interpreter is that it enables you to see the inner workings of C++ firsthand.

An Overview of Mini C++

Mini C++ consists of a large amount of code. Before beginning, it will be helpful for you to understand in general how Mini C++ is organized. Mini C++ contains three major subsystems: the expression parser, which handles numeric expressions; the interpreter, which actually executes the program; and a set of library functions.

The expression parser evaluates a numeric expression and returns the result. The expression can contain constants such as 10 or 88, variables, function calls, and, of course, operators. For example:

    x + num / 32

is an expression.

The interpreter module executes a C++ program. The interpreter works by reading the source code one token at a time. When it encounters a keyword, it does whatever that keyword requests. For example, when the interpreter reads an **if**, it processes the condition specified by the **if**. If that condition is true, the interpreter executes the block of code associated with the **if**. Interpretation continues until the end of the program is reached.

The library subsystem defines those functions that are built into Mini C++. Thus, they constitute the Mini C++ "standard library." Only a handful of library functions are included in this chapter, but you can easily add as many others as you like. In general, the Mini C++ library functions serve the same purpose as the real C++ library functions.

Mini C++ organizes these subsystems into the files shown here:

Subsystem	File Name
Parser	parser.cpp
Interpreter	minicpp.cpp
Library	libcpp.cpp

Mini C++ also uses the header file **mccommon.h**.

The Mini C++ Specifications

Despite the fact that C++ has relatively few keywords, it is a very rich and complicated language. It would take far more than a single chapter to describe and implement an interpreter for all of C++. Instead, Mini C++ understands a fairly narrow subset of the language. However, this particular subset includes many of C++'s most important features. For example, Mini C++ supports recursive functions, global and local variables, nested scopes, and most control statements. A list of all supported features is shown here:

- ▶ Parameterized functions with local variables
- ▶ Nested scopes
- ▶ Recursion
- ▶ The **if** statement
- ▶ The **switch** statement
- ▶ The **do-while**, **while**, and **for** loops
- ▶ The **break** statement
- ▶ Local and global variables of type **int** and **char**
- ▶ Function parameters of type **int** and **char**
- ▶ Integer and character constants
- ▶ String constants (limited implementation)
- ▶ The **return** statement, both with and without a value
- ▶ A handful of standard library functions
- ▶ The operators +, –, *, /, %, <, >, <=, >=, ==, !=, ++, – –, unary –, and unary +
- ▶ Functions returning integers
- ▶ /* and // comments
- ▶ Console I/O via **cin** and **cout**

Even though this list may seem short, it takes a relatively large amount of code to implement it. One reason for this is that a substantial "price of admission" must be paid when interpreting a language such as C++. Although the features just listed describe only a small subset of the C++ language, they do enable the interpreter to handle the core of the language, including its basic syntax, control statements, expressions, and function-call mechanisms. Thus, Mini C++ handles what one might call the "backbone" of the language.

As you no doubt noticed, Mini C++ does not support **class**. The reason for this is simply one of practicality. Supporting **class** implies that the interpreter also supports user-defined types, object instantiation, and the dot (.) operator. Furthermore, **class** requires that the interpreter understand **public** and **private**. Although these features are not in themselves difficult for an interpreter to handle, collectively they cause the code for the interpreter to grow to a size that is far too big to present in a single chapter. Once you understand how the interpreter works, you might find it enjoyable to add support for **class** on your own.

Other features not supported include function and operator overloading, templates, namespaces, exceptions, the preprocessor, structures, unions, and bitfields. Again, it is not difficult to interpret these features, but doing so causes the code to grow unacceptably long for use in a book format. Adding support for these features does make for an interesting project that you might enjoy on your own, however.

Some Mini C++ Restrictions

Even by implementing a relatively small subset of C++, the source code for Mini C++ is still quite long. In order to prevent it from growing even longer, a few restrictions have been imposed on the C++ grammar. The first is that the targets of **if, while, do,** and **for** must be blocks of code surrounded by beginning and ending braces. You cannot use a single statement. For example, Mini C++ will not correctly interpret code such as this:

```
for(a=0; a < 10; a++)
  for(b=0; b < 10; b++)
    for(c=0; c < 10; c++)
      cout << "hi";


if(...)
   if(...) x = 10;
```

Instead, you must write the code like this:

```
for(a=0; a < 10; a++) {
  for(b=0; b < 10; b++) {
    for(c=0; c < 10; c++) {
      cout << "hi";
    }
  }
}


if(...) {
  if(...) {
    x = 10;;
  }
}
```

This restriction makes it easier for the interpreter to find the end of the code that forms the target to one of these program control statements. However, because the objects of the program control statements are often blocks of code anyway, this restriction does not seem too harsh. (With a little effort, you can remove this restriction, if you like.)

Another restriction is that prototypes are not supported. All functions are assumed to return an integer type (**char** return types are allowed but elevated to **int**), and no parameter type checking is performed. Furthermore, because function overloading is not supported, there must be one and only one version of a function.

The **switch** statement is fully implemented except that it does not support the **default** statement. This restriction was made to reduce the size and complexity of the code needed to interpret a **switch** statement. (The **switch** is one of the more complex statements to interpret.) Support for **default** is something that you might want to try adding on your own.

Finally, all functions must be preceded by either an **int** or **char** type specifier. Therefore, the Mini C++ interpreter does not support a **void** return type. Thus, this declaration is valid:

```
int f()
{
  // ...
}
```

But this one isn't:

```
void f()
{
  // ...
}
```

An Informal Theory of C++

In order to best understand the operation of Mini C++, it is necessary to understand how the C++ language is structured. If you have ever seen a formal specification for the C++ language (such as that found in the ANSI/ISO C++ standard), you know that it is quite long and filled with rather cryptic statements. Don't worry—you won't need to deal this formally with the C++ language to understand Mini C++. The parts of C++ that Mini C++ interprets are easy to understand. That said, you will still need a basic understanding of how the C++ language is defined. For our purposes, the informal discussion that follows is sufficient. Keep in mind, however, that it intentionally simplifies a few concepts.

A C++ program consists of a collection of one or more functions, plus global variables (if any exist). A *function* is composed of a function name, its parameter list, and its body, which is a block of code. A *block* begins with a { , is followed by one or more statements, and ends with a }. A block (also called a compound statement) creates a scope. In general, a *statement* is either an expression, a nested code block, or begins with a keyword, such as **if**, **for**, or **int**. A nested block creates a nested scope.

NOTE

Although the preceding categories of statements (keyword, block, and expression) are sufficient for the purposes of understanding Mini C++, it is interesting to note that the ANSI/ISO standard for C++ uses a more finely grained definition. It defines statements as labeled, expression, compound, selection, iteration, jump, declaration, and try-block.

A C++ program begins with a call to **main( )**. It ends when either the last } or a **return** has been encountered in **main( )**—assuming that **exit( )** or **abort( )** has not been called elsewhere. Any other functions contained in the program must either be directly or indirectly called by **main( )**. Thus, when Mini C++ executes a program, it simply starts at the **main( )** function and stops when **main( )** ends.

C++ Expressions

At the foundation of C++ is the expression, because much of the action in a program takes place through one. To understand why, recall that C++ has three main categories of statements: keyword, block, and expression. This implies that any statement that is not based on a keyword or does not define a block is, by definition, an *expression statement*. Therefore, the following statements are all expressions:

```
count = 100;              // line 1
sample = i / 22 * (c-10); // line 2
num = abs(count) * 2;     // line 3
strcpy(str1, str2);       // line 4
```

Let's look more closely at each of these expression statements. In C++, the equal sign is an *assignment operator*. This is important. C++ does not treat assignment as a separate type of statement as some languages do. Instead, the equal sign is an assignment operator, and the value produced by the assignment operation is equal to that produced by the right side of the expression. Therefore, an assignment statement is actually an *assignment expression* in C++. Because it is an expression, it has a value. This is why it is legal to write expressions such as the following:

```
a = b = c = 100;
if( (a=4+5) == 0 ) ...;
```

The reason these work is that an assignment is an operation that produces a value.

Line 2 shows a more complex assignment expression. In this case, the value of the expression on the right is computed and assigned to **sample**.

In line 3, **abs( )** is called to return the absolute value of its argument. Thus, the use of a function in an expression causes that function to be called.

As line 4 shows, even a function call, by itself, is an expression. In this case, **strcpy( )** is called to copy the contents of one string to another. Even though the value returned by **strcpy( )** is ignored, the call to **strcpy( )** still constitutes an expression.

Defining an Expression

To handle the evaluation of expressions, Mini C++ uses an *expression parser*. Before you can understand the operation of the expression parser, you need to know how expressions are constructed. In virtually all computer languages, expressions are described using a set of *production rules*, which define the interaction of operands with operators. The production rules that define Mini C++ expressions are shown here:

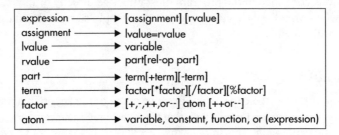

Here, *rel-op* refers to any of C++'s relational operators. The terms *lvalue* and *rvalue* refer to objects that can occur on the left side and right side of an assignment statement, respectively. The arrow means "produces." One thing that you should be aware of is that the precedence of the operators is built into the production rules. The higher the precedence, the further down the list the operator will be. As the production rules show, Mini C++ supports the following operators:

+	_	*	/	%	++	--
<	<=	>	>=	==	!=	()

To see how these rules work let's evaluate this C++ expression:

```
count = 10 - 5 * 3;
```

First, apply rule 1, which dissects the expression into these three parts:

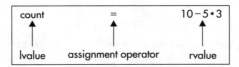

Since there are no relational operators in the "rvalue" part of the subexpression, the term production rule is invoked.

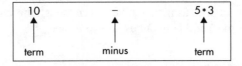

Of course, the second term is composed of the factors 5 and 3. These two factors are constants and represent the lowest level of the production rules. Next, begin moving back up the rules to compute the value of the expression. First, multiply 5*3, which yields 15. Next, subtract that value from 10, yielding −5. Finally, this value is assigned to **count** and is also the value of the entire expression. The Mini C++ expression parser evaluates expressions in the same way. It simply implements the production rules.

Because the expression parser is so important to Mini C++, it is where we will begin.

The Expression Parser

The piece of code that reads and analyzes expressions is called an *expression parser*. Without a doubt, the expression parser is the single most important subsystem needed by Mini C++. Because C++ defines expressions more broadly than do many other languages, a substantial amount of the code that constitutes a C++ program is executed by the expression parser.

There are several different ways to design an expression parser for C++. Many commercial compilers use a *table-driven parser*, which is usually created by a parser-generator program. While table-driven parsers are generally faster than other methods, they are hard to create by hand. Mini C++ uses a *recursive-descent parser*, which implements in logic the production rules discussed in the previous section.

A recursive-descent parser is essentially a collection of mutually recursive functions that process an expression. If the parser is used in a compiler, then it generates the proper object code that corresponds to the source code. However, in an interpreter, the parser evaluates a given expression. In this section, the Mini C++ parser is developed.

NOTE

I have written extensively about expression parsing over the years. For an in-depth look at the process as it relates to C++, refer to my book C++: The Complete Reference, McGraw-Hill/Osborne.

The Parser Code

The entire code for the Mini C++ recursive-descent parser is shown here. This code should be put into the file **parser.cpp**. The operation of the parser is explained in the sections that follow.

```
// Recursive descent parser for integer expressions.
//
#include <iostream>
#include <cstring>
#include <cstdlib>
#include <cctype>
#include "mccommon.h"

using namespace std;

// Keyword lookup table.
// Keywords must be entered lowercase.
struct commands {
  char command[20];
```

```
    token_ireps tok;
} com_table[] = {
  "if", IF,
  "else", ELSE,
  "for", FOR,
  "do", DO,
  "while", WHILE,
  "char", CHAR,
  "int", INT,
  "return", RETURN,
  "switch", SWITCH,
  "break", BREAK,
  "case", CASE,
  "cout", COUT,
  "cin", CIN,
  "", END  // mark end of table
};

// This structure links a library function name
// with a pointer to that function.
struct intern_func_type {
  char *f_name; // function name
  int (*p)();   // pointer to the function
} intern_func[] = {
  "getchar", call_getchar,
  "putchar", call_putchar,
  "abs", call_abs,
  "rand", call_rand,
  "", 0  // null terminate the list
};

// Entry point into parser.
void eval_exp(int &value)
{
  get_token();

  if(!*token) {
    throw InterpExc(NO_EXP);
  }

  if(*token == ';') {
    value = 0; // empty expression
    return;
  }
```

```
    eval_exp0(value);

    putback(); // return last token read to input stream
}

// Process an assignment expression.
void eval_exp0(int &value)
{
  // temp holds name of var receiving the assignment.
  char temp[MAX_ID_LEN+1];

  tok_types temp_tok;

  if(token_type == IDENTIFIER) {
    if(is_var(token)) { // if a var, see if assignment
      strcpy(temp, token);
      temp_tok = token_type;
      get_token();
      if(*token == '=') { // is an assignment
        get_token();
        eval_exp0(value); // get value to assign
        assign_var(temp, value); // assign the value
        return;
      }
      else { // not an assignment
        putback(); // restore original token
        strcpy(token, temp);
        token_type = temp_tok;
      }
    }
  }
  eval_exp1(value);
}

// Process relational operators.
void eval_exp1(int &value)
{
  int partial_value;
  char op;
  char relops[] = {
    LT, LE, GT, GE, EQ, NE, 0
  };

  eval_exp2(value);
```

```
    op = *token;
    if(strchr(relops, op)) {
      get_token();
      eval_exp2(partial_value);

      switch(op) { // perform the relational operation
        case LT:
          value = value < partial_value;
          break;
        case LE:
          value = value <= partial_value;
          break;
        case GT:
          value = value > partial_value;
          break;
        case GE:
          value = value >= partial_value;
          break;
        case EQ:
          value = value == partial_value;
          break;
        case NE:
          value = value != partial_value;
          break;
      }
    }
}

// Add or subtract two terms.
void eval_exp2(int &value)
{
  char  op;
  int partial_value;
  char okops[] = {
    '(', INC, DEC, '-', '+', 0
  };

  eval_exp3(value);

  while((op = *token) == '+' || op == '-') {
    get_token();

    if(token_type == DELIMITER &&
       !strchr(okops, *token))
        throw InterpExc(SYNTAX);
```

```cpp
    eval_exp3(partial_value);

    switch(op) { // add or subtract
      case '-':
        value = value - partial_value;
        break;
      case '+':
        value = value + partial_value;
        break;
    }
  }
}


// Multiply or divide two factors.
void eval_exp3(int &value)
{
  char  op;
  int partial_value, t;
  char okops[] = {
    '(', INC, DEC, '-', '+', 0
  };

  eval_exp4(value);

  while((op = *token) == '*' || op == '/'
        || op == '%') {
    get_token();

    if(token_type == DELIMITER &&
       !strchr(okops, *token))
         throw InterpExc(SYNTAX);

    eval_exp4(partial_value);

    switch(op) { // mul, div, or modulus
      case '*':
        value = value * partial_value;
        break;
      case '/':
        if(partial_value == 0)
          throw InterpExc(DIV_BY_ZERO);
        value = (value) / partial_value;
        break;
      case '%':
        t = (value) / partial_value;
```

```cpp
          value = value - (t * partial_value);
          break;
      }
    }
}


// Is a unary +, -, ++, or --.
void eval_exp4(int &value)
{
  char  op;
  char temp;

  op = '\0';
  if(*token == '+' || *token == '-' ||
     *token == INC || *token == DEC)
  {
    temp = *token;
    op = *token;
    get_token();
    if(temp == INC)
      assign_var(token, find_var(token)+1);
    if(temp == DEC)
      assign_var(token, find_var(token)-1);
  }

  eval_exp5(value);
  if(op == '-') value = -(value);
}

// Process parenthesized expression.
void eval_exp5(int &value)
{

  if((*token == '(')) {
    get_token();

    eval_exp0(value); // get subexpression

    if(*token != ')')
      throw InterpExc(PAREN_EXPECTED);
    get_token();
  }
  else
    atom(value);
}
```

```cpp
// Find value of number, variable, or function.
void atom(int &value)
{
  int i;
  char temp[MAX_ID_LEN+1];

  switch(token_type) {
    case IDENTIFIER:
      i = internal_func(token);
      if(i != -1) {
        // Call "standard library" function.
        value = (*intern_func[i].p)();
      }
      else if(find_func(token)) {
        // Call programmer-created function.
        call();
        value = ret_value;
      }
      else {
        value = find_var(token); // get var's value
        strcpy(temp, token); // save variable name

        // Check for ++ or --.
        get_token();
        if(*token == INC || *token == DEC) {
          if(*token == INC)
            assign_var(temp, find_var(temp)+1);
          else
            assign_var(temp, find_var(temp)-1);
        } else putback();
      }

      get_token();
      return;
    case NUMBER: // is numeric constant
      value = atoi(token);
      get_token();

      return;
    case DELIMITER: // see if character constant
      if(*token == '\'') {
        value = *prog;
        prog++;
        if(*prog!='\'')
          throw InterpExc(QUOTE_EXPECTED);
```

```
          prog++;
          get_token();

          return ;
        }
      if(*token==')') return; // process empty expression
      else throw InterpExc(SYNTAX);  // otherwise, syntax error
    default:
      throw InterpExc(SYNTAX); // syntax error
  }
}


// Display an error message.
void sntx_err(error_msg error)
{
  char *p, *temp;
  int linecount = 0;

  static char *e[]= {
    "Syntax error",
    "No expression present",
    "Not a variable",
    "Duplicate variable name",
    "Duplicate function name",
    "Semicolon expected",
    "Unbalanced braces",
    "Function undefined",
    "Type specifier expected",
    "Return without call",
    "Parentheses expected",
    "While expected",
    "Closing quote expected",
    "Division by zero",
    "{ expected (control statements must use blocks)",
    "Colon expected"
  };

  // Display error and line number.
  cout << "\n" << e[error];
  p = p_buf;
  while(p != prog) { // find line number of error
    p++;
    if(*p == '\r') {
      linecount++;
    }
```

```
  }
  cout << " in line " << linecount << endl;

  temp = p;
  while(p > p_buf && *p != '\n') p--;

  // Display offending line.
  while(p <= temp)
    cout << *p++;

  cout << endl;
}

// Get a token.
tok_types get_token()
{

  char *temp;

  token_type = UNDEFTT; tok = UNDEFTOK;

  temp = token;
  *temp = '\0';

  // Skip over white space.
  while(isspace(*prog) && *prog) ++prog;

  // Skip over newline.
  while(*prog == '\r') {
    ++prog;
    ++prog;
    // Again, skip over white space.
    while(isspace(*prog) && *prog) ++prog;
  }

  // Check for end of program.
  if(*prog == '\0') {
    *token = '\0';
    tok = END;
    return (token_type = DELIMITER);
  }

  // Check for block delimiters.
  if(strchr("{}", *prog)) {
    *temp = *prog;
```

```
    temp++;
    *temp = '\0';
    prog++;
    return (token_type = BLOCK);
  }

  // Look for comments.
  if(*prog == '/')
    if(*(prog+1) == '*') { // is a /* comment
      prog += 2;
      do { // find end of comment
        while(*prog != '*') prog++;
        prog++;
      } while (*prog != '/');
      prog++;
      return (token_type = DELIMITER);
    } else if(*(prog+1) == '/') { // is a // comment
      prog += 2;
      // Find end of comment.
      while(*prog != '\r' && *prog != '\0') prog++;
      if(*prog == '\r') prog +=2;
      return (token_type = DELIMITER);
    }

  // Check for double-ops.
  if(strchr("!<>=+-", *prog)) {
    switch(*prog) {
      case '=':
        if(*(prog+1) == '=') {
          prog++; prog++;
          *temp = EQ;
          temp++; *temp = EQ; temp++;
          *temp = '\0';
        }
        break;
      case '!':
        if(*(prog+1) == '=') {
          prog++; prog++;
          *temp = NE;
          temp++; *temp = NE; temp++;
          *temp = '\0';
        }
        break;
      case '<':
        if(*(prog+1) == '=') {
```

```
    prog++; prog++;
    *temp = LE; temp++; *temp = LE;
  }
  else if(*(prog+1) == '<') {
    prog++; prog++;
    *temp = LS; temp++; *temp = LS;
  }
  else {
    prog++;
    *temp = LT;
  }
  temp++;
  *temp = '\0';
  break;
case '>':
  if(*(prog+1) == '=') {
    prog++; prog++;
    *temp = GE; temp++; *temp = GE;
  } else if(*(prog+1) == '>') {
    prog++; prog++;
    *temp = RS; temp++; *temp = RS;
  }
  else {
    prog++;
    *temp = GT;
  }
  temp++;
  *temp = '\0';
  break;
case '+':
  if(*(prog+1) == '+') {
    prog++; prog++;
    *temp = INC; temp++; *temp = INC;
    temp++;
    *temp = '\0';
  }
  break;
case '-':
  if(*(prog+1) == '-') {
    prog++; prog++;
    *temp = DEC; temp++; *temp = DEC;
    temp++;
    *temp = '\0';
  }
  break;
```

```
    }

    if(*token) return(token_type = DELIMITER);
  }

  // Check for other delimiters.
  if(strchr("+-*^/%=;:(),'", *prog)) {
    *temp = *prog;
    prog++;
    temp++;
    *temp = '\0';
    return (token_type = DELIMITER);
  }

  // Read a quoted string.
  if(*prog == '"') {
    prog++;
    while(*prog != '"' && *prog != '\r' && *prog) {
      // Check for \n escape sequence.
      if(*prog == '\\') {
        if(*(prog+1) == 'n') {
          prog++;
          *temp++ = '\n';
        }
      }
      else if((temp - token) < MAX_T_LEN)
        *temp++ = *prog;

      prog++;
    }
    if(*prog == '\r' || *prog == 0)
      throw InterpExc(SYNTAX);
    prog++; *temp = '\0';
    return (token_type = STRING);
  }

  // Read an integer number.
  if(isdigit(*prog)) {
    while(!isdelim(*prog)) {
      if((temp - token) < MAX_ID_LEN)
        *temp++ = *prog;
      prog++;
    }
    *temp = '\0';
    return (token_type = NUMBER);
```

```
    }

    // Read identifier or keyword.
    if(isalpha(*prog)) {
      while(!isdelim(*prog)) {
        if((temp - token) < MAX_ID_LEN)
          *temp++ = *prog;
        prog++;
      }
      token_type = TEMP;
    }

    *temp = '\0';

    // Determine if token is a keyword or identifier.
    if(token_type == TEMP) {
      tok = look_up(token); // convert to internal form
      if(tok) token_type = KEYWORD; // is a keyword
      else token_type = IDENTIFIER;
    }

    // Check for unidentified character in file.
    if(token_type == UNDEFTT)
      throw InterpExc(SYNTAX);

    return token_type;
}

// Return a token to input stream.
void putback()
{
  char *t;

  t = token;
  for(; *t; t++) prog--;
}

// Look up a token's internal representation in the
// token table.
token_ireps look_up(char *s)
{
  int i;
  char *p;

  // Convert to lowercase.
```

```
  p = s;
  while(*p) { *p = tolower(*p); p++; }

  // See if token is in table.
  for(i=0; *com_table[i].command; i++) {
    if(!strcmp(com_table[i].command, s))
      return com_table[i].tok;
  }

  return UNDEFTOK; // unknown command
}

// Return index of internal library function or -1 if
// not found.
int internal_func(char *s)
{
  int i;

  for(i=0; intern_func[i].f_name[0]; i++) {
    if(!strcmp(intern_func[i].f_name, s))  return i;
  }
  return -1;
}

// Return true if c is a delimiter.
bool isdelim(char c)
{
  if(strchr(" !:;,+-<>'/*%^=()", c) || c == 9 ||
     c == '\r' || c == 0) return true;
  return false;
}
```

The parser uses the following global variables and enumerations (which are declared within the **mccommon.h** header file shown later in this chapter):

```
const int MAX_T_LEN  = 128;   // max token length
const int MAX_ID_LEN = 31;    // max identifier length

// Enumeration of token types.
enum tok_types { UNDEFTT, DELIMITER, IDENTIFIER,
                 NUMBER, KEYWORD, TEMP, STRING, BLOCK };

// Enumeration of internal representation of tokens.
enum token_ireps { UNDEFTOK, ARG, CHAR, INT, SWITCH,
                   CASE, IF, ELSE, FOR, DO, WHILE, BREAK,
                   RETURN, COUT, CIN, END };
```

```
// Enumeration of two-character operators, such as <=.
enum double_ops { LT=1, LE, GT, GE, EQ, NE, LS, RS, INC, DEC };

// These are the constants used when throwing a
// syntax error exception.
//
// NOTE: SYNTAX is a generic error message used when
// nothing else seems appropriate.
enum error_msg
     { SYNTAX, NO_EXP, NOT_VAR, DUP_VAR, DUP_FUNC,
       SEMI_EXPECTED, UNBAL_BRACES, FUNC_UNDEF,
       TYPE_EXPECTED, RET_NOCALL, PAREN_EXPECTED,
       WHILE_EXPECTED, QUOTE_EXPECTED, DIV_BY_ZERO,
       BRACE_EXPECTED, COLON_EXPECTED };

extern char *prog;  // current location in source code
extern char *p_buf; // points to start of program buffer

extern char token[MAX_T_LEN+1]; // string version of token
extern tok_types token_type; // contains type of token
extern token_ireps tok; // internal representation of token

extern int ret_value; // function return value

// Exception class for Mini C++.
class InterpExc {
  error_msg err;
public:
  InterpExc(error_msg e) { err = e; }
  error_msg get_err() { return err; }
};
```

The location in the source code at which execution is currently occurring is pointed to by **prog**. Thus, **prog** holds the address at which the next piece of the program will be read by the interpreter. The **p_buf** pointer is unchanged by the interpreter and always points to the start of the program being interpreted. The current token is stored in **token**. (A token is an indivisible unit of program code. It is more precisely defined by the following section.) The type of a token is stored in **token_type**. The **tok** variable holds the internal format of the token if that token is a keyword.

The enumeration **tok_types** declares the types of tokens recognized by Mini C++. The **token_ireps** enumeration specifies the internal format of tokens that represent keywords. Values that represent operators comprised of two characters, such as <=, are specified by the

double_ops enumeration. Various error codes are enumerated by **error_msg**. Finally, **InterpExc** is the exception class used to report syntax errors.

Tokenizing the Source Code

Fundamental to all interpreters (and compilers, for that matter) is a mechanism that reduces the source code into its constituent parts, which are referred to as *tokens*. A token is an indivisible piece of a program that represents one logical unit. For example, the {, +, = =, and **if** are all tokens. Even though the equality operator = = is comprised of two characters, they cannot be separated without changing the meaning. Thus, = = is a single logical unit, and therefore, a single token. Similarly, **if** is a token, but neither *i* nor *f* has any special meaning to C++.

The ANSI/ISO standard for C++ defines the following types of tokens:

keywords	identifiers	literal
operator	punctuator	

The *keywords* are those tokens that make up the C++ language, such as **while**. *Identifiers* are the names of variables, functions, and so on. *Literals* include strings and constant values, such as the number 10. *Operators* are self explanatory. *Punctuators* include such things as semicolons, commas, braces, and parentheses. (Some punctuators are also operators, depending upon their use.)

Although Mini C++ recognizes the same tokens as those specified by the ANSI/ISO C++ standard, it categorizes them a bit differently in order to make interpretation a bit easier. The token categories used by Mini C++ are shown here:

Token Type	Includes
delimiter	punctuators and operators
keyword	keywords
string	quoted strings
identifier	variable and function names
number	numeric constant
block	{ or }

Let's work through an example that illustrates how these token types are applied. Given the statement

```
for(x=0; x<10; x++) {
  num = num + x;
}
```

the following tokens are produced:

Token	Category
for	keyword
(	delimiter
x	identifier
=	delimiter
0	number
;	delimiter
x	identifier
<	delimiter
10	number
;	delimiter
x	identifier
++	delimiter
)	delimiter
{	block
num	identifier
=	delimiter
num	identifier
+	delimiter
x	identifier
;	delimiter
}	block

The function that returns tokens from the source code for the Mini C++ interpreter is called **get_token( )**, and it is shown here:

```
// Get a token.
tok_types get_token()
{

  char *temp;

  token_type = UNDEFTT; tok = UNDEFTOK;

  temp = token;
  *temp = '\0';

  // Skip over white space.
  while(isspace(*prog) && *prog) ++prog;

  // Skip over newline.
```

```
  while(*prog == '\r') {
    ++prog;
    ++prog;
    // Again, skip over white space.
    while(isspace(*prog) && *prog) ++prog;
  }

  // Check for end of program.
  if(*prog == '\0') {
    *token = '\0';
    tok = END;
    return (token_type = DELIMITER);
  }

  // Check for block delimiters.
  if(strchr("{}", *prog)) {
    *temp = *prog;
    temp++;
    *temp = '\0';
    prog++;
    return (token_type = BLOCK);
  }

  // Look for comments.
  if(*prog == '/')
    if(*(prog+1) == '*') { // is a /* comment
      prog += 2;
      do { // find end of comment
        while(*prog != '*') prog++;
        prog++;
      } while (*prog != '/');
      prog++;
      return (token_type = DELIMITER);
    } else if(*(prog+1) == '/') { // is a // comment
      prog += 2;
      // Find end of comment.
      while(*prog != '\r' && *prog != '\0') prog++;
      if(*prog == '\r') prog +=2;
      return (token_type = DELIMITER);
    }

  // Check for double-ops.
  if(strchr("!<>=+-", *prog)) {
    switch(*prog) {
      case '=':
```

```cpp
      if(*(prog+1) == '=') {
        prog++; prog++;
        *temp = EQ;
        temp++; *temp = EQ; temp++;
        *temp = '\0';
      }
      break;
    case '!':
      if(*(prog+1) == '=') {
        prog++; prog++;
        *temp = NE;
        temp++; *temp = NE; temp++;
        *temp = '\0';
      }
      break;
    case '<':
      if(*(prog+1) == '=') {
        prog++; prog++;
        *temp = LE; temp++; *temp = LE;
      }
      else if(*(prog+1) == '<') {
        prog++; prog++;
        *temp = LS; temp++; *temp = LS;
      }
      else {
        prog++;
        *temp = LT;
      }
      temp++;
      *temp = '\0';
      break;
    case '>':
      if(*(prog+1) == '=') {
        prog++; prog++;
        *temp = GE; temp++; *temp = GE;
      } else if(*(prog+1) == '>') {
        prog++; prog++;
        *temp = RS; temp++; *temp = RS;
      }
      else {
        prog++;
        *temp = GT;
      }
      temp++;
      *temp = '\0';
```

```
          break;
        case '+':
          if(*(prog+1) == '+') {
            prog++; prog++;
            *temp = INC; temp++; *temp = INC;
            temp++;
            *temp = '\0';
          }
          break;
        case '-':
          if(*(prog+1) == '-') {
            prog++; prog++;
            *temp = DEC; temp++; *temp = DEC;
            temp++;
            *temp = '\0';
          }
          break;
    }

    if(*token) return(token_type = DELIMITER);
  }

  // Check for other delimiters.
  if(strchr("+-*^/%=;:(),'", *prog)) {
    *temp = *prog;
    prog++;
    temp++;
    *temp = '\0';
    return (token_type = DELIMITER);
  }

  // Read a quoted string.
  if(*prog == '"') {
    prog++;
    while(*prog != '"' && *prog != '\r' && *prog) {
      // Check for \n escape sequence.
      if(*prog == '\\') {
        if(*(prog+1) == 'n') {
          prog++;
          *temp++ = '\n';
        }
      }
      else if((temp - token) < MAX_T_LEN)
        *temp++ = *prog;
```

```
      prog++;
    }
    if(*prog == '\r' || *prog == 0)
      throw InterpExc(SYNTAX);
    prog++; *temp = '\0';
    return (token_type = STRING);
  }

  // Read an integer number.
  if(isdigit(*prog)) {
    while(!isdelim(*prog)) {
      if((temp - token) < MAX_ID_LEN)
        *temp++ = *prog;
      prog++;
    }
    *temp = '\0';
    return (token_type = NUMBER);
  }

  // Read identifier or keyword.
  if(isalpha(*prog)) {
    while(!isdelim(*prog)) {
      if((temp - token) < MAX_ID_LEN)
        *temp++ = *prog;
      prog++;
    }
    token_type = TEMP;
  }

  *temp = '\0';

  // Determine if token is a keyword or identifier.
  if(token_type == TEMP) {
    tok = look_up(token); // convert to internal form
    if(tok) token_type = KEYWORD; // is a keyword
    else token_type = IDENTIFIER;
  }

  // Check for unidentified character in file.
  if(token_type == UNDEFTT)
    throw InterpExc(SYNTAX);

  return token_type;
}
```

The **get_token( )** function begins by skipping over all white space, including carriage returns and line feeds. Because no token contains a space (except for a quoted string or character constant), spaces must be bypassed. The **get_token( )** function also skips over comments. Then the next token in the program is read. Notice how each category of token is handled separately. For example, if the next character in the program is a digit, a number is read; if the next character is a letter, an identifier or keyword is obtained, and so on.

The string representation of the token is placed into **token**. Once read, the token's type (as enumerated by the **tok_types** enumeration) is put into **token_type** and, if the token is a keyword, its internal representation (as enumerated by **token_ireps**) is assigned to **tok** via the **look_up( )** function. (The reason for the internal representation of keywords will be explained later.) As you can see, **get_token( )** converts C++'s two-character operators, such as <= or ++, into their corresponding enumeration values. Although not technically necessary, this step makes the parser easier to implement.

Displaying Syntax Errors

If the parser encounters a syntax error, it throws an **InterpExc**, specifying an enumerated value that corresponds to the type of error found. (The other parts of Mini C++ also use **InterpExc**s to report errors.) The handler for **InterpExc** exceptions is found in **main( )**, which is part of the main interpreter file, **minicpp.cpp**, described later. This handler calls the **sntx_err( )** function, shown here, to report the error:

```
// Display an error message.
void sntx_err(error_msg error)
{
  char *p, *temp;
  int linecount = 0;

  static char *e[]= {
    "Syntax error",
    "No expression present",
    "Not a variable",
    "Duplicate variable name",
    "Duplicate function name",
    "Semicolon expected",
    "Unbalanced braces",
    "Function undefined",
    "Type specifier expected",
    "Return without call",
    "Parentheses expected",
    "While expected",
    "Closing quote expected",
    "Division by zero",
    "{ expected (control statements must use blocks)",
    "Colon expected"
```

```
};

// Display error and line number.
cout << "\n" << e[error];
p = p_buf;
while(p != prog) { // find line number of error
  p++;
  if(*p == '\r') {
    linecount++;
  }
}
cout << " in line " << linecount << endl;

temp = p;
while(p > p_buf && *p != '\n') p--;

// Display offending line.
while(p <= temp)
  cout << *p++;

cout << endl;
}
```

Notice that **sntx_err( )** displays a string that describes the error and the line number in which the error was detected (which may be one line after the error actually occurred). It also displays the line in which the error was detected.

Evaluating an Expression

The functions that begin with **eval_exp** and the **atom( )** function implement the production rules for Mini C++ expressions. To understand exactly how the parser evaluates an expression, work through the following expression. (Assume that **prog** points to the start of the expression.)

$$10 - 3 * 2$$

When **eval_exp( )**, the entry point into the parser, is called, it gets the first token. If the token is null, an exception is thrown that indicates that no expression was present. However, in this case, the token contains the number **10**. Since the token is not null, **eval_exp0( )** is called, which checks for an assignment operator. Because no assignment is present, **eval_exp1( )** is called, which in turn calls **eval_exp2( )**. Next, **eval_exp2( )** calls **eval_exp3( )** and **eval_exp3( )** calls **eval_exp4( )**. The **eval_exp4( )** handles the unary + and −, and the prefix ++ and − −. It then calls **eval_exp5( )**. At this point **eval_exp5( )** either recursively calls **eval_exp0( )** (in the case of a parenthesized expression) or **atom( )** to find a value. Because the token is not a left parenthesis, **atom( )** is executed and **value** is assigned the value 10.

Next, another token is retrieved, and the functions begin to return up the chain. The token is now the operator –, and the functions return up to **eval_exp2( )**.

What happens next is very important. Because the token is –, it is saved in **op**. The parser then gets the next token, which is 3, and the descent down the chain begins again. As before, **atom( )** is entered. The value 3 is returned in **value** and the operator * is read. This causes a return back up the chain to **eval_exp3( )**, where the final token 2 is read. At this point, the first arithmetic operation occurs—the multiplication of 2 and 3. The result is returned to **eval_exp2( )** and the subtraction is performed. The subtraction yields the answer 4. Although this process may seem complicated at first, working through some other examples on your own will clarify the parser's operation.

Now, let's look a bit more closely at the **atom( )** function. It finds the value of an integer constant or variable, a function, or a character constant. (It also handles postfix ++ and – –.) There are two kinds of functions that may be present in the source code: user-defined or library. If a user-defined function is encountered, its code is executed by the interpreter in order to determine its return value. (How Mini C++ actually achieves a function call is discussed in the next section.) If the function is a library function, first its address is looked up by the **internal_func( )** function, and then it is accessed via its interface function. The library functions and the addresses of their interface functions are held in the **intern_func** array, shown here:

```
// This structure links a library function name
// with a pointer to that function.
struct intern_func_type {
  char *f_name; // function name
  int (*p)();   // pointer to the function
} intern_func[] = {
  "getchar", call_getchar,
  "putchar", call_putchar,
  "abs", call_abs,
  "rand", call_rand,
  "", 0  // null terminate the list
};
```

As you can see, Mini C++ knows only a few library functions, but it is easy to add others that you might need. (The actual interface functions are contained in a separate file, which is discussed in the section "The Mini C++ Library Functions.")

One final point about the routines in the expression parser file: To correctly parse the C++ syntax, *one-token look-ahead* is occasionally required. For example, consider the following statement:

```
alpha = count();
```

In order for Mini C++ to know that **count** is a function and not a variable, it must read both **count** *and the next token*. If the next token is a parenthesis, as it is in this case, then the parser knows that **count** refers to a function. However, if the statement was

```
alpha = count * 10;
```

then the next token after **count** is the *****. Because it is not a parenthesis, it means that **count** must be a variable. Without one-token look-ahead, the parser has no way to make this determination. In both cases, the look-ahead token needs to be returned to the input stream for subsequent processing. For this reason, the expression parser file includes the **putback( )** function, which returns the last token read to the input stream.

The Mini C++ Interpreter

The engine that actually executes a C++ program is the interpreter. Before jumping right into the code, it will be helpful for you to understand in general how the interpreter operates. In many ways, the code for the interpreter is easier to understand than the expression parser because, conceptually, the act of interpreting a C++ program can be summed up by the following algorithm:

```
while(tokens_present) {
    get next token;
    take appropriate action;
}
```

This algorithm may seem unbelievably simple when compared to the expression parser, but this is exactly what all interpreters do! One thing to keep in mind is that the "take appropriate action" step may also involve reading additional tokens from the input stream and taking further appropriate action. Thus, the "take appropriate action" step can be recursive.

To understand how the algorithm actually works, let's manually interpret the following code fragment:

```
int a;

a = 10 * num;

if(a < 100) {
    cout << a;
}
```

Following the algorithm, read the first token, which is **int**. The appropriate action given this token is to read the next token in order to find out the name of the variable being declared (which, in this case, is **a**) and then to store its name. The next token is the semicolon that ends the line. The appropriate action here is to ignore it. Now, get the next token, which is **a**. Because this statement does not begin with a keyword, it must begin an expression. Here, the appropriate action is to evaluate the expression using the parser. This process eats up all the tokens in that statement. Next, read the **if** token. This signals the beginning of an **if** statement, so the appropriate action is to process the **if**, which means evaluating the conditional expression. If the outcome of the expression is true, then the block of code associated with the **if** is interpreted. Otherwise, it is skipped.

The process just described will take place for any C++ program. Interpretation stops only when the last token has been read or when a syntax error is encountered. With this basic algorithm in mind, let's examine the interpreter. The entire interpreter file, called **minicpp.cpp**, is shown here. The sections that follow examine it in detail.

```cpp
// A Mini C++ interpreter.

#include <iostream>
#include <fstream>
#include <new>
#include <stack>
#include <vector>
#include <cstring>
#include <cstdlib>
#include <cctype>
#include "mccommon.h"

using namespace std;

char *prog;  // current execution point in source code
char *p_buf; // points to start of program buffer

// This structure encapsulates the info
// associated with variables.
struct var_type {
  char var_name[MAX_ID_LEN+1]; // name
  token_ireps v_type; // data type
  int value; // value
};

// This vector holds info for global variables.
vector<var_type> global_vars;

// This vector holds info for local variables
// and parameters.
vector<var_type> local_var_stack;

// This structure encapsulates function info.
struct func_type {
  char func_name[MAX_ID_LEN+1]; // name
  token_ireps ret_type; // return type
  char *loc; // location of entry point in program
};

// This vector holds info about functions.
```

```cpp
vector<func_type> func_table;

// Stack for managing function scope.
stack<int> func_call_stack;

// Stack for managing nested scopes.
stack<int> nest_scope_stack;

char token[MAX_T_LEN+1]; // current token
tok_types token_type; // token type
token_ireps tok; // internal representation

int ret_value; // function return value

bool breakfound = false; // true if break encountered

int main(int argc, char *argv[])
{
  if(argc != 2) {
    cout << "Usage: minicpp <filename>\n";
    return 1;
  }

  // Allocate memory for the program.
  try {
    p_buf = new char[PROG_SIZE];
  } catch (bad_alloc exc) {
    cout << "Could Not Allocate Program Buffer\n";
    return 1;
  }

  // Load the program to execute.
  if(!load_program(p_buf, argv[1])) return 1;

  // Set program pointer to start of program buffer.
  prog = p_buf;

  try {
    // Find the location of all functions
    // and global variables in the program.
    prescan();

    // Next, set up the call to main().

    // Find program starting point.
```

```
    prog = find_func("main");

    // Check for incorrect or missing main() function.
    if(!prog) {
      cout << "main() Not Found\n";
      return 1;
    }

    // Back up to opening (.
    prog--;

    // Set the first token to main
    strcpy(token, "main");

    // Call main() to start interpreting.
    call();
  }
  catch(InterpExc exc) {
    sntx_err(exc.get_err());
    return 1;
  }
  catch(bad_alloc exc) {
    cout << "Out Of Memory\n";
    return 1;
  }

  return ret_value;
}

// Load a program.
bool load_program(char *p, char *fname)
{
  int i=0;

  ifstream in(fname, ios::in | ios::binary);
  if(!in) {
    cout << "Cannot Open file.\n";
    return false;
  }

  do {
    *p = in.get();
    p++; i++;
  } while(!in.eof() && i < PROG_SIZE);
```

```cpp
  if(i == PROG_SIZE) {
    cout << "Program Too Big\n";
    return false;
  }

  // Null terminate the program. Skip any EOF
  // mark if present in the file.
  if(*(p-2) == 0x1a) *(p-2) = '\0';
  else *(p-1) = '\0';

  in.close();

  return true;
}

// Find the location of all functions in the program
// and store global variables.
void prescan()
{
  char *p, *tp;
  char temp[MAX_ID_LEN+1];
  token_ireps datatype;
  func_type ft;

  // When brace is 0, the current source position
  // is outside of any function.
  int brace = 0;

  p = prog;

  do {
    // Bypass code inside functions
    while(brace) {
      get_token();
      if(tok == END) throw InterpExc(UNBAL_BRACES);
      if(*token == '{') brace++;
      if(*token == '}') brace--;
    }

    tp = prog; // save current position
    get_token();

    // See if global var type or function return type.
    if(tok==CHAR || tok==INT) {
      datatype = tok; // save data type
```

```
      get_token();

    if(token_type == IDENTIFIER) {
      strcpy(temp, token);
      get_token();

      if(*token != '(') { // must be global var
        prog = tp; // return to start of declaration
        decl_global();
      }
      else if(*token == '(') { // must be a function

        // See if function already defined.
        for(unsigned i=0; i < func_table.size(); i++)
          if(!strcmp(func_table[i].func_name, temp))
            throw InterpExc(DUP_FUNC);

        ft.loc = prog;
        ft.ret_type = datatype;
        strcpy(ft.func_name, temp);
        func_table.push_back(ft);

        do {
          get_token();
        } while(*token != ')');
        // Next token will now be opening curly
        // brace of function.
      }
      else putback();
    }
  }
  else {
    if(*token == '{') brace++;
    if(*token == '}') brace--;
  }
} while(tok != END);
if(brace) throw InterpExc(UNBAL_BRACES);
prog = p;
}

// Interpret a single statement or block of code. When
// interp() returns from its initial call, the final
// brace (or a return) in main() has been encountered.
void interp()
{
```

```cpp
int value;
int block = 0;

do {
  // Don't interpret until break is handled.
  if(breakfound) return;

  token_type = get_token();

  // See what kind of token is up.
  if(token_type == IDENTIFIER ||
     *token == INC || *token == DEC)
  {
    // Not a keyword, so process expression.
    putback();  // restore token to input stream for
                // further processing by eval_exp()
    eval_exp(value); // process the expression
    if(*token != ';') throw InterpExc(SEMI_EXPECTED);
  }
  else if(token_type==BLOCK) { // block delimiter?
    if(*token == '{') { // is a block
      block = 1; // interpreting block, not statement
      // Record nested scope.
      nest_scope_stack.push(local_var_stack.size());
    }
    else { // is a }, so reset scope and return
      // Reset nested scope.
      local_var_stack.resize(nest_scope_stack.top());
      nest_scope_stack.pop();
      return;
    }
  }
  else // is keyword
    switch(tok) {
      case CHAR:
      case INT:      // declare local variables
        putback();
        decl_local();
        break;
      case RETURN:  // return from function call
        func_ret();
        return;
      case IF:       // process an if statement
        exec_if();
        break;
```

```
          case ELSE:     // process an else statement
            find_eob(); // find end of else block
                        // and continue execution
            break;
          case WHILE:    // process a while loop
            exec_while();
            break;
          case DO:       // process a do-while loop
            exec_do();
            break;
          case FOR:      // process a for loop
            exec_for();
            break;
          case BREAK:    // handle break
            breakfound = true;

            // Reset nested scope.
            local_var_stack.resize(nest_scope_stack.top());
            nest_scope_stack.pop();
            return;
          case SWITCH:   // handle a switch statement
            exec_switch();
            break;
          case COUT:     // handle console output
            exec_cout();
            break;
          case CIN:      // handle console input
            exec_cin();
            break;
          case END:
            exit(0);
        }
  } while (tok != END && block);
  return;
}

// Return the entry point of the specified function.
// Return NULL if not found.
char *find_func(char *name)
{
  unsigned i;

  for(i=0; i < func_table.size(); i++)
    if(!strcmp(name, func_table[i].func_name))
      return func_table[i].loc;
```

```
    return NULL;
}

// Declare a global variable.
void decl_global()
{
  token_ireps vartype;
  var_type vt;

  get_token(); // get type

  vartype = tok; // save var type

  // Process comma-separated list.
  do {
    vt.v_type = vartype;
    vt.value = 0; // init to 0
    get_token(); // get name

    // See if variable is a duplicate.
    for(unsigned i=0; i < global_vars.size(); i++)
      if(!strcmp(global_vars[i].var_name, token))
        throw InterpExc(DUP_VAR);

    strcpy(vt.var_name, token);
    global_vars.push_back(vt);

    get_token();
  } while(*token == ',');

  if(*token != ';') throw InterpExc(SEMI_EXPECTED);
}

// Declare a local variable.
void decl_local()
{
  var_type vt;

  get_token(); // get var type
  vt.v_type = tok; // store type

  vt.value = 0; // init var to 0

  // Process comma-separated list.
  do {
```

```
    get_token(); // get var name

    // See if variable is already the name
    // of a local variable in this scope.
    if(!local_var_stack.empty())
    for(int i=local_var_stack.size()-1;
        i >= nest_scope_stack.top(); i--)
    {
      if(!strcmp(local_var_stack[i].var_name, token))
        throw InterpExc(DUP_VAR);
    }

    strcpy(vt.var_name, token);
    local_var_stack.push_back(vt);
    get_token();
  } while(*token == ',');

  if(*token != ';') throw InterpExc(SEMI_EXPECTED);
}

// Call a function.
void call()
{
  char *loc, *temp;
  int lvartemp;

  // First, find entry point of function.
  loc = find_func(token);

  if(loc == NULL)
    throw InterpExc(FUNC_UNDEF); // function not defined
  else {
    // Save local var stack index.
    lvartemp = local_var_stack.size();

    get_args(); // get function arguments
    temp = prog; // save return location

    func_call_stack.push(lvartemp); // push local var index

    prog = loc; // reset prog to start of function
    get_params(); // load the function's parameters with
                  // the values of the arguments

    interp(); // interpret the function
```

```
      prog = temp; // reset the program pointer

      if(func_call_stack.empty()) throw InterpExc(RET_NOCALL);

      // Reset local_var_stack to its previous state.
      local_var_stack.resize(func_call_stack.top());
      func_call_stack.pop();
  }
}


// Push the arguments to a function onto the local
// variable stack.
void get_args()
{
  int value, count, temp[NUM_PARAMS];
  var_type vt;

  count = 0;
  get_token();
  if(*token != '(') throw InterpExc(PAREN_EXPECTED);

  // Process a comma-separated list of values.
  do {
    eval_exp(value);
    temp[count] = value; // save temporarily
    get_token();
    count++;
  } while(*token == ',');
  count--;

  // Now, push on local_var_stack in reverse order.
  for(; count>=0; count--) {
    vt.value = temp[count];
    vt.v_type = ARG;
    local_var_stack.push_back(vt);
  }
}

// Get function parameters.
void get_params()
{
  var_type *p;
  int i;

  i = local_var_stack.size()-1;
```

```cpp
  // Process comma-separated list of parameters.
  do {
    get_token();
    p = &local_var_stack[i];
    if(*token != ')' ) {
      if(tok != INT && tok != CHAR)
        throw InterpExc(TYPE_EXPECTED);

      p->v_type = tok;
      get_token();

      // Link parameter name with argument already on
      // local var stack.
      strcpy(p->var_name, token);
      get_token();
      i--;
    }
    else break;
  } while(*token == ',');

  if(*token != ')') throw InterpExc(PAREN_EXPECTED);
}

// Return from a function.
void func_ret()
{
  int value;

  value = 0;

  // Get return value, if any.
  eval_exp(value);

  ret_value = value;
}

// Assign a value to a variable.
void assign_var(char *vname, int value)
{
  // First, see if it's a local variable.
  if(!local_var_stack.empty())
    for(int i=local_var_stack.size()-1;
        i >= func_call_stack.top(); i--)
    {
      if(!strcmp(local_var_stack[i].var_name,
```

```
                            vname))
      {
        if(local_var_stack[i].v_type == CHAR)
          local_var_stack[i].value = (char) value;
        else if(local_var_stack[i].v_type == INT)
          local_var_stack[i].value = value;
        return;
      }
    }

  // Otherwise, try global vars.
  for(unsigned i=0; i < global_vars.size(); i++)
    if(!strcmp(global_vars[i].var_name, vname)) {
      if(global_vars[i].v_type == CHAR)
        global_vars[i].value = (char) value;
      else if(global_vars[i].v_type == INT)
        global_vars[i].value = value;
      return;
    }

  throw InterpExc(NOT_VAR); // variable not found
}

// Find the value of a variable.
int find_var(char *vname)
{
  // First, see if it's a local variable.
  if(!local_var_stack.empty())
    for(int i=local_var_stack.size()-1;
        i >= func_call_stack.top(); i--)
    {
      if(!strcmp(local_var_stack[i].var_name, vname))
        return local_var_stack[i].value;
    }

  // Otherwise, try global vars.
  for(unsigned i=0; i < global_vars.size(); i++)
    if(!strcmp(global_vars[i].var_name, vname))
      return global_vars[i].value;

  throw InterpExc(NOT_VAR); // variable not found
}

// Execute an if statement.
void exec_if()
```

```
{
  int cond;

  eval_exp(cond); // get if expression.

  if(cond) { // if true, process target of IF
    // Confirm start of block.
    if(*token != '{')
      throw InterpExc(BRACE_EXPECTED);

    interp();
  }
  else {
    // Otherwise skip around IF block and
    // process the ELSE, if present.

    find_eob(); // find start of next line
    get_token();

    if(tok != ELSE) {
      // Restore token if no ELSE is present.
      putback();
      return;
    }

    // Confirm start of block.
    get_token();
    if(*token != '{')
      throw InterpExc(BRACE_EXPECTED);
    putback();

    interp();
  }
}

// Execute a switch statement.
void exec_switch()
{
  int sval, cval;
  int brace;

  eval_exp(sval); // Get switch expression.

  // Check for start of block.
  if(*token != '{')
```

```
      throw InterpExc(BRACE_EXPECTED);

// Record new scope.
nest_scope_stack.push(local_var_stack.size());

// Now, check case statements.
for(;;) {
  brace = 1;
  // Find a case statement.
  do {
    get_token();
    if(*token == '{') brace++;
    else if(*token == '}') brace--;
  } while(tok != CASE && tok != END && brace);

  // If no matching case found, then skip.
  if(!brace) break;

  if(tok == END) throw InterpExc(SYNTAX);

  // Get value of the case statement.
  eval_exp(cval);

  // Read and discard the :
  get_token();

  if(*token != ':')
    throw InterpExc(COLON_EXPECTED);

  // If values match, then interpret.
  if(cval == sval) {
    brace = 1;
    do {
      interp();

      if(*token == '{') brace++;
      else if(*token == '}') brace--;
    } while(!breakfound && tok != END && brace);

    // Find end of switch statement.
    while(brace) {
      get_token();
      if(*token == '{') brace++;
      else if(*token == '}') brace--;
    }
```

```cpp
      breakfound = false;

      break;
    }
  }
}

// Execute a while loop.
void exec_while()
{
  int cond;
  char *temp;

  putback(); // put back the while
  temp = prog; // save location of top of while loop

  get_token();
  eval_exp(cond); // check the conditional expression

  // Confirm start of block.
  if(*token != '{')
    throw InterpExc(BRACE_EXPECTED);

  if(cond)
    interp(); // if true, interpret
  else { // otherwise, skip to end of loop
    find_eob();
    return;
  }

  prog = temp; // loop back to top

  // Check for break in loop.
  if(breakfound) {
    // Find start of loop block.
    do {
      get_token();
    } while(*token != '{' && tok != END);

    putback();
    breakfound = false;
    find_eob(); // now, find end of loop
    return;
  }
}
```

```cpp
// Execute a do loop.
void exec_do()
{
  int cond;
  char *temp;


  // Save location of top of do loop.
  putback(); // put back do
  temp = prog;

  get_token(); // get start of loop block

  // Confirm start of block.
  get_token();
  if(*token != '{')
    throw InterpExc(BRACE_EXPECTED);
  putback();

  interp(); // interpret loop

  // Check for break in loop.
  if(breakfound) {
    prog = temp;
    // Find start of loop block.
    do {
      get_token();
    } while(*token != '{' && tok != END);

    // Find end of while block.
    putback();
    find_eob();

    // Now, find end of while expression.
    do {
      get_token();
    } while(*token != ';' && tok != END);
    if(tok == END) throw InterpExc(SYNTAX);

    breakfound = false;
    return;
  }

  get_token();
  if(tok != WHILE) throw InterpExc(WHILE_EXPECTED);
```

```
    eval_exp(cond); // check the loop condition

    // If true loop; otherwise, continue on.
    if(cond) prog = temp;
}

// Execute a for loop.
void exec_for()
{
  int cond;
  char *temp, *temp2;
  int paren ;

  get_token(); // skip opening (
  eval_exp(cond); // initialization expression

  if(*token != ';') throw InterpExc(SEMI_EXPECTED);
  prog++; // get past the ;
  temp = prog;

  for(;;) {
    // Get the value of the conditional expression.
    eval_exp(cond);

    if(*token != ';') throw InterpExc(SEMI_EXPECTED);
    prog++; // get past the ;
    temp2 = prog;

    // Find start of for block.
    paren = 1;
    while(paren) {
      get_token();
      if(*token == '(') paren++;
      if(*token == ')') paren--;
    }

    // Confirm start of block.
    get_token();
    if(*token != '{')
      throw InterpExc(BRACE_EXPECTED);
    putback();

    // If condition is true, interpret
    if(cond)
      interp();
```

```
    else { // otherwise, skip to end of loop
      find_eob();
      return;
    }

    prog = temp2; // go to increment expression

    // Check for break in loop.
    if(breakfound) {
      // Find start of loop block.
      do {
        get_token();
      } while(*token != '{' && tok != END);

      putback();
      breakfound = false;
      find_eob(); // now, find end of loop
      return;
    }

    // Evaluate the increment expression.
    eval_exp(cond);

    prog = temp; // loop back to top
  }
}

// Execute a cout statement.
void exec_cout()
{
  int val;

  get_token();
  if(*token != LS) throw InterpExc(SYNTAX);

  do {
    get_token();

    if(token_type==STRING) {
      // Output a string.
      cout << token;
    }
    else if(token_type == NUMBER ||
            token_type == IDENTIFIER) {
      // Output a number.
```

```cpp
          putback();
          eval_exp(val);
          cout << val;
        }
      else if(*token == '\'') {
        // Output a character constant.
          putback();
          eval_exp(val);
          cout << (char) val;
        }

      get_token();
    } while(*token == LS);

    if(*token != ';') throw InterpExc(SEMI_EXPECTED);
}

// Execute a cin statement.
void exec_cin()
{
    int val;
    char chval;
    token_ireps vtype;

    get_token();
    if(*token != RS) throw InterpExc(SYNTAX);

    do {
      get_token();
      if(token_type != IDENTIFIER)
        throw InterpExc(NOT_VAR);

        vtype = find_var_type(token);

        if(vtype == CHAR) {
          cin >> chval;
          assign_var(token, chval);
        }
        else if(vtype == INT) {
          cin >> val;
          assign_var(token, val);
        }

        get_token();
    } while(*token == RS);
```

```cpp
    if(*token != ';') throw InterpExc(SEMI_EXPECTED);
}

// Find the end of a block.
void find_eob()
{
  int brace;

  get_token();
  if(*token != '{')
    throw InterpExc(BRACE_EXPECTED);

  brace = 1;

  do {
    get_token();
    if(*token == '{') brace++;
    else if(*token == '}') brace--;
  } while(brace && tok != END);

  if(tok==END) throw InterpExc(UNBAL_BRACES);
}

// Determine if an identifier is a variable. Return
// true if variable is found; false otherwise.
bool is_var(char *vname)
{
  // See if vname is a local variable.
  if(!local_var_stack.empty())
    for(int i=local_var_stack.size()-1;
        i >= func_call_stack.top(); i--)
    {
      if(!strcmp(local_var_stack[i].var_name, vname))
        return true;
    }

  // See if vname is a global variable.
  for(unsigned i=0; i < global_vars.size(); i++)
    if(!strcmp(global_vars[i].var_name, vname))
      return true;

  return false;
}

// Return the type of variable.
```

```
token_ireps find_var_type(char *vname)
{
  // First, see if it's a local variable.
  if(!local_var_stack.empty())
    for(int i=local_var_stack.size()-1;
        i >= func_call_stack.top(); i--)
    {
      if(!strcmp(local_var_stack[i].var_name, vname))
        return local_var_stack[i].v_type;
    }

  // Otherwise, try global vars.
  for(unsigned i=0; i < global_vars.size(); i++)
    if(!strcmp(global_vars[i].var_name, vname))
        return local_var_stack[i].v_type;

  return UNDEFTOK;
}
```

The main( ) Function

The **main( )** function begins the interpretation of the program that you specify on the command line. It is shown here:

```
int main(int argc, char *argv[])
{
  if(argc != 2) {
    cout << "Usage: minicpp <filename>\n";
    return 1;
  }

  // Allocate memory for the program.
  try {
    p_buf = new char[PROG_SIZE];
  } catch (bad_alloc exc) {
    cout << "Could Not Allocate Program Buffer\n";
    return 1;
  }

  // Load the program to execute.
  if(!load_program(p_buf, argv[1])) return 1;

  // Set program pointer to start of program buffer.
  prog = p_buf;
```

```
  try {
    // Find the location of all functions
    // and global variables in the program.
    prescan();

    // Next, set up the call to main().

    // Find program starting point.
    prog = find_func("main");

    // Check for incorrect or missing main() function.
    if(!prog) {
      cout << "main() Not Found\n";
      return 1;
    }

    // Back up to opening (.
    prog--;

    // Set the first token to main
    strcpy(token, "main");

    // Call main() to start interpreting.
    call();
  }
  catch(InterpExc exc) {
    sntx_err(exc.get_err());
    return 1;
  }
  catch(bad_alloc exc) {
    cout << "Out Of Memory\n";
    return 1;
  }

  return ret_value;
}
```

The **main( )** function begins by allocating memory to hold the program being interpreted. Notice that the largest program that can be interpreted is specified by the constant **PROG_SIZE**. This value is arbitrarily set at 10,000, but you can increase it if you want. Next, the program is loaded by calling **load_program( )**. After the program has been loaded, **main( )** performs three primary actions:

1. It calls **prescan( )**, the interpreter prescanner.
2. It readies the interpreter for the call to **main( )** by finding its location in the program.

3. It executes **call( )**, which begins execution of the program at the start of **main( )**.

The **main( )** function also handles all **InterpExc** exceptions generated by Mini C++. This includes those thrown by the parser, too.

The following sections describe the key components of the interpreter in detail.

The Interpreter Prescan

Before the interpreter can start executing a program, two important clerical tasks must be performed:

1. All global variables must be found and initialized.
2. The location of each function defined in the program must be found.

These tasks are carried out by the *interpreter prescan*.

In Mini C++, all executable code exists *inside* functions, so there is no reason for the Mini C++ interpreter to go outside a function once execution has begun. However, global variable declaration statements lie outside all functions. Thus, it is necessary for the prescanner to handle these declarations. There is no other (efficient) way for the interpreter to know about them.

In the interest of execution speed, it is important (although not technically necessary) that the location of each function defined in the program be known so that a call to a function can be reasonably fast. If this step is not performed, a lengthy sequential search of the source code would be needed to find the entry point to a function each time it is called.

Finding the entry point of all functions also serves a second purpose. As you know, a C++ program does not begin execution at the physical top of the program. Instead, it begins at the **main( )** function. Furthermore, there is no requirement that **main( )** be the first function in the program. It is therefore necessary to find the location of the **main( )** function within the program's source code so that execution can begin at that point. (Remember also that global variables may precede **main( )**, so even if it is the first function, it is not necessarily the first line of code.) Because the prescanner finds the entry point of all functions, it also finds the entry point of **main( )**.

The function that performs the prescan is called **prescan( )**. It is shown here:

```
// Find the location of all functions in the program
// and store global variables.
void prescan()
{
  char *p, *tp;
  char temp[MAX_ID_LEN+1];
  token_ireps datatype;
  func_type ft;

  // When brace is 0, the current source position
  // is outside of any function.
```

```cpp
  int brace = 0;

  p = prog;

  do {
    // Bypass code inside functions
    while(brace) {
      get_token();
      if(tok == END) throw InterpExc(UNBAL_BRACES);
      if(*token == '{') brace++;
      if(*token == '}') brace--;
    }

    tp = prog; // save current position
    get_token();

    // See if global var type or function return type.
    if(tok==CHAR || tok==INT) {
      datatype = tok; // save data type
      get_token();

      if(token_type == IDENTIFIER) {
        strcpy(temp, token);
        get_token();

        if(*token != '(') { // must be global var
          prog = tp; // return to start of declaration
          decl_global();
        }
        else if(*token == '(') { // must be a function

          // See if function already defined.
          for(unsigned i=0; i < func_table.size(); i++)
            if(!strcmp(func_table[i].func_name, temp))
              throw InterpExc(DUP_FUNC);

          ft.loc = prog;
          ft.ret_type = datatype;
          strcpy(ft.func_name, temp);
          func_table.push_back(ft);

          do {
            get_token();
          } while(*token != ')');
          // Next token will now be opening curly
```

```
          // brace of function.
      }
      else putback();
    }
  }
  else {
    if(*token == '{') brace++;
    if(*token == '}') brace--;
  }
} while(tok != END);
if(brace) throw InterpExc(UNBAL_BRACES);
prog = p;
}
```

The **prescan( )** function works like this. Each time an opening curly brace is encountered, **brace** is incremented. Whenever a closing curly brace is read, **brace** is decremented. Therefore, whenever **brace** is greater than zero, the current token is being read from within a function. However, if **brace** equals zero when a variable is found, then the prescanner knows it must be a global variable. By the same method, if a function name is encountered when **brace** equals zero, then it must be that function's definition. (Remember, Mini C++ does not support function prototypes.)

Global variables are stored in a vector called **global_vars**, which holds structures of type **var_type**, shown here:

```
// This structure encapsulates the info
// associated with variables.
struct var_type {
  char var_name[MAX_ID_LEN+1]; // name
  token_ireps v_type; // data type
  int value; // value
};
```

This structure stores the name, value, and type of a variable.

Global variables are entered into the **global_vars** vector by **decl_global( )**, shown next:

```
// Declare a global variable.
void decl_global()
{
  token_ireps vartype;
  var_type vt;

  get_token(); // get type

  vartype = tok; // save var type

  // Process comma-separated list.
```

```
  do {
    vt.v_type = vartype;
    vt.value = 0; // init to 0
    get_token(); // get name

    // See if variable is a duplicate.
    for(unsigned i=0; i < global_vars.size(); i++)
      if(!strcmp(global_vars[i].var_name, token))
        throw InterpExc(DUP_VAR);

    strcpy(vt.var_name, token);
    global_vars.push_back(vt);

    get_token();
  } while(*token == ',');

  if(*token != ';') throw InterpExc(SEMI_EXPECTED);
}
```

In essence, **decl_global( )** obtains the type and name of a variable, initializes it to zero and then puts it on the end of **global_vars**. However, first a check is performed to ensure that a variable with that name has not already been declared.

The location of each user-defined function is put into a vector called **func_table**, which stores structures of type **func_type**, shown here:

```
// This structure encapsulates function info.
struct func_type {
  char func_name[MAX_ID_LEN+1]; // name
  token_ireps ret_type; // return type
  char *loc; // location of entry point in program
};
```

Each function entry contains the return type, name, and location in the source code of the function's entry point. Before a function is entered into the table, **prescan( )** checks that one by the same name does not already exist. Notice that no parameter information is stored. This information is obtained at runtime, when a function is actually called.

The interp( ) Function

The **interp( )** function is the heart of the interpreter. It is the function that decides what action to take based on the next token in the input stream. The function is designed to interpret one unit of code and then return. If the unit consists of a single statement, then that statement is interpreted and **interp( )** returns. However, if an opening brace is read, then all statements within that block are interpreted. This is managed by the **block** flag, which is set to 1 if an opening brace is read. This causes the function to continue to interpret statements until a closing brace is read. The **interp( )** function is shown here:

```cpp
// Interpret a single statement or block of code. When
// interp() returns from its initial call, the final
// brace (or a return) in main() has been encountered.
void interp()
{
  int value;
  int block = 0;

  do {
    // Don't interpret until break is handled.
    if(breakfound) return;

    token_type = get_token();

    // See what kind of token is up.
    if(token_type == IDENTIFIER ||
       *token == INC || *token == DEC)
    {
      // Not a keyword, so process expression.
      putback();  // restore token to input stream for
                  // further processing by eval_exp()
      eval_exp(value); // process the expression
      if(*token != ';') throw InterpExc(SEMI_EXPECTED);
    }
    else if(token_type==BLOCK) { // block delimiter?
      if(*token == '{') { // is a block
        block = 1; // interpreting block, not statement
        // Record nested scope.
        nest_scope_stack.push(local_var_stack.size());
      }
      else { // is a }, so reset scope and return
        // Reset nested scope.
        local_var_stack.resize(nest_scope_stack.top());
        nest_scope_stack.pop();
        return;
      }
    }
    else // is keyword
      switch(tok) {
        case CHAR:
        case INT:      // declare local variables
          putback();
```

```
        decl_local();
        break;
      case RETURN:  // return from function call
        func_ret();
        return;
      case IF:      // process an if statement
        exec_if();
        break;
      case ELSE:    // process an else statement
        find_eob(); // find end of else block
                    // and continue execution
        break;
      case WHILE:   // process a while loop
        exec_while();
        break;
      case DO:      // process a do-while loop
        exec_do();
        break;
      case FOR:     // process a for loop
        exec_for();
        break;
      case BREAK:   // handle break
        breakfound = true;

        // Reset nested scope.
        local_var_stack.resize(nest_scope_stack.top());
        nest_scope_stack.pop();
        return;
      case SWITCH:  // handle a switch statement
        exec_switch();
        break;
      case COUT:    // handle console output
        exec_cout();
        break;
      case CIN:     // handle console input
        exec_cin();
        break;
      case END:
        exit(0);
    }
  } while (tok != END && block);
  return;
}
```

Calls to functions like **exit( )** excepted, a C++ program ends when the last brace (or a **return**) in **main( )** is encountered—not necessarily at the last line of source code. This is one reason that **interp( )** executes only a statement or a block of code and not the entire program. Also, conceptually, C++ consists of blocks of code. Therefore, **interp( )** is called each time a new block of code is encountered. This includes function blocks and blocks begun by various C++ statements, such as **if**. In the process of executing a program, Mini C++ may call **interp( )** recursively.

The **interp( )** function works like this. First, it checks if a **break** statement has been encountered in the program. If one has, the global variable **breakfound** will be true. This variable remains set until it is cleared by another part of the interpreter, as you will see when the interpretation of the control statements are described.

Assuming that **breakfound** is false, **interp( )** reads the next token from the program. If the token is an identifier, the statement must be an expression, so the expression parser is called. Because the expression parser expects to read the first token in the expression itself, the token is returned to the input stream via a call to **putback( )**. When **eval_exp( )** returns, **token** will hold the last token read by the expression parser, which must be a semicolon if the statement is syntactically correct. If **token** does not contain a semicolon, an error is reported.

If the next token from the program is an opening brace, **block** is set to 1 and the current size of **local_var_stack** is pushed onto **nest_scope_stack**. **local_var_stack** holds all local variables, including those declared in nested block scopes. Conversely, if the next token is a closing brace, **local_var_stack** is truncated to the size specified by the top of **nest_scope_stack**. This effectively removes any local variables that may have been declared inside that scope. Thus, a { causes the size of the local variable stack to be saved, and a } causes the local variable stack to be reset to its previous size. This mechanism supports nested, local scopes.

Finally, if the token is a keyword, the **switch** statement is executed, calling the appropriate routine to handle the statement. The reason that keywords are given integer equivalents by **get_token( )** is to allow the use of the **switch** statement instead of requiring a sequence of **if** statements involving string comparisons (which are quite slow).

Handling Local Variables

When the interpreter encounters an **int** or **char** keyword, it calls **decl_local( )** to create storage for a local variable. As stated earlier, no global variable declaration statement will be encountered by the interpreter once the program is executing because only code within a function is executed. Therefore, if a variable declaration statement is found, it must be for a local variable (or a parameter, which will be discussed in the next section). As a general rule, local variables are stored on a stack. If the language is compiled, the system stack is generally used; however, in an interpreted mode, the stack for local variables must be maintained by the interpreter.

In Mini C++, **local_var_stack** provides the stack for local variables. Somewhat unexpectedly, **local_var_stack** is a **vector** rather than a **stack** container. The reason for this is that although local variables are managed in a stack-like fashion, the container must be able to be searched sequentially when access to a variable's value is needed. The **stack** container does not conveniently allow such a sequential search, but **vector** does.

The **decl_local( )** function is shown here:

```
// Declare a local variable.
void decl_local()
{
  var_type vt;

  get_token(); // get var type
  vt.v_type = tok; // store type

  vt.value = 0; // init var to 0

  // Process comma-separated list.
  do {
    get_token(); // get var name

    // See if variable is already the name
    // of a local variable in this scope.
    if(!local_var_stack.empty())
    for(int i=local_var_stack.size()-1;
        i >= nest_scope_stack.top(); i--)
    {
      if(!strcmp(local_var_stack[i].var_name, token))
        throw InterpExc(DUP_VAR);
    }

    strcpy(vt.var_name, token);
    local_var_stack.push_back(vt);
    get_token();
  } while(*token == ',');

  if(*token != ';') throw InterpExc(SEMI_EXPECTED);
}
```

Each time a local variable is encountered, its name, type, and value (initially zero) are pushed onto the stack. The process works like this. The **decl_local( )** function first reads the type of the variable or variables being declared and sets the initial value to zero. Next, it enters a loop, which reads the names of a comma-separated list of identifiers. Each time through the loop, the information about each variable is pushed onto the local variable stack. In the process, a check is made to ensure that a variable by the same name is not already existent in the current scope. (Variables declared within the current scope are found between the current top of **local_var_stack** and the index saved on the top of **nest_scope_stack**.) At the end, the final token is checked to make sure that it contains a semicolon.

Calling User-Defined Functions

Probably the most difficult part of implementing an interpreter for C++ is managing the execution of user-defined functions. Not only does the interpreter need to begin reading the source code at a new location and then return to the calling routine after the function terminates, but it must also deal with these three tasks: the passing of arguments, the allocation of parameters, and the return value of the function.

All function calls (except the initial call to **main( )**) take place through the expression parser from the **atom( )** function by a call to **call( )**. It is the **call( )** function that actually handles the details of calling a function. The **call( )** function is shown here. Let's examine it closely:

```cpp
// Call a function.
void call()
{
  char *loc, *temp;
  int lvartemp;

  // First, find entry point of function.
  loc = find_func(token);

  if(loc == NULL)
    throw InterpExc(FUNC_UNDEF); // function not defined
  else {
    // Save local var stack index.
    lvartemp = local_var_stack.size();

    get_args(); // get function arguments
    temp = prog; // save return location

    func_call_stack.push(lvartemp); // push local var index

    prog = loc; // reset prog to start of function
    get_params(); // load the function's parameters with
                  // the values of the arguments

    interp(); // interpret the function

    prog = temp; // reset the program pointer

    if(func_call_stack.empty()) throw InterpExc(RET_NOCALL);

    // Reset local_var_stack to its previous state.
    local_var_stack.resize(func_call_stack.top());
    func_call_stack.pop();
  }
}
```

The first thing that **call( )** does is find the location of the entry point in the source code to the specified function by calling **find_func( )**. Next, it saves the current size of the local variable stack into the **lvartemp** variable. Then it calls **get_args( )** to process any function arguments. The **get_args( )** function reads a comma-separated list of expressions and pushes them onto the local variable stack in reverse order. (The expressions are pushed in reverse order so that they can be more easily matched with their corresponding parameters when the function is interpreted.) When the values are pushed, they are not given names. The names of the parameters are given to them by the **get_params( )** function, which will be discussed in a moment.

Once the function arguments have been processed, the current value of **prog** is saved in **temp**. This location is the return point of the function. Next, the value of **lvartemp** is pushed onto the function call stack, **func_call_stack**. Its purpose is to store the index of the top of the local variable stack each time a function is called. This value represents the starting point on the local variable stack for variables (and parameters) relative to the function being called. The value on the top of the function call stack is used to prevent a function from accessing any local variables other than those it declares.

The next two lines of code set the program pointer to the start of the function and link the name of its formal parameters with the values of the arguments already on the local variable stack with a call to **get_params( )**. To do this, **get_params( )** reads each parameter and copies its name to the corresponding argument already stored in **local_var_stack**.

The actual execution of the function is performed through a call to **interp( )**. When **interp( )** returns, the program pointer (**prog**) is reset to its return point, and the local variable stack index is reset to its value before the function call. This final step effectively removes all of the function's local variables and parameters from the stack.

If the function being called contains a **return** statement, then **interp( )** calls **func_ret( )** prior to returning to **call( )**. This function processes any return value. It is shown here:

```
// Return from a function.
void func_ret()
{
  int value;

  value = 0;

  // Get return value, if any.
  eval_exp(value);

  ret_value = value;
}
```

The global variable **ret_value** is an integer that holds the return value of a function. At first glance you might wonder why the local variable **value** receives the return value from **eval_exp( )**, rather than **ret_value**. The reason is that functions can be recursive and **eval_exp( )** may need to call the same function in order to obtain its value. In this situation, a global variable cannot be used to receive the value because it will be overwritten.

Assigning Values to Variables

Let's return briefly to the expression parser. When an assignment statement is encountered, the value of the right side of the expression is computed, and this value is assigned to the variable on the left using a call to **assign_var( )**. However, C++ supports various scopes, including the global scope (formally called *namespace scope*) and local scope. Furthermore, local scopes can be nested. This is important because it affects the way that Mini C++ finds the value of variables. To understand why, consider the following Mini C++ program:

```
int count;

int main()
{
  int count, i;

  count = 100;

  i = f();

  return 0;
}

int f()
{
  int count;

  count = 99;

  return count;
}
```

When **count** is assigned a value, how does the **assign_var( )** function know which variable is being referred to? Is it the global **count** or one of the local **count**s? The answer is simple. In C++, local variables take priority over global variables of the same name. Furthermore, local variables are not known outside their own block. To see how these rules can be used to resolve the preceding assignments, examine the **assign_var( )** function, shown here:

```
// Assign a value to a variable.
void assign_var(char *vname, int value)
{
  // First, see if it's a local variable.
  if(!local_var_stack.empty())
    for(int i=local_var_stack.size()-1;
        i >= func_call_stack.top(); i--)
    {
```

```
      if(!strcmp(local_var_stack[i].var_name,
               vname))
      {
        if(local_var_stack[i].v_type == CHAR)
          local_var_stack[i].value = (char) value;
        else if(local_var_stack[i].v_type == INT)
          local_var_stack[i].value = value;
        return;
      }
    }

  // Otherwise, try global vars.
  for(unsigned i=0; i < global_vars.size(); i++)
    if(!strcmp(global_vars[i].var_name, vname)) {
      if(global_vars[i].v_type == CHAR)
        global_vars[i].value = (char) value;
      else if(global_vars[i].v_type == INT)
        global_vars[i].value = value;
      return;
    }

  throw InterpExc(NOT_VAR); // variable not found
}
```

As explained in the previous section, each time a function is called, the current index of the top of the local variable stack (**local_var_stack**) is pushed onto the function call stack (**func_call_stack**). This means that any local variables (or parameters) defined by the function will be pushed onto the stack above that point. Therefore, the **assign_var( )** function first searches **local_var_stack**, beginning with the current top-of-stack and stopping when the index reaches that saved by the latest function call. This mechanism ensures that only those variables local to the function are examined. (It also helps support recursive functions because the current top-of-stack value is saved each time a function is invoked.) Therefore, in the example, the line

```
count = 100;
```

in **main( )** causes **assign_var( )** to find the local variable **count** inside **main( )**. In **f( )**, the statement

```
count = 99;
```

causes **assign_var( )** to find the **count** declared within **f( )**.

If no local variable matches the name of a variable, then the global variable list is searched. If neither the local or global variable list contains the variable, a syntax error results.

Now, consider the case in which a variable is declared within a nested scope, such as shown here:

```
int f(int n)
{
  int count;

  count = 99

  if(n > 0) {
    int count; // this count is local to the if

    count = 100; // refers to count in if block
    // ...
  }

  return count; // refers to outer count.
}
```

In this situation, the outer **count** (which is declared at the start of the function code) is pushed onto **local_var_stack** first. Then the **count** that is local to the **if** block is pushed onto **local_var_stack**. Thus, when the following line executes:

```
count = 100; // refers to count in if block
```

assign_var( ) looks up **count** and finds the copy of **count** that is local to the **if** block first, just as it should.

One last point, within the **interp( )** function, each time a block is left, **local_var_stack** is truncated to the size is was before entering the block. This effectively removes all local variables declared within that block from the stack. **local_var_stack** is also truncated each time a function returns, which removes all local variables and parameters associated with the function.

Executing an if Statement

Now that the basic structure of the Mini C++ interpreter has been described, it is time to see how the control statements are implemented. In general, each time a keyword statement is encountered, **interp( )** calls a function that processes that statement. The functions that interpret the various control statements all begin with the prefix **exec_**. For example, a **for** is interpreted by **exec_for( )**, a **switch** is interpreted by **exec_switch( )**, and so on.

One of the easiest control statements to interpret is the **if**. The **if** statement is processed by **exec_if( )**, shown here:

```
// Execute an if statement.
void exec_if()
{
```

```
  int cond;

  eval_exp(cond); // get if expression.

  if(cond) { // if true, process target of IF
    // Confirm start of block.
    if(*token != '{')
      throw InterpExc(BRACE_EXPECTED);

    interp();
  }
  else {
    // Otherwise skip around IF block and
    // process the ELSE, if present.

    find_eob(); // find start of next line
    get_token();

    if(tok != ELSE) {
      // Restore token if no ELSE is present.
      putback();
      return;
    }

    // Confirm start of block.
    get_token();
    if(*token != '{')
      throw InterpExc(BRACE_EXPECTED);
    putback();

    interp();
  }
}
```

Let's look closely at the operation of this function.

First, **exec_if( )** calls **eval_exp( )** to compute the value of the conditional expression. If the condition is true (nonzero), the function calls **interp( )**, which executes the code within the **if** block. If the condition is false, **find_eob( )** is called, which advances the program pointer to the location immediately after the end of the **if** block. If an **else** is present, the block of code associated with the **else** is executed. Otherwise, execution simply begins with the next line of code.

If the **if** block executes and there is an **else** block present, there must be some way for the **else** block to be bypassed. This is accomplished in **interp( )** when an **else** statement is encountered. In this case, **interp( )** simply calls **find_eob( )** to bypass the **else** block. After that, execution resumes with the first statement after the **else** block. Remember, the only time an **else** will be processed by **interp( )** (in a syntactically correct program) is after an **if** block is executed.

One other point: notice that **exec_if( )** confirms that the code that is the target of the **if** and **else** is contained within a block. As explained, to simplify the interpreter, the targets of all control statements must be blocks of code. This restriction streamlines the interpreter code.

The switch and break Statements

Interpreting the **switch** statement requires more work than does the **if** statement. One reason is that its syntax is more complicated. Another reason is that it relies on the **break** statement. Thus, to handle a **switch** statement implies that **break** must also be handled. Both are examined here.

Handling **break** is actually fairly easy because it performs the same action whether it is used in a **switch** statement or in a loop: it causes the block associated with that statement to be exited. Mini C++ handles **break** by use of a global flag variable called **breakfound**, which is initially set to false. When a **break** is found, **breakfound** is set to true. This variable is then checked by the **switch** statement (and the loop statements described later) to determine if a **break** has been executed. If **breakfound** is true, the current block is terminated and **breakfound** is reset to false.

The **break** statement is handled inside **interp( )** by the code shown here:

```
case BREAK:    // handle break
  breakfound = true;

  // Reset nested scope.
  local_var_stack.resize(nest_scope_stack.top());
  nest_scope_stack.pop();
  return;
```

As you can see, in addition to setting **breakfound** to true, the local variable stack is reset to its state prior to the start of the block being terminated. Recall that variables can be declared within any block and are local to that block. Thus, when **break** is found, any local variables associated with the enclosing block must be removed.

The **switch** statement is handled by the **exec_switch( )** function shown here:

```
// Execute a switch statement.
void exec_switch()
{
  int sval, cval;
  int brace;

  eval_exp(sval); // Get switch expression.

  // Check for start of block.
  if(*token != '{')
    throw InterpExc(BRACE_EXPECTED);
```

```
// Record new scope.
nest_scope_stack.push(local_var_stack.size());

// Now, check case statements.
for(;;) {
  brace = 1;
  // Find a case statement.
  do {
    get_token();
    if(*token == '{') brace++;
    else if(*token == '}') brace--;
  } while(tok != CASE && tok != END && brace);

  // If no matching case found, then skip.
  if(!brace) break;

  if(tok == END) throw InterpExc(SYNTAX);

  // Get value of the case statement.
  eval_exp(cval);

  // Read and discard the :
  get_token();

  if(*token != ':')
    throw InterpExc(COLON_EXPECTED);

  // If values match, then interpret.
  if(cval == sval) {
    brace = 1;
    do {
      interp();

      if(*token == '{') brace++;
      else if(*token == '}') brace--;
    } while(!breakfound && tok != END && brace);

    // Find end of switch statement.
    while(brace) {
      get_token();
      if(*token == '{') brace++;
      else if(*token == '}') brace--;
    }
    breakfound = false;
```

```
      break;
    }
  }
}
```

First, **exec_switch( )** obtains the value of the **switch** expression and stores this value in **sval**. Next, it checks for the start of the **switch** block and stores the top of the local variable stack on **nest_scope_stack**. This step is necessary because the **switch** statement creates a nested scope. Next, the value of each **case** statement is examined until either a match with the value in **sval** is found, or the end of the **switch** is reached. (Recall that, for the sake of simplicity, Mini C++ does not support the **default** statement.) If a match is found, the statements associated with that case are executed until a **break** statement is encountered (that is, until **breakfound** is true), or until the end of the **switch** block is found. After a **break** is encountered, **exec_switch( )** ends by finding the end of the **switch** block and then setting **breakfound** to false.

Processing a while Loop

A **while** loop is quite easy to interpret. The function that performs this task is **exec_while( )**, shown here:

```
// Execute a while loop.
void exec_while()
{
  int cond;
  char *temp;

  putback(); // put back the while
  temp = prog; // save location of top of while loop

  get_token();
  eval_exp(cond); // check the conditional expression

  // Confirm start of block.
  if(*token != '{')
    throw InterpExc(BRACE_EXPECTED);

  if(cond)
    interp(); // if true, interpret
  else { // otherwise, skip to end of loop
    find_eob();
    return;
  }

  prog = temp; // loop back to top
```

```
  // Check for break in loop.
  if(breakfound) {
    // Find start of loop block.
    do {
      get_token();
    } while(*token != '{' && tok != END);

    putback();
    breakfound = false;
    find_eob();
    return;
  }
}
```

The **exec_while( )** function works like this. First, the **while** token is put back into the input stream, and the location of the **while** in the program is saved into the **temp** pointer. This address is used to allow the interpreter to loop back to the top of the **while**. Next, the **while** is reread to remove it from the input stream, and **eval_exp( )** is called to compute the value of the **while**'s conditional expression. If the conditional expression is true, **interp( )** is called to interpret the **while** code block. When **interp( )** returns, **prog** (the program pointer) is loaded with the location of the start of the **while** loop, which causes program execution to resume at the top of the loop when control returns to **interp( )**. This results in the next iteration of the loop. However, if **interp( )** returns because of a **break** statement being found within the loop, iteration stops, the end of the **while** block is found, and **exec_while( )** returns. When the conditional expression is false, the end of the **while** block is found and the function returns.

Processing a do-while Loop

A **do-while** loop is processed much like the **while**. When **interp( )** encounters a **do** statement, it calls **exec_do( )**, shown here:

```
// Execute a do loop.
void exec_do()
{
  int cond;
  char *temp;


  // Save location of top of do loop.
  putback(); // put back do
  temp = prog;

  get_token(); // get start of loop block

  // Confirm start of block.
```

```
  get_token();
  if(*token != '{')
    throw InterpExc(BRACE_EXPECTED);
  putback();

  interp(); // interpret loop

  // Check for break in loop.
  if(breakfound) {
    prog = temp;
    // Find start of loop block.
    do {
      get_token();
    } while(*token != '{' && tok != END);

    // Find end of while block.
    putback();
    find_eob();

    // Now, find end of while expression.
    do {
      get_token();
    } while(*token != ';' && tok != END);
    if(tok == END) throw InterpExc(SYNTAX);

    breakfound = false;
    return;
  }

  get_token();
  if(tok != WHILE) throw InterpExc(WHILE_EXPECTED);

  eval_exp(cond); // check the loop condition

  // If true loop; otherwise, continue on.
  if(cond) prog = temp;
}
```

The main difference between the **do-while** and the **while** loops is that the **do-while** always executes its block of code at least once because the conditional expression is at the bottom of the loop. Therefore, **exec_do( )** first saves the location of the top of the loop into **temp** and then calls **interp( )** to interpret the block of code associated with the loop. When **interp( )** returns, the corresponding **while** is retrieved and the conditional expression is evaluated. If the condition is true, **prog** is reset to the top of the loop; otherwise, execution will continue on. If a **break** is encountered, iteration stops and the end of the loop block is found.

The for Loop

The interpretation of the **for** loop poses a more difficult challenge than the other loops. Part of the reason for this is that the structure of the C++ **for** is definitely designed with compilation in mind. The main trouble is that the conditional expression of the **for** must be checked at the top of the loop, but the increment portion occurs at the bottom of the loop. Therefore, even though these two pieces of the **for** loop occur next to each other in the source code, their interpretation is separated by the block of code being iterated. With a little effort, though, the **for** can be correctly interpreted.

When **interp( )** encounters a **for** statement, **exec_for( )** is called. This function is shown here:

```
// Execute a for loop.
void exec_for()
{
  int cond;
  char *temp, *temp2;
  int paren ;

  get_token(); // skip opening (
  eval_exp(cond); // initialization expression

  if(*token != ';') throw InterpExc(SEMI_EXPECTED);
  prog++; // get past the ;
  temp = prog;

  for(;;) {
    // Get the value of the conditional expression.
    eval_exp(cond);

    if(*token != ';') throw InterpExc(SEMI_EXPECTED);
    prog++; // get past the ;
    temp2 = prog;

    // Find start of for block.
    paren = 1;
    while(paren) {
      get_token();
      if(*token == '(') paren++;
      if(*token == ')') paren--;
    }

    // Confirm start of block.
    get_token();
    if(*token != '{')
      throw InterpExc(BRACE_EXPECTED);
```

```
    putback();

    // If condition is true, interpret
    if(cond)
      interp();
    else { // otherwise, skip to end of loop
      find_eob();
      return;
    }

    prog = temp2; // go to increment expression

    // Check for break in loop.
    if(breakfound) {
      // Find start of loop block.
      do {
        get_token();
      } while(*token != '{' && tok != END);

      putback();
      breakfound = false;
      find_eob();
      return;
    }

    // Evaluate the increment expression.
    eval_exp(cond);

    prog = temp; // loop back to top
  }
}
```

This function begins by processing the initialization expression in the **for**. The initialization portion of the **for** is executed only once and does not form part of the loop. Next, the program pointer is advanced to a point immediately after the semicolon that ends the initialization statement, and this address is assigned to **temp**. This location is the start of the conditional expression. An infinite loop is then entered that checks the conditional portion of the loop and assigns **temp2** the address of the start of the increment expression. Then, the beginning of the loop code is found. Finally, if the conditional expression is true, the loop block is interpreted. Otherwise, the end of the block is found and execution continues on after the **for** loop. Assuming that the loop executes, when the call to **interp( )** returns, the increment expression is evaluated, and the process repeats. Of course, this process stops if a **break** is encountered within the loop block.

Handling cin and cout Statements

Because I/O via **cin** and **cout** is a fundamental part of C++, it seems only proper for Mini C++ to support them. However, Mini C++ does not handle I/O through **cin** and **cout** the way that it is handled by a commercial compiler. As you know, **cin** and **cout** are predefined identifiers that correspond to streams that are linked to standard input and standard output. They are used to input and output information at the console through the use of the I/O operators << and >>. Thus, << and >> are overloaded for I/O. However, Mini C++ does not support operator overloading. In fact, to keep Mini C++ as simple as possible, it does not even support the << or >> shift operators! (However, **get_token( )** *will* recognize these operators.) Despite these restrictions, it is still quite easy to interpret **cin** and **cout** statements.

Console output through **cout** is handled by the **exec_cout( )** function, shown here:

```
// Execute a cout statement.
void exec_cout()
{
  int val;

  get_token();
  if(*token != LS) throw InterpExc(SYNTAX);

  do {
    get_token();

    if(token_type==STRING) {
      // Output a string.
      cout << token;
    }
    else if(token_type == NUMBER ||
            token_type == IDENTIFIER) {
      // Output a number.
      putback();
      eval_exp(val);
      cout << val;
    }
    else if(*token == '\'') {
      // Output a character constant.
      putback();
      eval_exp(val);
      cout << (char) val;
    }

    get_token();
  } while(*token == LS);
```

```
    if(*token != ';') throw InterpExc(SEMI_EXPECTED);
}
```

When a **cout** identifier is encountered, the next token is read. If it is not a <<, then a syntax error is reported. Otherwise, a loop is entered that obtains and then outputs the value of the string or expression on the right side of the <<. This process continues until the end of the **cout** statement is reached.

The **cin** statement is handled by **exec_cin( )**, shown next:

```
// Execute a cin statement.
void exec_cin()
{
  int val;
  char chval;
  token_ireps vtype;

  get_token();
  if(*token != RS) throw InterpExc(SYNTAX);

  do {
    get_token();
    if(token_type != IDENTIFIER)
      throw InterpExc(NOT_VAR);

    vtype = find_var_type(token);

    if(vtype == CHAR) {
      cin >> chval;
      assign_var(token, chval);
    }
    else if(vtype == INT) {
      cin >> val;
      assign_var(token, val);
    }

    get_token();
  } while(*token == RS);

  if(*token != ';') throw InterpExc(SEMI_EXPECTED);
}
```

When a **cin** identifier is encountered, the next token is read. If it is not a >>, then a syntax error is reported. Otherwise, a loop is entered that obtains the variable that will receive input, reads input from the console, and stores that input into the variable. Notice that the type of the variable determines whether integer or character data is read. This process continues until the end of the **cout** statement is reached.

The Mini C++ Library Functions

Because the programs executed by Mini C++ are never compiled and linked, any library routines they use must be handled directly by Mini C++. The best way to do this is to create an interface function that Mini C++ calls when a library function is encountered. This interface function sets up the call to the actual library function and handles any return values.

Because of space limitations, Mini C++ supports only four "library" functions: **getchar( )**, **putchar( )**, **abs( )**, and **rand( )**. These functions are translated into calls to the actual library functions of the same name. The Mini C++ library routines are in the file **libcpp.cpp**. It is shown here:

```cpp
// ***** Internal Library Functions *****

// Add more of your own, here.

#include <iostream>
#include <cstdlib>
#include <cstdio>
#include "mccommon.h"

using namespace std;

// Read a character from the console.
// If your compiler supplies an unbuffered
// character intput function, feel free to
// substitute it for the call to cin.get().
int call_getchar()
{
  char ch;

  ch = getchar();

  // Advance past ()
  get_token();
  if(*token != '(')
    throw InterpExc(PAREN_EXPECTED);

  get_token();
  if(*token != ')')
    throw InterpExc(PAREN_EXPECTED);

  return ch;
}

// Write a character to the display.
```

```
int call_putchar()
{
  int value;

  eval_exp(value);

  putchar(value);

  return value;
}

// Return absolute value.
int call_abs()
{
  int val;

  eval_exp(val);

  val = abs(val);

  return val;
}

// Return a random integer.
int call_rand()
{

  // Advance past ()
  get_token();
  if(*token != '(')
    throw InterpExc(PAREN_EXPECTED);

  get_token();
  if(*token != ')')
    throw InterpExc(PAREN_EXPECTED);

  return rand();
}
```

To add more library functions of your own choosing, first enter their names and the addresses of their interface functions into the **intern_func** array (which is declared in **parser.cpp**). Next, following the lead of the functions shown previously, create appropriate interface functions. Finally, add their prototypes to **mccommon.h**.

The mccommon.h Header File

All three source files for Mini C++, **minicpp.cpp**, **parser.cpp**, and **libcpp.cpp**, include the header file **mccommon.h**, shown here:

```
// Common declarations used by parser.cpp, minicpp.cpp,
// or libcpp.cpp, or by other files that you might add.
//
const int MAX_T_LEN  = 128;   // max token length
const int MAX_ID_LEN = 31;    // max identifier length
const int PROG_SIZE  = 10000; // max program size
const int NUM_PARAMS = 31;    // max number of parameters

// Enumeration of token types.
enum tok_types { UNDEFTT, DELIMITER, IDENTIFIER,
                 NUMBER, KEYWORD, TEMP, STRING, BLOCK };

// Enumeration of internal representation of tokens.
enum token_ireps { UNDEFTOK, ARG, CHAR, INT, SWITCH,
                   CASE, IF, ELSE, FOR, DO, WHILE, BREAK,
                   RETURN, COUT, CIN, END };

// Enumeration of two-character operators, such as <=.
enum double_ops { LT=1, LE, GT, GE, EQ, NE, LS, RS, INC, DEC };

// These are the constants used when throwing a
// syntax error exception.
//
// NOTE: SYNTAX is a generic error message used when
// nothing else seems appropriate.
enum error_msg
    { SYNTAX, NO_EXP, NOT_VAR, DUP_VAR, DUP_FUNC,
      SEMI_EXPECTED, UNBAL_BRACES, FUNC_UNDEF,
      TYPE_EXPECTED, RET_NOCALL, PAREN_EXPECTED,
      WHILE_EXPECTED, QUOTE_EXPECTED, DIV_BY_ZERO,
      BRACE_EXPECTED, COLON_EXPECTED };

extern char *prog;  // current location in source code
extern char *p_buf; // points to start of program buffer

extern char token[MAX_T_LEN+1]; // string version of token
extern tok_types token_type; // contains type of token
extern token_ireps tok; // internal representation of token

extern int ret_value; // function return value
```

```cpp
extern bool breakfound; // true if break encountered

// Exception class for Mini C++.
class InterpExc {
  error_msg err;
public:
  InterpExc(error_msg e) { err = e; }
  error_msg get_err() { return err; }
};

// Interpreter prototypes.
void prescan();
void decl_global();
void call();
void putback();
void decl_local();
void exec_if();
void find_eob();
void exec_for();
void exec_switch();
void get_params();
void get_args();
void exec_while();
void exec_do();
void exec_cout();
void exec_cin();
void assign_var(char *var_name, int value);
bool load_program(char *p, char *fname);
int find_var(char *s);
void interp();
void func_ret();
char *find_func(char *name);
bool is_var(char *s);
token_ireps find_var_type(char *s);

// Parser prototypes.
void eval_exp(int &value);
void eval_exp0(int &value);
void eval_exp1(int &value);
void eval_exp2(int &value);
void eval_exp3(int &value);
void eval_exp4(int &value);
void eval_exp5(int &value);
void atom(int &value);
void sntx_err(error_msg error);
```

```
void putback();
bool isdelim(char c);
token_ireps look_up(char *s);
int find_var(char *s);
tok_types get_token();
int internal_func(char *s);
bool is_var(char *s);

// "Standard library" prototypes.
int call_getchar();
int call_putchar();
int call_abs();
int call_rand();
```

Compiling and Linking the Mini C++ Interpreter

To use Mini C++, you must compile and link **minicpp.cpp**, **parser.cpp**, and **libcpp.cpp**. You can use just about any modern C++ compiler, including Borland C++ and Visual C++. For example, for Visual C++, you can use the following command line:

```
cl -GX minicpp.cpp parser.cpp libcpp.cpp
```

For Borland C++, this command line can be used:

```
bcc32 minicpp.cpp parser.cpp libcpp.cpp
```

If you use a different compiler, simply follow the instructions that come with it.

NOTE

For some older versions of Visual C++, Mini C++ may not be given sufficient stack space. You can use the /Fsize option to increase the stack.

To run a program, specify its name after minicpp on the command line. For example, this runs a program called **test.cpp**:

```
minicpp test.cpp
```

Demonstrating Mini C++

In this section, several C++ programs are shown that demonstrate the features and capabilities of Mini C++. The first demonstrates all features supported by Mini C++:

```
/* Mini C++ Demonstration Program #1.

   This program demonstrates all features
```

```
   of C++ that are recognized by Mini C++.
*/

int i, j; // global vars
char ch;

int main()
{
  int i, j; // local vars

  // Call a "standard library' function.
  cout << "Mini C++ Demo Program.\n\n";

  // Call a programmer-defined function.
  print_alpha();

  cout << "\n";

  // Demonstrate do and for loops.
  cout << "Use loops.\n";
  do {
    cout << "Enter a number (0 to quit): ";
    cin >> i;

    // Demonstrate the if
    if(i < 0 ) {
      cout << "Numbers must be positive, try again.\n";
    }
    else {
      for(j = 0; j <= i; ++j) {
        cout << j << " summed is ";
        cout << sum(j) << "\n";
      }
    }
  } while(i != 0);

  cout << "\n";

  // Demonstrate the break in a loop.
  cout << "Break from a loop.\n";
  for(i=0; i < 100; i++) {
    cout << i << "\n";
    if(i == 5) {
      cout << "Breaking out of loop.\n";
      break;
```

```
      }
    }

    cout << "\n";

    // Demonstrate the switch
    cout << "Use a switch.\n";
    for(i=0; i < 6; i++) {
      switch(i) {
        case 1: // can stack cases
        case 0:
          cout << "1 or 0\n";
          break;
        case 2:
          cout << "two\n";
          break;
        case 3:
          cout << "three\n";
          break;
        case 4:
          cout << "four\n";
          cout << "4 * 4 is "<< 4*4 << "\n";
//        break; // this break is optional
        // no case for 5
      }
    }
    cout << "\n";

    cout << "Use a library function to generate "
         << "10 random integers.\n";
    for(i=0; i < 10; i++) {
      cout << rand() << " ";
    }

    cout << "\n";
    cout << "Done!\n";

    return 0;
}

// Sum the values between 0 and num.
// This function takes a parameter.
int sum(int num)
{
  int running_sum;
```

```
    running_sum = 0;

  while(num) {
    running_sum = running_sum + num;
    num--;
  }
  return running_sum;
}

// Print the alphabet.
int print_alpha()
{
  cout << "This is the alphabet:\n";

  for(ch = 'A'; ch<='Z'; ch++) {
    putchar(ch);
  }
  cout << "\n";

  return 0;
}
```

Here is a sample run:

```
Mini C++ Demo Program.

This is the alphabet:
ABCDEFGHIJKLMNOPQRSTUVWXYZ

Use loops.
Enter a number (0 to quit): 10
0 summed is 0
1 summed is 1
2 summed is 3
3 summed is 6
4 summed is 10
5 summed is 15
6 summed is 21
7 summed is 28
8 summed is 36
9 summed is 45
10 summed is 55
Enter a number (0 to quit): 0
0 summed is 0
```

```
Break from a loop.
0
1
2
3
4
5
Breaking out of loop.

Use a switch.
1 or 0
1 or 0
two
three
four
4 * 4 is 16

Use a library function to generate 10 random integers.
130 10982 1090 11656 7117 17595 6415 22948 31126 9004
Done!
```

The next example demonstrates nested loops:

```
// Nested loop example.
int main()
{
  int i, j, k;

  for(i = 0; i < 5; i = i + 1) {
    for(j = 0; j < 3; j = j + 1) {
      for(k = 3; k ; k = k - 1) {
        cout << i <<", ";
        cout << j << ", ";
        cout << k << "\n";
      }
    }
  }

  cout << "done";

  return 0;
}
```

A portion of its output is shown here:

```
0, 0, 3
0, 0, 2
0, 0, 1
0, 1, 3
0, 1, 2
0, 1, 1
0, 2, 3
0, 2, 2
0, 2, 1
.
.
.
```

The next program exercises the assignment operator:

```cpp
// Assignments as operations.
int main()
{
  int a, b;

  a = b = 5;

  cout << a << " " << b << "\n";

  while(a=a-1) {
    cout << a << " ";
    do {
      cout << b << " ";
    } while((b=b-1) > -5);
    cout << "\n";
  }

  return 0;
}
```

The output from this program is shown next:

```
5 5
4 5 4 3 2 1 0 -1 -2 -3 -4
3 -5
2 -6
1 -7
```

Recursive functions are demonstrated by the next program. In it, the function **factr( )** computes the factorial of a number.

```
// This program demonstrates a recursive function.

// A recursive function that returns the
// factorial of i.
int factr(int i)
{
  if(i<2) {
    return 1;
  }
  else {
    return i * factr(i-1);
  }
}

int main()
{
  cout << "Factorial of 4 is: ";
  cout << factr(4) << "\n";

  cout << "Factorial of 6 is: ";
  cout << factr(6) << "\n";

  return 0;
}
```

The output is shown here:

```
Factorial of 4 is: 24
Factorial of 6 is: 720
```

The next program fully demonstrates function arguments:

```
// A more rigorous example of function arguments.

int f1(int a, int b)
{
  int count;

  cout << "Args for f1 are ";
  cout << a << " " << b << "\n";

  count = a;
  do {
```

```
    cout << count << " ";
  } while(count=count-1);

  cout << a << " " << b
       << " " << a*b << "\n";

  return a*b;
}

int f2(int a, int x, int y)
{
  cout << "Args for f2 are ";
  cout << a << " " << x << " "
       << y << "\n";
  cout << x / a << " ";
  cout << y*x << "\n";

  return 0;
}

int main()
{
  f2(10, f1(10, 20), 99);

  return 0;
}
```

The output from this program is shown here:

```
Args for f1 are 10 20
10 9 8 7 6 5 4 3 2 1 10 20 200
Args for f2 are 10 200 99
20 19800
```

The following program exercises each loop statement:

```
// Exercise the loop statements.
int main()
{
  int a;
  char ch;

  // The while.
  cout << "Enter a number: ";
  cin >> a;
  while(a) {
```

```
    cout << a*a << " ";
    --a;
  }
  cout << "\n";

  // The do-while.
  cout << "\nEnter characters, 'q' to quit.\n";
  do {
    // Use two "standard library" functions.
    ch = getchar();
    putchar(ch);
  } while(ch != 'q');
  cout << "\n\n";

  // the for.
  for(a=0; a<10; ++a) {
    cout << a << " ";
  }

  cout << "\n\nDone!\n";

  return 0;
}
```

Here is a sample run:

```
Enter a number: 10
100 81 64 49 36 25 16 9 4 1

Enter characters, 'q' to quit.
This is a test. q
This is a test. q

0 1 2 3 4 5 6 7 8 9

Done!
```

Notice that the built-in library function **getchar( )** is line-buffered in this run, which causes no characters to be displayed by **putchar( )** until ENTER has been pressed. This behavior is the result of the real **getchar( )** function that is called by Mini C++. As you know, most compilers implement **getchar( )** as line-buffered. The point is that the built-in, Mini C++ function exhibits the same behavior as the library function that underlies it.

The final program demonstrates the use of nested scopes. In it, the variable **x** is declared three times: first as a global variable, then as a variable local to the **if** block, and finally, again within the **while** block. All three are separate and distinct from each other.

```cpp
// Demonstrate nested scopes.

int x; // global x

int main()
{
  int i;

  i = 4;

  x = 99; // global x is 99

  if(i == 4) {
    int x; // local x
    int num; // local to if statement

    x = i * 2;
    cout << "Outer local x before loop: "
         << x << "\n";

    while(x--) {
      int x; // another local x

      x = 18;
      cout << "Inner local x: " << x << "\n";
    }

    cout << "Outer local x after loop: "
         << x << "\n";
  }

  // Can't refer to num here because it is local
  // to the preceding if block.
// num = 10;

  cout << "Global x: " << x << "\n";
}
```

The output is shown here. Notice that all three **x**'s are separate.

```
Outer local x before loop: 8
Inner local x: 18
```

```
Inner local x: 18
Inner local x: 18
Inner local x: 18
Inner local x: 18
Inner local x: 18
Inner local x: 18
Inner local x: 18
Outer local x after loop: -1
Global x: 99
```

Improving Mini C++

Mini C++ was designed with transparency of operation in mind. The goal was to develop an interpreter that could be easily understood with the least amount of effort. It was also designed in such a way that it could be easily expanded. As such, Mini C++ is not particularly fast or efficient; however, the basic structure of the interpreter is in place, and you can increase its speed of execution by following these steps.

Virtually all commercial interpreters expand the role of the prescanner. The entire source program being interpreted is converted from its human-readable form into an internal format. In this internal form, all but quoted strings and constants are transformed into integer tokens, much the way that Mini C++ converts the C++ keywords into integer tokens. It may have occurred to you that Mini C++ performs a number of string comparisons. For example, each time a variable or function is searched for, several string comparisons take place. String comparisons are very costly in terms of time; however, if each identifier in the source program is converted into an integer, then much faster integer comparisons can be used. In general, the conversion of the source program into an internal form is the *single most important change* you can make to Mini C++ to improve its efficiency. The increase in speed will be dramatic.

Another area for improvement, meaningful mostly for large programs, is the lookup routines for variables and functions. Even if you convert these items into integer tokens, the current approach to searching for them relies upon a sequential search. You could, however, substitute some other faster method. For example, you might try using a **map** container, or perhaps some sort of hashing method or tree structure.

As stated earlier, one restriction that Mini C++ has relative to the full C++ grammar is that the targets of the control statements, such as **if**, must be blocks of code enclosed between curly braces. The reason for this is that it greatly simplifies the **find_eob( )** function, which is used to find the end of a block of code after one of the control statements executes. The **find_eob( )** function need look only for a closing curly brace to match the one that starts the block. You might find it an interesting exercise to remove this restriction.

Expanding Mini C++

There are two general areas in which you can expand and enhance the Mini C++ interpreter: C++ features and ancillary features. Some of these are discussed briefly in the following sections.

Adding New C++ Features

There are two basic categories of statements you can add to Mini C++. The first is additional action statements, such as the **goto** and **continue**. You might also want to add support for the **default** statement to the **switch**. You should have little trouble adding any of these if you study the way that Mini C++ interprets the other statements. If something doesn't work the first time, try finding the problem by displaying the contents of each token as it is processed.

The second category of statement you can add is support for additional data types. Mini C++ already contains the basic "hooks" for additional data types. For example, the **var_type** structure already contains a field for the type of variable. To add other built-in types (for example, **float**, **double**, and **long**), simply increase the size of the value field to the size of the largest element you wish to hold.

The addition of classes poses a greater challenge. First, you will need to design ways to instantiate objects. To do this, you will need to allocate memory large enough to hold the data members of the class and store a reference to this memory in another new field that you will need to add to **var_type**. You will also need to handle the concepts of public and private.

Supporting pointers is no more difficult than supporting any other data type. However, you will need to add support for the pointer operators to the expression parser. Once you have implemented pointers, arrays will be easy. Space for an array should be allocated dynamically using **new**, and a pointer to the array should be stored in a new field added to **var_type** for this purpose.

To handle different return types for functions, you will need to make use of the **ret_type** field in the **func_type** structure. This field defines what type of data a function returns. It is currently set but otherwise unused.

One easy addition you might try adding is support for **#include**. This preprocessor directive can be easily handled during the prescan process.

One final thought: if you like to experiment with language constructs, don't be afraid to add a non-C++ extension. For example, you can easily add a **foreach** loop like the one described in Chapter 4.

Adding Ancillary Features

Interpreters give you the opportunity to add several interesting and useful features. For example, you can add a trace facility that displays each token as it is executed. You can also add the ability to display the contents of each variable as the program executes. Another feature you might want to add is an integrated editor so that you can "edit and go" instead of having to use a separate editor to create your C++ programs.

Index

INTERNATIONAL CONTACT INFORMATION

AUSTRALIA
McGraw-Hill Book Company
Australia Pty. Ltd.
TEL +61-2-9900-1800
FAX +61-2-9878-8881
http://www.mcgraw-hill.com.au
books-it_sydney@mcgraw-hill.com

CANADA
McGraw-Hill Ryerson Ltd.
TEL +905-430-5000
FAX +905-430-5020
http://www.mcgraw-hill.ca

GREECE, MIDDLE EAST, & AFRICA
(Excluding South Africa)
McGraw-Hill Hellas
TEL +30-210-6560-990
TEL +30-210-6560-993
TEL +30-210-6560-994
FAX +30-210-6545-525

MEXICO (Also serving Latin America)
McGraw-Hill Interamericana Editores
S.A. de C.V.
TEL +525-1500-5108
FAX +525-117-1589
http://www.mcgraw-hill.com.mx
carlos_ruiz@mcgraw-hill.com

SINGAPORE (Serving Asia)
McGraw-Hill Book Company
TEL +65-6863-1580
FAX +65-6862-3354
http://www.mcgraw-hill.com.sg
mghasia@mcgraw-hill.com

SOUTH AFRICA
McGraw-Hill South Africa
TEL +27-11-622-7512
FAX +27-11-622-9045
robyn_swanepoel@mcgraw-hill.com

SPAIN
McGraw-Hill/
Interamericana de España, S.A.U.
TEL +34-91-180-3000
FAX +34-91-372-8513
http://www.mcgraw-hill.es
professional@mcgraw-hill.es

UNITED KINGDOM, NORTHERN,
EASTERN, & CENTRAL EUROPE
McGraw-Hill Education Europe
TEL +44-1-628-502500
FAX +44-1-628-770224
http://www.mcgraw-hill.co.uk
emea_queries@mcgraw-hill.com

ALL OTHER INQUIRIES Contact:
McGraw-Hill/Osborne
TEL +1-510-420-7700
FAX +1-510-420-7703
http://www.osborne.com
omg_international@mcgraw-hill.com

Sound Off!

Visit us at **www.osborne.com/bookregistration** and let us know what you thought of this book. While you're online you'll have the opportunity to register for newsletters and special offers from McGraw-Hill/Osborne.

We want to hear from you!

Sneak Peek

Visit us today at **www.betabooks.com** and see what's coming from McGraw-Hill/Osborne tomorrow!

Based on the successful software paradigm, Bet@Books™ allows computing professionals to view partial and sometimes complete text versions of selected titles online. Bet@Books™ viewing is free, invites comments and feedback, and allows you to "test drive" books in progress on the subjects that interest you the most.